CONTEMPORARY ISSUES IN CLIMATE CHANGE LAW AND POLICY: ESSAYS INSPIRED BY THE IPCC

by

Robin Kundis Craig and Stephen R. Miller,

Editors

ENVIRONMENTAL LAW INSTITUTE
Washington, D.C.

ELI publishes books that contribute to education of the profession and disseminate diverse points of view and opinion to stimulate a robust and creative exchange of ideas. These publications, which express opinions of the authors and not necessarily those of the Institute, its Board of Directors, or funding organizations, exemplify ELI's commitment to dialogue with all sectors. ELI welcomes suggestions for book topics and encourages the submission of draft manuscripts and book proposals.

Published April 2016.

Cover design by Davonne Flannagan.
Cover photograph courtesy of NASA/Michael Studinger

Printed in the United States of America.
ISBN 978-1-58576-177-7

*To all those who are helping to mold the law
to the Anthropocene*
— R.K.C.

*To Birgitt, Isolde, Nils,
and the future generations*
—S.R.M.

Contents

Preface

This is the second book published by the Environmental Law Collaborative (ELC), an affiliation of environmental law professors that began in 2011. The aspirations of the ELC were well-summarized by Profs. Jessica Owley and Keith Hirokawa in their preface to the ELC's first book, *Rethinking Sustainability to Meet the Climate Change Challenge* (ELI Press 2015):

> Inspired by early conferences at Airlie House (particularly the 1969 conference that gave birth to the Environmental Law Institute), the group created a forum to bring together our fellow researchers to discuss and make progress on pressing environmental concerns. The ELC seeks to foster progress toward an adaptive, conscious, and equitable governance of actions that impact local and global ecologies by engaging the contemporary discourse. To advance society and secure welfare, locally and globally, we must be prepared to face divisive issues that confront our environment. Assuming our strength lies in the democratic development and confirmation of values and priorities, our citizenry must be willing and capable of understanding the circumstances and alternatives that face our natural surroundings. It has become increasingly apparent that although environmental policy is benefited by a robust drive for the dissemination of information, environmental policy is also influenced by strategic misinformation and effective use of persuasive communication.
>
> The ELC facilitates dialog among thought leaders on sustainable policy priorities, practical implementation strategies, assessment mechanism, and cooperative analysis of science, economics, and ethics. The core functions served by this group are: (1) collaborative research and analysis of law and policy questions that implicate the integrity of ecosystems; (2) production of literature that reflects the insights from the collaboration and makes laws and policy recommendations that may be targeted to specific entities or for broad-based consideration; and (3) effective dissemination of work product when and where it may produce meaningful and considered action.[1]

Since the ELC's creation, it has engaged in two significant series of collaborations. The first series of collaborations arose out of the ELC's first meeting in July 2012 in Chester, Connecticut. Over three days, the ELC participants discussed the meaning of sustainability in the face of climate change. Participants spurred these discussions by raising issues of significance from a

---

1. Jessica Owley & Keith H. Hirokawa, Rethinking Sustainability to Meet the Climate Change Challenge ix-xi (2015).

number of scholarly and practical perspectives that reflected the broad range of attending scholars' respective interests and expertise. These discussions sparked a series of short essays that the ELC participants published in May 2013 as a collective article on the topic of "Rethinking Sustainability to Meet the Climate Change Challenge" in the *Environmental Law Reporter*.[2] These ELC participants then expanded their essays into full book chapters, publishing them in our 2015 book quoted above.

The second series of collaborations began with the ELC's July 2014 meeting in Jackson, Wyoming. Over three days in residence at the Teton Science School, the 2014 ELC participants—a mix of returning and new scholars—focused on the relationship between law and the Intergovernmental Panel on Climate Change's (IPCC's) most recent set of reports, generally referred to collectively as the Fifth Assessment Report, or AR5. The IPCC's Fifth Assessment is comprised of three substantive publications, the first of which focuses on the physical science basis for climate change[3]; a second report that focuses on adaptation and climate change[4]; and a third report that focuses on mitigation and climate change.[5] In addition, the Fifth Assessment includes a synthesis report that summarizes the three substantive reports.[6] For consistency throughout this volume, we refer to these reports, respectively, as the *2013 IPCC Physical Science Report*; the *2014 IPCC Adaptation Report*; the *2014 IPCC Mitigation Report*; and the *2014 IPCC Synthesis Report*.

At the ELC's second meeting, scholars engaged in considerable debate about the Fifth Assessment. In an effort to memorialize some of that discussion, the participants decided to produce a second collection of short essays in which each author responded to a passage from the Fifth Assessment and used that passage to investigate broader themes regarding the role of law in addressing and responding to climate change. In January 2015, that collection of essays was published in the *Environmental Law Reporter*.[7]

This book's collection of chapters represents the final project of this second collaboration, focused around law and the Fifth Assessment. Some of the contributions to this book remain directly tied to the text of the IPCC's

---

2.   Michael Burger et al., *Rethinking Sustainability to Meet the Climate Change Challenge*, 43 ELR 10342 (Apr. 2013).

3.   Intergovernmental Panel on Climate Change, Climate Change 2013: The Physical Science Basis (2013) [hereinafter 2013 IPCC Physical Science Report].

4.   Intergovernmental Panel on Climate Change, Climate Change 2014: Impacts, Adaptation, and Vulnerability (2014) [hereinafter 2014 IPCC Adaptation Report].

5.   Intergovernmental Panel on Climate Change, Climate Change 2014: Mitigation of Climate Change (2014) [hereinafter 2014 IPCC Mitigation Report].

6.   Intergovernmental Panel on Climate Change, Climate Change 2014: Synthesis Report (2014) [hereinafter 2014 IPCC Synthesis Report].

7.   Sarah J. Adams-Schoen et al., *A Response to the IPCC Fifth Assessment*, 45 ELR 10027 (Jan. 2015).

reports, while others focus on climate change more generally. Viewed as a whole, this book's chapters are illustrative of the overwhelming number of legal issues that climate change creates. Some chapters focus on overarching themes of law and sustainable development in the Fifth Assessment,[8] while many chapters chose to focus on legal- and policy-oriented tools for climate change mitigation and adaptation efforts.[9] Several chapters theorize better approaches to climate change decisionmaking and adaptation,[10] while others focus on how court procedure affects climate change cases[11] as well as the national security implications of climate change.[12]

The third meeting of the ELC is currently planned for summer 2016 in Monterey, California. At that time, the ELC will turn its attention to the issue of "Beyond Zero-Sum Environmentalism," seeking, through both scholarship and a commitment to social change, innovative ways to avoid framing environmental protection, and necessarily incurring negative repercussions in other sectors.

---

8.   *See infra* Chapter 1.
9.   *See infra* Chapters 2-6.
10. *See infra* Chapters 7 and 8.
11. *See infra* Chapter 9.
12. *See infra* Chapter 10.

About the Authors

Robin Kundis Craig is the William H. Leary Professor of Law at the University of Utah S.J. Quinney College of Law. After earning a Ph.D. at U.C. Santa Barbara in English Literature and an independent master's degree from the Johns Hopkins University's Writing Seminars in Writing About Science, Professor Craig attended the Lewis & Clark School of Law in Portland, Oregon, from which she graduated summa cum laude and first in her class. At the University of Utah, Professor Craig is also affiliated with the College of Law's Stegner Center for Land, Resources, and Environment and a faculty affiliate of the University of Utah's Global Change & Sustainability Center. Professor Craig's research focuses on "all things water," especially the impact of climate change on freshwater resources and the oceans, the Clean Water Act, and the intersection of water and energy law. She also has written several articles and book chapters on constitutional environmental law, administrative law, and statutory interpretation. She is the author, co-author, or editor of 10 books and the author or co-author of over 100 law review articles and book chapters.

Stephen R. Miller is Associate Professor of Law at the University of Idaho College of Law. Professor Miller's academic works have been published by or are forthcoming from Cambridge University Press, the *Harvard Environmental Law Review*, the *Harvard Journal on Legislation*, and a number of other law reviews and professional journals. His article, "Legal Neighborhoods," was selected to be reprinted in the *Land Use and Environmental Law Review*, an annual, peer-selected compendium of the 10 best land use and environmental law articles of the year. He is also the director of the College of Law's Economic Development Clinic, through which he is principal investigator on a three-year, $240,000 grant from the U.S. Forest Service and the Idaho Department of Lands to develop legal and code-based strategies to reduce the impact of wildfire on the built environment. Professor Miller received his undergraduate degree from Brown University, an M.A. in City and Regional Planning from the University of California, Berkeley, and his J.D. from the University of California, Hastings College of Law.

***

Sarah J. Adams-Schoen is an Assistant Professor of Law at the Touro College Jacob D. Fuchsberg Law Center, where she also directs the Institute on Land Use & Sustainable Development Law. She teaches courses on environmental law, land use law, property law and related subjects, manages research projects related to land use and sustainability, and is a principal investigator on a New York Sea Grant project involving local law and coastal resilience. Her scholarship currently focuses on state and local law and policy related to climate resilience. After receiving her M.S. in Public Policy with distinction from the London School of Economics, Professor Adams-Schoen worked as a senior policy analyst for Portland, Oregon's Metro Regional Government, where she continued to work while earning her J.D. magna cum laude from Lewis & Clark Law School. After that, she worked in private law practice for nearly a decade handling primarily complex environmental and other regulatory matters. Professor Adams-Schoen is currently the co-editor-in-chief of *Municipal Lawyer*, a publication of the New York State Bar Association, and is Vice Chair of the Land Use Committee of the State and Local Government Law Section of the American Bar Association.

Cinnamon Piñon Carlarne is a Professor of Law at the Ohio State University Moritz College of Law. Prior to joining the Moritz faculty, she was an Assistant Professor of Law at the University of South Carolina School of Law. From 2006-2008, Professor Carlarne was the Harold Woods Research Fellow in Environmental Law at Wadham College, Oxford, where she was a member of the law faculty and the Centre for Socio-Legal Studies. She previously taught at the University of Cincinnati Center for Environmental Studies. Prior to that, she was an associate attorney in the Energy, Land Use, and Environment section at Akin Gump Strauss Hauer & Feld in Washington, D.C. Professor Carlarne's scholarship focuses on the evolution of systems of domestic and international environmental governance and includes a book on comparative climate change law and policy with Oxford University Press; a forthcoming text, the Oxford Handbook of International Climate Change Law; a series of journal articles and book chapters exploring questions of domestic and international environmental law; and a textbook on oceans and human health and human well-being. She is on the editorial board *Transnational Environmental Law* (Cambridge University Press) and she is on the Academic Board for *Climate Law* (IOS Press). Professor Carlarne earned her law degree from the University of California at Berkeley. She also holds a B.C.L. and an M.A. in Environmental Change and Management from the University of Oxford.

John C. Dernbach, a nationally and internationally recognized authority on sustainable development, climate change, and environmental law, is Distinguished Professor of Law at Widener University Commonwealth Law School, and director of its Environmental Law and Sustainability Center. Professor Dernbach writes and lectures widely on sustainable development, climate change, and environmental law. He has written more than 40 articles for law reviews and peer-reviewed journals, and has authored, coauthored, or contributed chapters to 30 books. He leads the only national project that comprehensively assesses U.S. sustainability efforts and makes recommendations for future efforts. As part of that project, he is the principal author of *Acting as if Tomorrow Matters: Accelerating the Transition to Sustainability* (ELI Press 2012) and the editor of *Agenda for a Sustainable America* (ELI Press 2009) and *Stumbling Toward Sustainability* (ELI Press 2002). He also was a member of the National Research Council Committee that, in *Sustainability and the U.S. Environmental Protection Agency* (2011), made recommendations on how to institutionalize sustainability at EPA. Previously, he worked in a variety of positions at the Pennsylvania Department of Environmental Protection, most recently as that agency's policy director.

Keith H. Hirokawa joined the faculty at Albany Law School in 2009. He teaches courses involving environmental and natural resources law, land use planning, property law, and jurisprudence. Professor Hirokawa's scholarship has explored convergences in ecology, ethics, economics, and law, with particular attention given to local environmental law, ecosystem services policy, watershed management, and environmental impact analysis. He has authored dozens of professional and scholarly articles in these areas and has co-edited (with Patricia Salkin) *Greening Local Government* (2012). Prior to joining the faculty at Albany Law, Professor Hirokawa was an Associate Professor at Texas Wesleyan University School of Law and an Adjunct Professor at the University of Oregon School of Law. Professor Hirokawa practiced land use and environmental law in Oregon and Washington and was heavily involved with community groups and nonprofit organizations. Professor Hirokawa studied philosophy and law at the University of Connecticut, where he earned his J.D. and M.A. degrees. He earned his LL.M. in Environmental and Natural Resources Law from Lewis & Clark Law School.

Katrina Fischer Kuh is Professor of Law and Associate Dean for Intellectual Life at the Maurice A. Deane School of Law at Hofstra University. Professor Kuh teaches Environmental Law, Torts, Administrative Law, Global

Change and U.S. Law, and International Environmental Law. Her scholarship, which has been published in journals including the *Duke Law Journal* and *Vanderbilt Law Review*, focuses on climate change, sustainability, and second-generation environmental challenges. Professor Kuh is the co-editor of *The Law of Adaptation to Climate Change: United States and International Aspects*. Prior to joining the Hofstra faculty in 2007, Professor Kuh worked in the Environmental and Litigation practice groups in the New York office of Arnold & Porter LLP and served as an advisor on natural resource policy in the U.S. Senate. She received her law degree from the Yale Law School and served as a law clerk to Judge Charles S. Haight of the District Court for the Southern District of New York and Judge Diana Gribbon Motz of the U.S. Court of Appeals for the Fourth Circuit.

Jessica Owley teaches Environmental Law, Property, and Federal Indian Law. She joined the SUNY Buffalo Law in 2010 after serving as an assistant professor at Pace Law School. She is an expert on land conservation and conservation easements in particular. Her work has been published in the *Ecology Law Quarterly*, *Harvard Environmental Law Review*, *Land Use Policy*, *Stanford Environmental Law Journal*, *Vermont Law Review*, and many other places. Though her general research is on land conservation and property rights, her current scholarship focuses on using property tools for conservation in the context of climate change. Professor Owley is one of the founding members of the Environmental Law Collaborative and co-edited the first book produced by the organization, *Rethinking Sustainability to Meet the Climate Change Challenge*. Before entering academia, Professor Owley practiced in the Land Use and Environment Law group at Morrison & Foerster in San Francisco. Prior to private practice, Professor Owley clerked for Hon. Harry Pregerson of the U.S. Court of Appeals for the Ninth Circuit and Hon. Dean D. Pregerson of the Central District of California. Professor Owley received her undergraduate degree in Physics from Wellesley College and four graduate degrees from the University of California-Berkeley: J.D., Ph.D., and M.S. in Environmental Science, Policy, and Management, and an M.L.A. in Environmental Planning.

Shannon Roesler is Professor of Law at the Oklahoma City University School of Law. Professor Roesler served as a law clerk to the Hon. Deanell Reece Tacha on the U.S. Court of Appeals for the Tenth Circuit. She was also a staff attorney and teaching fellow in the International Women's Human Rights Clinic at Georgetown University Law Center and a visiting faculty member at the University of Kansas School of Law. Professor Roesler received her B.A. and J.D. from the University of Kansas, her M.A. in English Literature from the University of Chicago, her M.A. in Political Science from the University of Wisconsin, and her LL.M. from Georgetown University Law Center. Her current scholarship focuses on the intersection of environmental laws and policies with a range of topics, including distributive justice, information disclosure, multijurisdictional governance, and the federal courts.

Jonathan Rosenbloom is a Professor of Law and Director of Environmental and Sustainability Programming at Drake University Law School, teaching in the areas of environmental law, sustainability, and state and local government. His research focuses on collective action challenges, particularly environmental challenges, facing local governments and has been published in *Hastings Law Journal, Brigham Young University Law Review, Harvard Environmental Law Review* and others. Professor Rosenbloom founded the Drake Fellowship in Sustainability Law for two Drake law students each year. Fully supported by external funds, the fellowship focuses on drafting model local ordinances on issues relevant to sustainability. Professor Rosenbloom received his Bachelors in Architecture from the Rhode Island School of Design, J.D. from New York Law School, and LL.M. from Harvard Law School. Prior to teaching, he worked as an attorney for the federal government, for a nonprofit urban research institute, and for Reed Smith LLP, where he co-managed a real estate division. Immediately prior to entering academia, he founded a nonprofit that worked with state and local governments on becoming more sustainable and clerked for the Hon. Rosemary Barkett on the U.S. Court of Appeals for the Eleventh Circuit. He is a commissioner on the Des Moines Plan and Zoning Commission and serves on a number of state and local environmental boards, including as chair of central Iowa's regional economic development and sustainability committee, representing over 4,700 businesses. He was named Drake Law School 2013 Outstanding Professor of the Year and is currently writing a textbook with Shelley Saxer (Pepperdine), called *Resilience & Sustainability: From Theory to Practice.*

Inara Scott teaches courses on environmental law, social enterprise, and sustainable business at Oregon State University's College of Business. Professor Scott's research at Oregon State centers on clean energy, the electric power system, legal and policy implications of climate change, and sustainability in business. Professor Scott received her J.D., summa cum laude, from Lewis & Clark Law School in Portland, Oregon, and her B.A. from Duke University, summa cum laude. Her work on energy policy, utility regulation reform, and sustainable business practices has been published in the *Harvard Environmental Law Review*, *Environmental Law*, and the *American Business Law Journal*, among others. Prior to teaching, Professor Scott practiced law for over a decade, specializing in utility and administrative law.

David Takacs is a newly tenured professor of law at the University of California, Hastings College of Law. He holds a J.D. from UC Hastings, an LL.M. from the School of Oriental & African Studies at the University of London, and a B.S. (Biology), M.A., and Ph.D. (Science & Technology Studies) from Cornell University. He has been a consultant for international NGOs and U.S. government agencies, analyzing legal and policy issues pertaining to REDD (Reducing Emissions From Deforestation and Forest Degradation) and global climate change. His scholarly work addresses carbon offsetting, biodiversity conservation law, and the human right to water. He is the author of *The Idea of Biodiversity* (Johns Hopkins Univ. Press). Before his legal career, Professor Takacs was a professor in Earth Systems Science & Policy at CSU Monterey Bay, a lecturer in the John S. Knight Writing Program at Cornell, and a Peace Corps Forestry Volunteer in Senegal.

Chapter 1
Climate Change, Sustainable Development, and the IPCC's Fifth Assessment Report

Robin Kundis Craig

What does climate change mean for sustainable development? According to the Intergovernmental Panel on Climate Change (IPCC) in its Fifth Assessment Report (AR5),[1] climate change threatens sustainable development goals. The AR5 represents a first strong international consensus caution that failure to address climate change may well undermine the pursuit of sustainable development. As such, the AR5 subtly underscores the critical importance of a functional environment and ecological systems to human thriving—and perhaps even to human survival—a reality that sustainable development in practice often ignores.

I. Three Models of Sustainable Development and the Role of the Environment

Sustainable development emerged at about the same time as scientists were becoming convinced that climate change was occurring and that humans had something to do with it. While the International Union for the Conservation of Nature (IUCN) dates the concept of sustainable development to its 1969 mandate and the 1972 United Nations Conference on the Human

---

1. As used in this volume, the "Fifth Assessment Report" and "AR5" refer collectively to the four reports that the IPCC published in 2013 and 2014: INTERGOVERNMENTAL PANEL ON CLIMATE CHANGE, CLIMATE CHANGE 2013: THE PHYSICAL SCIENCE BASIS (2013), *available at* https://www.ipcc.ch/report/ar5/wg1/ [hereinafter 2013 IPCC PHYSICAL SCIENCE REPORT]; INTERGOVERNMENTAL PANEL ON CLIMATE CHANGE, CLIMATE CHANGE 2014: IMPACTS, ADAPTATION, AND VULNERABILITY (2014), *available at* https://www.ipcc.ch/report/ar5/wg2/ [hereinafter 2014 IPCC ADAPTATION REPORT]; INTERGOVERNMENTAL PANEL ON CLIMATE CHANGE, CLIMATE CHANGE 2014: MITIGATION OF CLIMATE CHANGE (2014), *available at* https://www.ipcc.ch/report/ar5/wg3/ [hereinafter 2014 IPCC MITIGATION REPORT]; and INTERGOVERNMENTAL PANEL ON CLIMATE CHANGE, CLIMATE CHANGE 2014: SYNTHESIS REPORT (2014), *available at* https://www.ipcc.ch/report/ar5/syr/ [hereinafter 2014 IPCC SYNTHESIS REPORT].

Environment (Stockholm),[2] the World Commission on Environment and Development's (also known as the Brundtland Commission's) 1987 report, *Our Common Future*, is generally credited with launching sustainable development as an international governance goal.[3] Indeed, that report provided the most common definition of sustainable development: "Development that meets the needs of the present without compromising the ability of future generations to meet their own needs."[4] Sustainable development goals were further operationalized in 1992 at the "Earth Summit" in Rio de Janeiro, Brazil, particularly in Agenda 21.[5] Sustainable development also became one of the United Nations' eight Millennium Development Goals in 2000.[6]

Sustainable development has been defined and redefined a number of times in a number of ways.[7] Literally, as sustainable development textbook author Jennifer Elliott has noted, "sustainable development refers to maintaining development over time."[8] More importantly, pursuers of sustainable development make different assumptions about the relationship between human beings and the environment.[9] Such differing assumptions are evident in the three models of sustainable development—the "three pillars" model, the "interlocking circles" model, and the "nested circles" model—all three of which describe the relationships among society and social welfare, the environment, and economic development.[10]

The three pillars model (Figure 1) "confirm[s] the need to consider the social, ecological and economic arenas together and equally" to achieve sustainable development, but it does not clearly depict the interconnections among the three pillars.[11] In particular, the three pillars model does not acknowledge that economic development and social well-being, as well as sustainable development, depend upon well-functioning ecosystems that can continue to deliver goods and services. In other words, the three pillars

---

2.   W.M. Adams, IUCN, The World Conservation Union, The Future of Sustainability: Re-Thinking Environment and Development in the Twenty-first Century 1 (May 2006), *available at* http://cmsdata.iucn.org/downloads/iucn_future_of_sustanability.pdf.
3.   Jennifer A. Elliott, An Introduction to Sustainable Development 8 (4th ed. 2013); *see also* Adams, *supra* note 2, at 1 (also noting the Brundtland Commission and the Earth Summit).
4.   U.N. World Commission on Environment and Development, *Our Common Future*, U.N. Doc. A/42/427, Annex (1987), *available at* http://www.un-documents.net/our-common-future.pdf.
5.   Elliott, *supra* note 3, at 9.
6.   *Id.* at 10, 12-14 tbl. 1.2.
7.   *Id.* at 16. Even the IUCN has admitted that the Brundtland Commission's definition was "vague" and that "the definition of sustainable development evolved" over time. Adams, *supra* note 2, at 1-2.
8.   Elliott, *supra* note 3, at 16.
9.   *Id.* at 18 (quoting K. Lee et al. eds., Global Sustainable Development in the Twenty-First Century 9 (2000)).
10.   *See* Adams, *supra* note 2, at 2 fig. 1 (presenting the three models).
11.   *Id.* at 20-21.

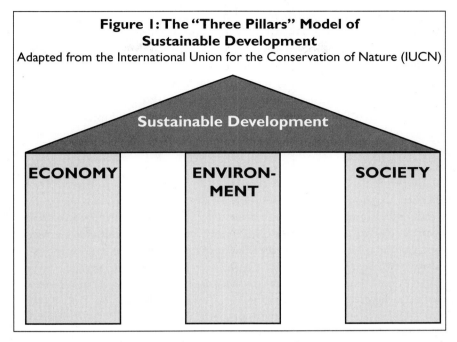

Figure 1: The "Three Pillars" Model of Sustainable Development
Adapted from the International Union for the Conservation of Nature (IUCN)

Sustainable Development

ECONOMY   ENVIRON-   SOCIETY
               MENT

model suggests that social and economic systems (or socioeconomic systems) can exist and function independently of the environment, when in fact all social and economic systems are socio-ecological systems.

This conceptual view of the social and economic pillars as independent helps to explain the difference between "weak" and "strong" sustainability. "Weak" interpretations of sustainable development view human and physical capital as adequate substitutes for natural capital in the environment in terms of "the total capital stock passed onto the next generation. . . ."[12] In this view, for example, an increase in roads might be deemed an adequate substitute for loss of wetlands in terms of resources left to the next generation.[13] Weak sustainability perspectives thus underplay the ultimate dependence of all human societies and economies on functional ecosystems. In contrast, "[s]trong sustainability demands the protection of critical natural capital because once lost, these assets are lost forever, and they cannot be recreated."[14] "Critical natural capital" are the natural resources "required for survival," including

12.   *Id.* at 23 Box 1.1.
13.   *Id.*
14.   *Id.*

both functional resources such as the ozone layer and valued resources such as rare species or species helpful to medical care.[15]

Unlike the three pillars model, the interlocking circles model of sustainable development (Figure 2) more clearly communicates "the need to integrate thinking and action in sustainable development across traditional disciplinary boundaries and established policy-making departments. . . ."[16] Indeed, the IUCN, in its Programme for 2005-2008, adopted "the interlocking circles model to demonstrate that the three objectives need to be better integrated, with action to redress the balance between dimensions of sustainability. . . ."[17] The middle area of overlap represents the area in which the goals of all three spheres are all maximized—i.e., "the possibility of mutually supportive ('win-win-win') gains" in all three areas (economic, social, and environmental) simultaneously.[18] Moreover, "[t]he small area of overlap relative to the whole sphere portrays the unsustainable nature of much activity, but also opens the idea of the potential to expand this area of positive overlap."[19]

An important but often overlooked aspect of the overlapping spheres model is the concept of trade offs. Specifically, the small area in the center representing true sustainable development is the product of trade offs among the three areas. As such,

> this model supports understandings that achieving sustainable development in practice regularly involves trade-offs across the different spheres; that difficult choices have to be made at particular points in time and at particular scales as to what is being pursued and how; that certain goals can be compromised in the achievement of others; and that any action will carry unequal impacts for particular interests and for groups of people.[20]

The interlocking circles model thus also supports the idea that sustainable development requires systems thinking[21]—that is, an approach that acknowledges that society, economic development, and the environment exist as complex interactions rather than isolated arenas. The IUCN, for example, has identified "two fundamental issues" for sustainable development, "the problem of environmental degradation that so commonly accompanies economic growth, and yet the need for such growth to alleviate poverty."[22]

---

15. *Id.*
16. *Id.* at 21.
17. ADAMS, *supra* note 2, at 2.
18. ELLIOTT, *supra* note 3, at 21.
19. *Id.*
20. *Id.*
21. *Id.*
22. ADAMS, *supra* note 2, at 2.

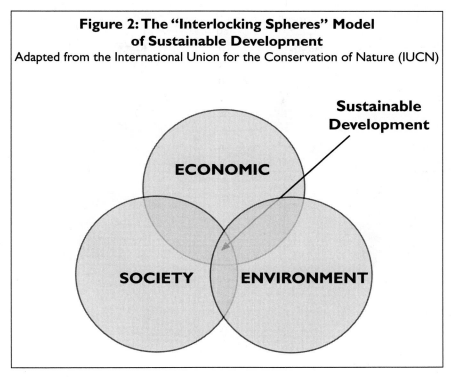

**Figure 2: The "Interlocking Spheres" Model
of Sustainable Development**
Adapted from the International Union for the Conservation of Nature (IUCN)

However, like the three pillars model, the interlocking circles model treats the three areas of focus as equal and somewhat commensurable—i.e., it suggests no limits on humans' ability to trade improvements in one sphere (say, economic development) for degradations in another (say, the environment). As such, the interlocking spheres model, like the three pillars model, can support a weak sustainability approach that undermines the environmental "bottom line" of human existence.

Environmental limits do emerge, however, in the third model of sustainable development, the nested circles model (Figure 3). In this model, "the spheres of economy and society are shown as embedded in a wider circle of ecology," portraying "an understanding of environmental limits setting boundaries within which a sustainable society and economy must be sought."[23] Furthermore, this model acknowledges that "activities that damage the functioning of natural systems ultimately weaken the basis of human existence itself."[24] Thus, this model underscores that the societal and eco-

---

23. *Id.*
24. *Id.*

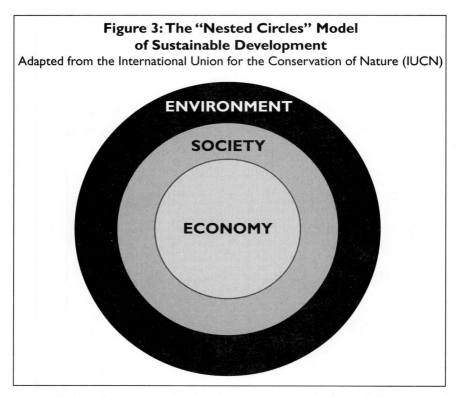

**Figure 3: The "Nested Circles" Model
of Sustainable Development**
Adapted from the International Union for the Conservation of Nature (IUCN)

ENVIRONMENT

SOCIETY

ECONOMY

nomic goals within sustainable development ultimately depend on a rich and well-functioning environment that supplies at the very least critical natural capital and preferably more extensive ecosystem goods and services.

II.   Sustainable Development and the Anthropocene

Humans are pervasively altering planetary ecological function. While these alterations derive from many causes—consumption of natural resources, pollution and waste disposal, and a growing human population—climate change is among the most recently acknowledged, most pervasive, and most complex of these human drivers. Indeed, human influence on world ecological processes and the resulting rapid increase of species extinctions may prompt the International Union of Geological Sciences—the international scientific organization that is in charge of officially designating and naming geological time periods—to recognize our current interval as a new epoch, the Anthropocene ('the new age of humans").[25]

In a world increasingly dominated by anthropogenic change, concern about the implications of climate change, in particular its implications for sustainable development, are mounting. Notably, in 2006, the IUCN acknowledged that "the evidence is that the global human enterprise is rapidly becoming less sustainable and not more."[26] It recognized several problems with sustainable development as currently being implemented. First, an ambiguous definition of "sustainable development" allows governments to pursue what are effectively very different overall goals:

> Environmentalists, governments, economic and political planners and business people use "sustainability" or "sustainable development" to express sometimes very diverse visions of how economy and environment should be managed. The Brundtland definition was neat but inexact. The concept is holistic, attractive, elastic but imprecise. The idea of sustainable development may bring people together but it does not necessarily help them to agree on goals. In implying everything sustainable development arguably ends up meaning nothing.[27]

Second, failure to privilege environmental protection effectively perpetuates the degradation of the ecological in pursuit of economic growth and development.[28] Instead, the IUCN emphasized:

> The three "pillars" cannot be treated as if equivalent. First, the economy is an institution that emerges from society: these are in many ways the same, the one a mechanism or set of rules created by society to mediate the exchange of economic goods or value. The environment is different, since it is not created by society. Thinking about trade-offs rarely acknowledges this. Second, the environment underpins both society and economy. The resources available on earth and the solar system effectively present a finite limit on human activity. Effective limits are often much more specific and framing, in that the capacity of the biosphere to absorb pollutants, provide resources and services is clearly limited in space and time. In many areas (e.g. warm shallow coastal waters adjacent to industrialised regions) that capacity is close to its limits.[29]

---

25. Joseph Stromberg, *What Is the Anthropocene and Are We in It?*, Smithsonian Mag., Jan. 2013, *at* http://www.smithsonianmag.com/science-nature/what-is-the-anthropocene-and-are-we-in-it-164801414/?no-ist; Subcommission on Quaternary Stratigraphy, International Union of Geological Sciences, *Working Group on the "Anthropocene,"* http://quaternary.stratigraphy.org/workinggroups/anthropocene/ (last visited June 17, 2015).
26. Adams, *supra* note 2, at 3.
27. *Id.*
28. *Id.* at 3-4.
29. *Id.* at 4.

A globalized economy based on consumerism adds to the problem, because it separates consumers from the environmental impacts of production.[30] As a result, the human footprint on the world, in terms of consumption, degradation, and waste, is large and extremely damaging, raising concerns that we may be exceeding the planet's capacity to adapt to human activity.[31]

This is the critical question for the Anthropocene: Is long-term sustainable development still even possible, or are humans driving ecological systems across thresholds from which they might never return, endangering the survival of all in the process? As the IUCN noted in 2006:

> The velocity of environmental change is fast, and increasing. As Peter Vitousek and colleagues comment, tellingly, 'we are changing the earth more rapidly than we are understanding it'. Rates of human transformation of the earth are increasing, particularly in countries undergoing rapid industrialization or de-industrialisation. The human capacity to destroy life-support systems (ecosystem services) is new. Humanity is burning through natural assets and their capacity to support life and quality of human life without thought to the future and the rights and needs of today's people.[32]

Undermining sustainable development even further is the increasing reality that humans can no longer depend on past environmental conditions—or hope to restore those conditions[33]—because of climate change.[34] Climate change results from the cumulative emissions of greenhouse gases from numerous human activities, and it is altering—in some cases transforming—ecological and socio-ecological systems. As ecosystems enter this new era of continual, complex, unprecedented, and often unpredictable change, it is worth asking what climate change might therefore mean for the sustainable development goals that policymakers are increasingly incorporating into the world's governance systems. Indeed, even the notably conservative IPCC is becoming increasingly alarmed about the future of sustainable development—and the increase is quite notable in comparing its 2007 Fourth Assessment Report to its 2014 Fifth Assessment Report.

---

30. *Id.* at 8 (citing J.L. Newton & Eric T. Freyfogle, *Sustainability: A Dissent*, 19 CONSERVATION BIOLOGY 23-32 (2004)).
31. *Id.* at 4-5, 6 Box 1.
32. *Id.* at 7 (quoting Peter M. Vitousek et al., *Human Domination of Earth's Ecosystems*, 277 SCIENCE 494, 494-99 (July 25, 1997)).
33. *See id.* at 9:
      Developments in ecological restoration offer novel and inspiriting opportunities to enhance and reinstate biodiversity and ecosystem services, yet human skills in ecosystem assembly remain limited. For this reason, any argument for a strategy of "develop now and restore damaged ecosystems later," based on extrapolation of the logic of the "environmental Kutznets curve" is fundamentally flawed. "Critical natural capital" cannot be replaced within realistic timeframes.
34. *Id.*

III.   The IPCC, Sustainable Development, and Climate Change: The Fourth Assessment Report (2007)

In 2007, in its Fourth Assessment Report, the IPCC and its Working Groups were mildly concerned, but not particularly worried, about the future of sustainable development. Instead, the IPCC emphasized that climate change mitigation and adaptation are consistent with sustainable development goals. Thus, for example, "[t]here is growing understanding of the possibilities to choose and implement climate response options in several sectors to realise synergies and avoid conflicts with other dimensions of sustainable development."[35] The IPCC also highlighted several specific synergies between climate change and sustainable development goals: government taxes, subsidies, fiscal policies, and regulatory regimes to encourage sustainable development could potential reduce global greenhouse gas emissions; forest conservation and sustainable management practices could decrease greenhouse gas emissions from deforestation; renewable energy requirements and increased efficiencies in electricity transmission and distribution could reduce carbon dioxide emissions from the electric power sector; and insurance benefits for green building and green transportation could reduce those sectors' greenhouse gas emissions.[36]

Over the longer term, however, the Fourth Assessment Report did illuminate the need for integrated adaptive management—that is, that "[r]esponding to climate change involves an iterative risk management process that includes both mitigation and adaptation, taking into account actual and avoided climate change damages, co-benefits, sustainability, equity and attitudes to risk."[37] In particular, it emphasized risks to unique and threatened systems, such as coral reefs; risks of extreme weather events; distribution of impacts and vulnerabilities, emphasizing the precarious position of many of the world's most impoverished nations; aggregate impacts, especially at higher temperatures; and the risks of large-scale singularities, such as cessation of ocean currents or the collapse of the Greenland or Antarctic ice sheets.[38] It also emphasized the critical role of climate change mitigation, because "[u]nmitigated climate change would, in the long term, be *likely* to exceed the capacity of natural, managed and human systems to adapt. Reliance on adaptation alone could eventually lead to a magnitude of climate

35.   INTERGOVERNMENTAL PANEL ON CLIMATE CHANGE: CLIMATE CHANGE 2007: SYNTHESIS REPORT 61 (2007) [hereinafter 2007 IPCC SYNTHESIS REPORT].
36.   *Id.* at 62 tbl. 4-3.
37.   *Id.* at 64.
38.   *Id.* at 64-65.

change to which effective adaptation is not possible, or will only be available at very high social, environmental and economic costs."[39]

In the long run, moreover, unmitigated climate change could impede sustainable development—although sustainable development could also reduce societies' vulnerability to climate change.[40] Specifically, "[i]t is *very likely* that climate change can slow the pace of progress toward sustainable development either directly through increased exposure to adverse impacts or indirectly through erosion of the capacity to adapt. Over the next half-century, climate change could impede achievement of the Millennium Development Goals."[41] Conversely, "[b]oth adaptive and mitigative capacities can be enhanced through sustainable development. Sustainable development can, thereby, reduce vulnerability to climate change by reducing sensitivities (through adaptation) and/or exposure (through mitigation)."[42]

The Working Group II report, *Climate Change 2007: Impacts, Adaptation, and Vulnerability,*[43] dug more deeply into sustainability in Chapter 20 but did not offer a fundamentally different picture of the relationship between climate change and sustainable development. For example, the Working Group concluded that:

> Efforts to cope with the impacts of climate change and attempts to promote sustainable development share common goals and determinants including access to resources (including information and technology), equity in the distribution of resources, stocks of human and social capital, access to risk-sharing mechanisms and abilities of decision-support mechanisms to cope with uncertainty . . . (very high confidence). Nonetheless, some development activities exacerbate climate-related vulnerabilities . . . (very high confidence).[44]

Moreover, a nation's capacity to pursue sustainable development largely paralleled its capacity to adapt to climate change, with the Working Group underscoring "the fundamental observation that the factors that determine a country's ability to promote (sustainable) development coincide with the factors that influence adaptive capacity relative to climate change, climate variability and climatic extremes."[45] Indeed, the Working Group also emphasized

39.   *Id.* at 65.
40.   *Id.* at 70 ("Sustainable development can reduce vulnerability to climate change, and climate change could impede nations' abilities to achieve sustainable development pathways.").
41.   *Id.*
42.   *Id.*
43.   Intergovernmental Panel on Climate Change, Climate Change 2007: Impacts, Adaptation, and Vulnerability (2007), *available at* http://www.ipcc.ch/publications_and_data/publications_ipcc_fourth_assessment_report_wg2_report_impacts_adaptation_and_vulnerability.htm [hereinafter 2007 IPCC Adaptation Report].
44.   *Id.* at 813.
45.   *Id.* at 816.

the "two-way causality" between climate change adaptation and sustainable development and the fact that the two goals could reinforce each other.[46] Nevertheless, "[d]espite these synergies, few discussions about promoting sustainability have thus far explicitly included adapting to climate impacts, reducing hazard risks and/or promoting adaptive capacity."[47] As such, a key problem in 2007 was incorporating climate change responses into sustainable development actions—not the effects of climate change per se.[48]

Viewed in the longer term, however, climate change could become an increasing problem for sustainable development goals. In the near term, "[i]t is very likely that climate change . . . will not be a significant extra impediment to nations reaching their 2015 Millennium Development Targets since many other obstacles with more immediate impacts stand in the way."[49] However, "[o]ver the next half-century, it is very likely that climate change will make it more difficult for nations to achieve the Millennium Development Goals for the middle of the century."[50] Moreover, "by 2100, climate change will likely produce significant impacts across the globe, even if aggressive mitigation were implemented in combination with significantly enhanced adaptive capacity."[51] Nevertheless, Working Group II most clearly advocated a risk management approach to the problem, concluding that "[v]iewing the climate problem from a risk perspective can offer climate policy deliberations and negotiations new insight into the synergies by which governments can promote sustainable development, reduce the risk of climate-related damages and take advantage of climate-related opportunities."[52]

Working Group III, in its report entitled *Climate Change 2007: Mitigation of Climate Change*,[53] also discussed the relationship between climate change and sustainable development. Like Working Group II, it noted "the two-way relationship between climate change mitigation and sustainable development. . . . Development that is sustainable in many other respects can create conditions in which mitigation can be effectively pursued (development first) (*high agreement, much evidence*)."[54] Working Group III reviewed case stud-

---

46. *Id.* at 817-19.
47. *Id.* at 813.
48. *See id.* at 835-36 (discussing ways to integrate the two).
49. *Id.* at 813.
50. *Id.*
51. *Id.*
52. *Id.* at 837.
53. Intergovernmental Panel on Climate Change, Climate Change 2007: Mitigation of Climate Change (2007), *available at* http://www.ipcc.ch/publications_and_data/publications_ipcc_fourth_assessment_report_wg3_report_mitigation_of_climate_change.htm [hereinafter 2007 IPCC Mitigation Report].
54. *Id.* at 693; *see also id.* at 695-96 (discussing this relationship).

ies showing how development choice could reduce greenhouse gas emissions and emphasized that:

> There is a growing understanding of the possibilities to choose mitigation options and their implementation such that there is no conflict with other dimensions of sustainable development; or, where trade-offs are inevitable, to allow a rational choice to be made. The sustainable development benefits of mitigation options vary within a sector and over regions (*high agreement, much evidence*). . . .[55]

Moreover, Working Group III also suggested that nations retain considerable flexibility in their approaches to sustainable development even in a climate change era, noting that "[m]aking development more sustainable recognizes that there are many ways in which societies balance the economic, social, and environmental, including climate change, dimensions of sustainable development."[56] While Working Group III recognized that certain choices for mitigating climate change can undermine other sustainable development goals, such as economic development in particular sectors like coal,[57] the clear implication was that climate change, and the environment more generally, can be balanced against these other societal and sustainable development goals.

Nevertheless, like Working Group II, Working Group III emphasized that climate change needed to be part of the sustainable development discussion. For example, one pervasive problem in development is that "[d]ecisions about the development of the most significant sectors that shape emission profiles—energy, industry, transportation and land use—are made by ministries and companies that do not regularly attend to climate risks."[58] Indeed, incorporating climate change considerations into development policy is critical because "[c]limate policy alone will not solve the climate problem. Making development more sustainable by changing development paths can make a major contribution to climate goals."[59] Working Group III recommended mainstreaming climate change considerations into development policies and noted the possible benefits of mitigation strategies for sustainable development: "Generally, mitigation options that improve productivity of resource use, whether it is energy, water, or land, yield positive benefits across all three dimensions of sustainable development."[60] Overall,

---

55. *Id.* at 694.
56. *Id.* at 695.
57. *Id.* at 726 (citation omitted).
58. *Id.* at 700.
59. *Id.*
60. *Id.* at 726.

Working Group III concluded that "development-oriented scenarios could be enriched by taking global climate change explicitly into account,"[61] that "the capacity to mitigate is rooted in development paths,"[62] and that "[u]nderstanding of the sustainable development implications in each of many sectors is growing, but further analysis will be needed for key sectors and where least information is available."[63]

IV.   The IPCC, Sustainable Development, and Climate Change: The Fifth Assessment Report (2014)

The IPCC was notably more concerned about the future of sustainable development in the Anthropocene in its 2014 AR5, although it still avoids alarmist rhetoric, especially in the Summaries for Policymakers. For example, the Summary for Policymakers in the Synthesis Report[64] warns that:

> Continued emission of greenhouse gases will cause further warming and long-lasting changes in all components of the climate system, increasing the likelihood of severe, pervasive and irreversible impacts for people and ecosystems. Limiting climate change would require substantial and sustained reductions in greenhouse gas emissions which, together with adaptation, can limit climate change risks.[65]

Moreover, "[c]limate change will amplify existing risks and create new risks for natural and human systems. Risks are unevenly distributed and are generally greater for disadvantaged people and communities in countries at all levels of development."[66] These risks, moreover, are long-term: "Many aspects of climate change and associated impacts will continue for centuries, even if anthropogenic emissions of greenhouse gases are stopped. The risks of abrupt or irreversible changes increase as the magnitude of the warming increases."[67]

In its more specific discussion of sustainable development, the AR5 downplayed the two-way relationship between climate change policies and sustainable development to emphasize instead how necessary climate policies are for sustainable development to occur. In broadest strokes:

> Adaptation and mitigation are complementary strategies for reducing and managing the risks of climate change. Substantial emissions reductions over

---

61. *Id.* at 733.
62. *Id.*
63. *Id.* at 734.
64. 2014 IPCC Synthesis Report, *supra* note 1, at 1-32.
65. *Id.* at 8.
66. *Id.* at 13.
67. *Id.* at 16.

the next few decades can reduce climate risks in the 21st century and beyond, increase prospects for effective adaptation, reduce the costs and challenges of mitigation in the longer term and contribute to climate-resilient pathways for sustainable development.[68]

More specifically, "Limiting the effects of climate change is necessary to achieve sustainable development and equity, including poverty eradication."[69] However, adaptation policies are limited in their effectiveness, and "[t]aking a longer-term perspective, in the context of sustainable development, increases the likelihood that more immediate adaptation actions will also enhance future options and preparedness."[70]

Nevertheless, the last highlighted message that the Summary for Policymakers conveys is that "[c]limate change is a threat to sustainable development."[71] While "[s]trategies and actions can be pursued now which will move towards climate-resilient pathways for sustainable development [and] at the same time helping to improve livelihoods, social and economic well-being and effective environmental management," "[d]elaying global mitigation actions may reduce options for climate-resilient pathways and adaptation in the future. Opportunities to take advantage of positive synergies between adaptation and mitigation may decrease with time, particularly if limits to adaptation are exceeded."[72] For the IPCC, this is a fairly serious call to action.

Climate change, the IPCC emphasizes repeatedly in the AR5, threatens humanity's future choices. In addition to the discussion quoted above, Working Group II in its report, *Climate Change 2014: Impacts, Adaptation, and Vulnerability*, stresses that:

> **Prospects for climate-resilience pathways for sustainable development are related fundamentally to what the world accomplishes with climate change mitigation (*high confidence*).** Since mitigation reduces the rate as well as the magnitude of warming, it also increases the time available for adaptation to a particular level of climate change, potentially by several decades. Delaying mitigation may reduce options for climate-resilient pathways in the future.[73]

On first read, this is a fairly obvious statement: Getting serious about climate change mitigation now will reduce humanity's need to adapt to cli-

68. *Id.* at 17.
69. *Id.*
70. *Id.* at 19.
71. *Id.* at 31.
72. *Id.*
73. 2014 IPCC ADAPTATION REPORT, *supra* note 1, at 28.

mate change in the future and give us more time to adapt overall. However, as in the final Summary for Policymakers, the last sentence also suggests that delayed mitigation efforts may also reduce humanity's future options— including options for *any* development, let alone sustainable development.

This suggestion begins to align the IPCC with the IUCN, which acknowledged in 2006 that "[t]he uncomfortable bottom line of sustainability is the insight that the biosphere is limited."[74] Especially in an era of climate change,

> The earth's capacity to yield products for human consumption, to absorb or sequestrate human wastes (especially novel compounds), and to yield ecosystem services are all of them limited. The idea that that there is always somewhere to absorb externalities is flawed, and it is a myth of progress that living systems will always recover from human demands.[75]

If, as many scientists and the IUCN suspect, we are approaching (or passing) a suite of ecological limits, humans' options for future development are narrowing, or perhaps disappearing altogether.

As the IPCC emphasizes, moreover, the potential loss of future options poses risks to societies and socio-ecological systems that should already be modifying how we think about development goals, even sustainable development goals. All human societies ultimately depend on ecosystems and the goods and services that those ecosystems provide, but climate change directly threatens the current states of most of the world's ecosystems. Change an ecosystem too much in a bad way, and you retard the economic and social development (and ultimately survival) of the societies that depend on that ecosystem.

The climate change extremes of this new reality, such as the predicted disappearance of island nations as a result of sea-level rise,[76] have been well-publicized but not yet incorporated into global development goals. In part, these kinds of extreme, existential, threats to island (and Arctic) cultures and nations may not seem generalizable; indeed, they are currently generally portrayed as tragic but somewhat unusual climate change fates for particular kinds of human societies, with the implication that the rest of us will still be able to muddle along in our pursuit of continuous development.

Ecological dependence, however, is more insidious than that. In particular, there are a suite of ecological changes that can thoroughly undermine development goals in a particular society *without* completely wiping it out.

---

74.   ADAMS, *supra* note 2, at 11.
75.   *Id.*
76.   *E.g., Climate Change: The "Greatest Threat" to the Peoples of the Pacific,* DW.COM., July 30, 2014, http://www.dw.com/en/climate-change-the-greatest-threat-to-the-peoples-of-the-pacific/a-17822235.

The *BBC News* recently published a particularly poignant example of the human tragedies that can result from ecosystem decline, tracing how the loss of terrestrial food species and especially freshwater and offshore fisheries has led to increased slavery—especially child slavery—in Somalia, Burma, Cambodia, and Thailand.[77] Fewer fisheries and other food species make it highly labor-intensive to get food, promoting the enslavement of children and others to carry out this task.[78] At some point, in other words, a society's dependence on a failing or radically changing ecosystem drastically retards, even reverses, economic and social development. Climate change is making it all the more likely that a variety of ecosystems will experience such changes, or crash completely.

Moving past the Summary for Policymakers into Chapter 20 of Working Group II's 2014 report, the IPCC now concludes that "[c]limate change poses a moderate threat to current sustainable development and a severe threat to future sustainable development."[79] Thus, although the IPCC still hews to sustainable development as a global goal, it acknowledges that climate change could substantially vitiate that goal. As it notes in its classically reserved tone, "[a]dded to other stresses such as poverty, inequality, or diseases, the effects of climate change will make sustainable development objectives such as food and livelihood security, poverty reduction, health, and access to clean water more difficult to achieve for many locations, systems, and affected populations."[80]

For societies that lose their homelands, food supply, or water supply, this statement does not go nearly far enough. Sustainable development goals—indeed, *any* development goals—presume that the relevant society will continue to have the basic ecological requisites for development—a place to inhabit, a source or sources of food, water that is or can be made potable. Climate change calls those assumptions into question and limits the future development options for current societies—particularly in conjunction with an ever-rising global human population.

Nor is the potential loss of development options, or developmental retardation, limited to developing nations. Europe's remaining ecosystems cannot support the human population of that continent at their current levels of affluence. Indeed, in 2005, the World Wildlife Fund estimated that Europe's consumption footprint more than doubles its own biological productive

---

77.   Matt McGrath, *Global Decline of Wildlife Linked to Child Slavery*, BBC NEWS SCI. &. ENV'T, July 24, 2014, http://www.bbc.com/news/science-environment-28463036.
78.   *Id.*
79.   2014 IPCC ADAPTATION REPORT, *supra* note 1, at 1104.
80.   *Id.*

capacity, and hence "Europe's well being depends on ecological capacity from elsewhere."[81] The United States' ecological footprint is even greater. While consumption patterns in Europe and the United States raise valid climate change issues in their own right, the point here is much more limited: We cannot assess the United States' and European Union's climate change vulnerability *or* development futures by looking only at those nations' capacity to respond to the climate change impacts within their borders. These two sets of societies are intimately dependent on the health of ecosystems elsewhere, and climate change impacts on *those* ecosystems potentially limit the United States' and E.U.'s future options as much as they limit the options of much more physically proximate societies.

The IPCC, however, is just beginning to wrestle with what climate change could truly mean for future human development, sustainable or otherwise. Notably, reduced and changing resources alter not only a particular society's development options but also its adaptive capacity, potentially creating a vicious cycle of ever-diminishing resilience and ability to cope with climate change, let alone achieve economic or social progress. Clearly, as the IPCC does emphasize, a strong, immediate, and effective climate change mitigation strategy is our first-best approach to preserving as many options as possible for the future.

V.   Incorporating Resilience and Transformation

One does not have to read anything into the IPCC's AR5 to conclude that humanity needs to start to reconsider what "development goals" can look like in an option-constrained—and in many places under many scenarios, *severely* option-limited—future. As Working Group II stated in its 2014 report, "[c]limate change calls for new approaches to sustainable development that take into account complex interactions between climate and social and ecological systems."[82]

The IUCN has recommended a greater incorporation of resilience thinking, noting that "[t]he capacity of nature to meet human needs depends on both its internal dynamics and its dynamic responses to human stresses. The resilience of the biosphere is critical to the sustainability of human enterprise on earth."[83] It also emphasizes that "[t]he solution to unsustainable planetary

81. World Wildlife Fund, Europe 2005: The Ecological Footprint 3 (June 2005), *available at* http://www2.wwf.fi/wwf/www/uploads/pdf/ekologinen_jalanjalki_june05.pdf.
82. 2014 IPCC Adaptation Report, *supra* note 1, at 1104.
83. Adams, *supra* note 2, at 12. The IUCN also emphasized the ecological perspective on resilience, which acknowledges that irreversible transformations of ecological systems are part of the resilience response:

management demands a move beyond both 'business as usual' and 'politics as usual'. There is nothing usual about the situation humankind is in: nobody has ever been here before."[84]

The IPCC similarly has increased its reliance on resilience as a response to climate change. Specifically, in its AR5 it promoted what it calls "climate-resilient pathways."[85] "Climate-resilient pathways are development trajectories that combine adaptation and mitigation to realize the goal of sustainable development. They can be seen as iterative, continually evolving processes for managing change within complex systems."[86] As the IPCC envisions the future:

> Prospects for climate-resilient pathways are related fundamentally to what the world accomplishes with climate change mitigation, but both mitigation and adaptation are essential for climate change risk management at all scales (high confidence; medium evidence, high agreement). As the magnitude of climate change increases and the consequences become increasingly significant to many areas, systems, and populations, the challenges to sustainable development increase. Beyond some magnitudes and rates of climate change, the impacts on most systems would be great enough that sustainable development may no longer be possible for many systems and locations. At the local scale, governments, businesses, communities, and individuals in many developing regions have limited capacities to mitigate climate change because they contribute very little to global emissions. They may also have relatively limited capacities to adapt for reasons of income, education, health, security, political power, or access to technology. At all scales, however, mitigation and adaptation actions are fundamental for effective implementation of climate risk management and reduction.[87]

Significantly, however, transformations are also likely to be part of our future. As Working Group II summarized,

To promote sustainable development within the context of climate change, climate-resilient pathways may involve significant transformations (*high confidence; medium evidence, high agreement*). Transformations in

---

Non-linear dynamics are accepted as an inherent element in ecosystem function. Polluted lakes do not necessarily return to their former state when pollution stops; climate can not be expected to vary around some mean approximating to the conditions of the last 30 years; it is highly likely that extinction of certain species will change the amplitude and frequency of ecosystem change in ways that constrain human opportunities; novel compounds and broad-taxon genetic manipulation may well generate shifts in ecosystem form and function.
    Id.
84. *Id.* at 14.
85. *Id.* at 1104–05.
86. *Id.* at 1104.
87. *Id.* at 1104–05.

economic, social, technological, and political decisions and actions can enable climate-resilient pathways. Although transformations may be reactive, forced, or induced by random factors, they may also be deliberately created through social and political processes.[88]

The IPCC is, essentially, looking for a sea change in nations' approaches both to climate change and to sustainable development, emphasizing that "[r]estricting adaptation responses to incremental changes to existing systems and structures without considering transformational change may increase costs and losses and miss opportunities."[89] The question, however, will be whether humans can successfully transform themselves before anthropogenic climate change too thoroughly transforms the environment upon which development depends.

VI. Conclusion

The IPCC, in its 2014 AR5, joins the IUCN in concluding that: (1) climate change represents a significant threat to sustainable development, particularly from 2050 onwards; and (2) nations and the international community need to transform their current plodding approaches to sustainable development to embrace more climate-resilient pathways. Such worldwide transformation is an ambitious goal, but it does reflect the reality that the environment is the ultimate limit to human development and that climate change is almost certainly shrinking our ecological boundaries. Whether we can both slow that shrinking and live comfortably and equitably within our ecological limits will remain the great question for the 21st century, but current trajectories suggest that sustainable development—and maybe *any* development—will rapidly become an impossible dream.

---

88. *Id.* at 1105.
89. 2014 IPCC Synthesis Report, *supra* note 1, at 80.

Chapter 2
Creating Legal Pathways to a Zero-Carbon Future
John C. Dernbach

What do we need to do to have a decent chance of preventing large and growing emissions and atmospheric concentrations of greenhouse gases from dangerously interfering with the climate system? The answer, according to the Intergovernmental Panel on Climate Change (IPCC), is that the world needs to reduce greenhouse gas emissions by at least 40% to 70% by 2050, and to zero or below by 2100.[1] Other scientific reports would say we must proceed faster.[2] The IPCC and others indicate that the many paths to this reduction should all be guided by sustainable development.[3] That is, nations must find ways to dramatically reduce greenhouse gas emissions that also foster equitable economic and social development and promote security.

The task, then, can be succinctly stated as follows: starting now, we must rapidly reduce greenhouse gas emissions to zero or below, creating as much social, environmental, economic, and security benefit as we can, and on an equitable basis. The IPCC reports don't say so as succinctly or directly, but that is among the most essential tasks of our time.

This chapter provides an overview of the challenge of achieving a zero-carbon future, as well as the way in which sustainable development would frame the decisionmaking process for doing so. It then reviews two major reports that describe overall approaches at the global and national levels for meeting the zero-carbon objective. Finally, it describes ways to identify and create legal pathways to that objective, building on the insights of these two

Author's Note: I would like to thank Austin Langon for helpful research assistance.

1. INTERGOVERNMENTAL PANEL ON CLIMATE CHANGE, CLIMATE CHANGE 2013: THE PHYSICAL SCIENCE BASIS 13 (2013), *available at* https://www.ipcc.ch/report/ar5/wg1/ [hereinafter 2013 IPCC PHYSICAL SCIENCE REPORT].
2. *See infra* notes 16-19 and accompanying text.
3. INTERGOVERNMENTAL PANEL ON CLIMATE CHANGE, CLIMATE CHANGE 2014: MITIGATION OF CLIMATE CHANGE, ch. 4 (2014), *available at* https://www.ipcc.ch/report/ar5/wg3/ [hereinafter 2014 IPCC MITIGATION REPORT].

reports. Creating legal pathways could help accelerate the transition the transition to a sustainable energy future.

I.   The Challenge of the Carbon Budget

The challenge posed by climate change is both urgent and enormous. It is also daunting: it requires that the world, as a whole, move as soon as possible from the current situation of increasing greenhouse gas emissions to rapid reductions in greenhouse gas emissions. A recently developed concept—the carbon budget[4]—provides a way of understanding both the magnitude of this challenge and possible pathways for an effective response.

The objective of the U.N. Framework Convention on Climate Change is "stabilization of greenhouse gas concentrations in the atmosphere at a level that would prevent dangerous anthropogenic interference with the climate system."[5] In 2010, the Conference of the Parties to the Convention translated the stabilization objective into a maximum permissible surface temperature increase—2 degrees Celsius (C) (or 3.6 degrees Fahrenheit) above preindustrial levels.[6] Parties, it said, "should take urgent action to meet this long-term goal, consistent with science and on the basis of equity."[7] In addition, it stated the importance of "strengthening the long-term global goal on the basis of the best available scientific knowledge, including in relation to a global average temperature rise of 1.5°C."[8] The Paris Agreement, which was adopted unanimously by the Conference of the Parties in December 2015, stated the objective in terms of both temperatures—to hold "the increase in the global average temperature to well below 2°C above pre-industrial levels," and to "pursue efforts to limit the temperature increase to 1.5°C above pre-industrial levels, recognizing that this would significantly reduce the risks and impacts of climate change."[9]

4.   Fred Pearce, *What Is the Carbon Limit? That Depends Who You Ask*, ENVIRONMENT360, Nov. 6, 2014, http://e360.yale.edu/feature/what_is_the_carbon_limit_that_depends_who_you_ask/2825/.
5.   United Nations Framework Convention on Climate Change, art. 2, May 29, 1992, S. Treaty Doc. No. 102-38, 1771 U.N.T.S. 107. U.N. Doc. A/AC.237/18 (Part II)/Add.1; 31 I.L.M. 849 [hereinafter Framework Convention].
6.   Conference of the Parties, United Nations Framework Convention on Climate Change, Decision 1/CP.16 (The Cancun Agreements: Outcome of the Work of the Ad Hoc Working Group on Long-Term Cooperative Action Under the Convention) ¶ 4, *in* Report of the Conference of the Parties on Its Sixteenth Session, Held in Cancun From 29 November to 10 December 2010, Addendum, Part Two: Action Taken by the Conference of the Parties at Its Sixteenth Session, FCCC/CP/2010/7/Add.1 (2011), *available at* http://unfccc.int/resource/docs/2010/cop16/eng/07a01.pdf.
7.   *Id.*
8.   *Id.* That translates to 2.7 degrees Fahrenheit.
9.   United Nations Framework Convention on Climate Change, Conference of the Parties, Paris Agreement, art. 2.1(a), *in* Decision 1/CP.21 (Adoption of the Paris Agreement) (2015), U.N. Doc.

The IPCC has translated the 2°C limit into a carbon "budget"—a numerical limit on all additional emissions, cumulatively, for the rest of the century. It concluded that this budget is between 630 and 1,180 gigatons of carbon dioxide equivalent.[10] That range represents the cumulative total of all new emissions of carbon dioxide equivalent between 2011 and 2100.[11] If cumulative emissions do not exceed the figures in that range, the IPCC states, it is "likely" that global average temperatures will stay below a 2°C increase.[12] To have a "likely" chance of staying within this budget, IPCC says, global greenhouse gas emissions need to be 40% to 70% lower by 2050 and "near zero" gigatons of carbon dioxide equivalent or "below" by 2100.[13]

Several points of caution are needed to understand this carbon budget. First, there is a one in three chance that, on its own terms, the budget will not succeed. The term "likely"—as used by both the Conference of the Parties and the IPCC—means that the chance of a particular outcome is greater than 66%,[14] or two out of three. To put this probability in perspective, it helps to recall that the U.S. Environmental Protection Agency (EPA) has traditionally regulated chemicals under its major statutes when they create a risk of cancer of between one in 10,000 and one in 10 million.[15] Cancer risks from chemicals are different from the risks of climate change, of course, but the contrasting probabilities are striking nonetheless. Even in Russian roulette, a player has only a one-in-six chance of dying.

Second, other calculations of a carbon budget provide even less time to reduce emissions that low. The writers of a frequently cited 2009 paper in *Nature*, for example, focused on the time period between 2000 and 2050, not 2000 and 2100, and calculated carbon budgets to avoid exceeding a 2°C increase based on cumulative emissions in the first half of this century.[16] Given past and projected emissions, they conclude, "we would exhaust the

FCCC/CP/2015/L.9/Rev.1, *available at* https://unfccc.int/resource/docs/2015/cop21/eng/l09r01. pdf [hereinafter Paris Agreement].

10. 2014 IPCC MITIGATION REPORT, *supra* note 3, at 431. A gigaton is one billion tons. Carbon dioxide equivalent includes all greenhouses gases measured according to the warming potential of carbon dioxide.

11. *Id.*

12. *Id.* at 441. Working Group I reached a slightly different estimate about the budget—1,010 additional gigatons of carbon dioxide equivalent. 2013 IPCC PHYSICAL SCIENCE REPORT, *supra* note 1, at 27. Working Group I used a slightly different methodology and did not use ranges. 2014 IPCC MITIGATION REPORT, *supra* note 3, at 441.

13. 2014 IPCC MITIGATION REPORT, *supra* note 3, at 13.

14. *Id.* at 4, note 2.

15. JOHN D. GRAHAM, THE LEGACY OF ONE IN A MILLION, RISK IN PERSPECTIVE 1-2 (1993) (Harvard Center for Risk Analysis), *available at* http://www.hsph.harvard.edu/wp-content/uploads/sites/1273/2013/06/ The-Legacy-of-One-in-a-Million-March-1993.pdf.

16. Malte Meinshausen et al., *Greenhouse-Gas Emission Targets for Limiting Global Warming to 2°C*, 458 NATURE 1158 (2009).

CO_2 emission budget by 2024, 2027 or 2039, depending on the probability accepted for exceeding 2°C (respectively 20%, 25% or 50%)."[17] The International Energy Agency states that, with business-as-usual emissions, the remaining carbon budget (based on a 50% chance of keeping the temperature increase below 2°C) will be exhausted around 2040.[18] Others, including James Hansen, are less certain that the world can increase global temperatures by 2°C without severe adverse consequences. They argue that 1.5°C, or an even lower temperature limit, would be even better.[19] The Paris Agreement appears to be based on a recognition of these concerns, aiming to keep the temperature increase "well below 2°C" and indicating the desirability of holding the increase to 1.5°C. Of course, the carbon budget to stay below a 1.5°C increase is even smaller, and hence it is more likely that the world will exceed it.

Third, operationalizing this budget requires that it be allocated by nation based on population, historical contribution to global atmospheric greenhouse gas concentrations, development status (developed vs. developing), equity, and other factors. The question of each nation's "fair share" of the budget is both essential and highly contested.[20]

At the same time, if business as usual continues, and the growth of greenhouse gas emissions continues to accelerate, the world will simply blow by the budget and considerably exceed global average temperature increases of 2°C. According to the IPCC, emissions of carbon dioxide equivalent are increasing by about 1 gigaton annually, were the highest in human history between 2000 and 2010, and in 2010 alone reached 49 gigatons.[21] Half of cumulative anthropogenic (human-caused) carbon dioxide emissions have occurred in the last 40 years.[22] These increases are occurring in spite of the efforts that have been made thus far to reduce greenhouse gas emissions.[23] The IPCC thus concludes:

---

17. *Id.* at 1159.
18. INTERNATIONAL ENERGY AGENCY, ENERGY AND CLIMATE CHANGE: WORLD ENERGY OUTLOOK SPECIAL REPORT, EXECUTIVE SUMMARY 2 (2015), *available at* http://www.iea.org/publications/freepublications/publication/WEO2015SpecialReportonEnergyandClimateChangeExecutiveSummaryUKversion-WEB.PDF.
19. James Hansen et al., *Assessing "Dangerous Climate Change": Required Reduction of Carbon Emissions to Protect Young People, Future Generations and Nature*, 8 PLOS ONE e81648 (2013). *See also* Jeff Tollefson, *Global-Warming Limit of 2°C Hangs in the Balance*, 520 NATURE 14 (Apr. 2, 2015).
20. DONALD A. BROWN, CLIMATE CHANGE ETHICS: NAVIGATING THE PERFECT MORAL STORM (2012); Fred Pearce, *The Trillion-Ton Cap: Allocating The World's Carbon Emissions*, ENVIRONMENT360, Oct. 23, 2013, *at* http://e360.yale.edu/feature/the_trillion-ton_cap_allocating_the_worlds_carbon_emissions/2703/.
21. 2013 IPCC PHYSICAL SCIENCE REPORT, *supra* note 1, at 6.
22. *Id.* at 7.
23. *Id.* at 6.

Without additional efforts to reduce GHG [greenhouse gas] emissions beyond those in place today, emissions growth is expected to persist driven by growth in global population and economic activities. Baseline scenarios, those without additional mitigation, result in global mean surface temperature increases in 2100 from 3.7°C to 4.8°C compared to pre-industrial levels. . . .[24]

A variety of other projections based on business-as-usual emissions growth also put the world on track for a temperature increase of at least 4°C.[25]

A 2012 report for the World Bank by the Potsdam Institute for Climate Impact Research and Climate Analytics describes the impact of a 4°C temperature increase by 2100 as disastrous.[26] Such a world, the report said, would be "one of unprecedented heat waves, severe drought, and major floods in many regions, with serious impacts on ecosystems and associated services."[27] The report adds:

[G]iven that uncertainty remains about the full nature and scale of impacts, there is also no certainty that adaptation to a 4°C world is possible. A 4°C world is likely to be one in which communities, cities and countries would experience severe disruptions, damage, and dislocation, with many of these risks spread unequally. It is likely that the poor will suffer most and the global community could become more fractured, and unequal than today.[28]

In the 2015 Paris Agreement, "Parties aim to reach global peaking of greenhouse gas emissions as soon as possible . . . and to undertake rapid reductions thereafter . . . so as to achieve a balance between anthropogenic emissions by sources and removals by sinks of greenhouse gases in the second half of this century . . . ."[29] This "balance" means that net greenhouse gas emissions should be zero by that time. Serious efforts to address the carbon budget must begin as soon as possible. As economist Nicholas Stern summarizes the available scientific literature, the window for keeping temperatures under 2°C "is still open, but is closing rapidly."[30]

---

24. *Id.* at 8.
25. Sustainable Development Solutions Network & Institute for Sustainable Development and International Relations, Pathways to Deep Decarbonization 4 (2014), *available at* http://unsdsn.org/wp-content/uploads/2014/09/DDPP_Digit_updated.pdf.
26. International Bank for Reconstruction and Development/World Bank, Turn Down the Heat: Why a 4°C Warmer World Must Be Avoided (2012), *available at* http://www-wds.world-bank.org/external/default/WDSContentServer/WDSP/IB/2015/07/17/090224b0828c33e7/1_0/Rendered/PDF/Turn0down0the00orld0must0be0avoided.pdf.
27. *Id.* at ix.
28. *Id.* at xviii.
29. Paris Agreement, *supra* note 9, art. 4.1.
30. Nicholas Stern, Why Are We Waiting? The Logic, Urgency, and Promise of Tackling Climate Change 32 (2015).

II. Sustainable Development as a Framework for Addressing the Carbon Budget

Sustainable development is a decisionmaking framework to foster human well-being by ensuring that societies achieve development and environment goals at the same time.[31] It is not simply an academic or policy idea; it is the internationally accepted framework[32] for maintaining and improving human quality of life and well-being for the present generation as well as future generations.[33] The United Nations Framework Convention on Climate Change specifically provides: "The Parties have a right to, and should, promote sustainable development."[34] Sustainable development provides an essential decisionmaking framework for addressing the carbon budget and is superior to conventional development.

A.   A Decisionmaking Framework

Sustainable development is a framework for making decisions; it is not a mere goal or sentiment, and it is not simply another word for green. The key action principle of sustainable development is integrated decisionmak-

---

31. John C. Dernbach & Federico Cheever, *Sustainable Development and Its Discontents*, 4 Transnat'l Envtl. L. 247 (2015); John C. Dernbach, *Sustainable Development as a Framework for National Governance*, 49 Case W. Res. L. Rev. 1 (1998).

32. G.A. Res. 70/1, Transforming Our World: The 2030 Agenda for Sustainable Development, preamble & ¶ 2, U.N. Doc. A/RES/70/1 (Oct. 21, 2015) ("We are determined to ensure that all human beings can enjoy prosperous and fulfilling lives and that economic, social and technological progress occurs in harmony with nature."); ("We are committed to achieving sustainable development in its three dimensions—economic, social and environmental—in a balanced and integrated manner."). *See also* U.N. Conference on Sustainable Development, *The Future We Want*, U.N. Doc. A/66/L.56, July 24, 2012, ¶ 1, *available at* http://daccess-dds-ny.un.org/doc/UNDOC/LTD/N12/436/88/PDF/N1243688.pdf?OpenElement (in which world's nations agreed to "renew our commitment to sustainable development and to ensuring the promotion of an economically, socially and environmentally sustainable future for our planet and for present and future generations."). The 2012 conference renewed the commitment originally made at the U.N. Conference on Environment and Development in 1992—to a "global partnership for sustainable development." U.N. Conference on Environment and Development (UNCED), Agenda 21, U.N. Doc. A/CONF.151.26, 1992, ¶ 1.1, *available at* http://www.un.org/esa/dsd/agenda21/.

33. At the U.N. Conference on Environment and Development in 1992, countries agreed to a statement of 27 principles for sustainable development called the Rio Declaration on Environment and Development. U.N. Conference on Environment and Development, U.N. Doc. A/CONF.151/26/Rev.1 (Vol. I), June 14, 1992, *available at* http://www.un.org/documents/ga/conf151/aconf15126-1annex1.htm [hereinafter Rio Declaration]. These principles have proven to have enduring significance in understanding what sustainable development means for law. *See* The Rio Declaration on Environment and Development: A Commentary (Jorge E. Viñuales ed., 2015) (detailed explanation of each principle of Rio Declaration). One provides: "Human beings are at the centre of concerns for sustainable development. They are entitled to a healthy and productive life in harmony with nature." Rio Declaration, prin. 1. According to another: "The right to development must be fulfilled so as to equitably meet developmental and environmental needs of present and future generations." *Id.* prin. 3.

34. Framework Convention, *supra* note 5, art. 3.4.

ing.[35] Essentially, decisionmakers must consider and advance environmental protection at the same time as they consider and advance their economic and social development goals.[36] By contrast, in conventional development, the environment tends to be an afterthought in a decisionmaking process in which economic development is the primary if not sole objective.[37] Sustainable development is thus not just about environmental law; it is about how the entire development process is conducted. This matters in three ways.

First, for developing countries, sustainable development provides a way of reconciling their equally daunting and otherwise irreconcilable objectives of economic development and reduction and elimination of carbon emissions. As recently as 2000, developed countries consumed more energy overall than developing countries.[38] By 2040, however, developing country energy consumption is projected to be more than twice as much as that in developed countries.[39] In fact, more than 85% of the growth in energy consumption over that period will come from developing countries.[40] Given the rising demand for energy in those countries, sustainable development of energy, including the greatest possible use of energy efficiency and renewable energy, provides the only realistic way of keeping temperatures "well below 2°C."

For developed countries, where there already tends to be a significant fossil-fuel-based energy infrastructure, the challenge is more one of converting that infrastructure to sustainable energy. However, for all countries, the challenge is to build "a new energy-industrial revolution."[41] This job requires a decisionmaking framework for integrating development and environmental considerations and goals; mere environmental goals will not get the job done. Thus, the parties to the Framework Convention agreed to integrate climate change mitigation and adaptation into their national development plans and processes.[42] Sustainable development requires public and private decisions that, taken together, actually keep global average temperature increases within 2°C.

Second, sustainable development is based on an understanding that problems have multiple dimensions and need to be understood as such. Thus,

---

35. John C. Dernbach, *Achieving Sustainable Development: The Centrality and Multiple Facets of Integrated Decisionmaking*, 10 IND. J. GLOBAL LEG. STUD. 247 (2003); Rio Declaration, *supra* note 33, prin. 4 ("In order to achieve sustainable development, environmental protection shall constitute an integral part of the development process and cannot be considered in isolation from it.").
36. *Id.*
37. WORLD COMMISSION ON ENVIRONMENT AND DEVELOPMENT, OUR COMMON FUTURE 28-29 (1987).
38. U.S. ENERGY INFORMATION ADMINISTRATION, INTERNATIONAL ENERGY OUTLOOK 2013, at 9 (2013).
39. *Id.*
40. *Id.*
41. STERN, *supra* note 30, at 30.
42. Framework Convention, *supra* note 5, art. 4.1(f).

climate change has environmental, economic, social, and security dimensions—all of which need to be taken seriously. In a conventional development setting, environmental problems tend to be undervalued because there is less certainty about the likelihood and significance of adverse environmental impacts than there is about the economic and perhaps social benefits of a project. Thus, the precautionary approach, in which "cost-effective measures to prevent environmental degradation" can and should proceed in spite of the lack of complete scientific certainty about environmental problems,[43] is intended to help ensure that environmental impacts are not undervalued. The precautionary approach is also embedded in the Framework Convention.[44]

The precautionary approach provides a way of resolving uncertainties about the size of the budget and what actions should be taken to avoid exceeding 2°C. Quite simply, as the Paris Agreement suggests, governmental, business, and nongovernmental actors should take all possible actions to keep the temperature increase as far below that level as they can.

Third, the effectiveness of sustainable development actions is not measured simply by their contribution to Gross Domestic Product (GDP), as tends to be the case with conventional development. Instead, the effectiveness of sustainable development actions is measured by their economic, environmental, security, and social benefits.[45] More broadly, they are measured by their contribution to human well-being or quality of life. For the carbon budget challenge, these measures of sustainable development make it possible for nations to consider and achieve a range of benefits beyond reduction of greenhouse gas emissions. Because greenhouse gases are distributed fairly evenly through the global atmosphere, the greenhouse gas benefits of reductions are also distributed globally.

As U.S. states discovered more than a decade ago, the other benefits (called co-benefits) of addressing climate change—including new jobs; growing businesses; greater stability in energy production; reduced emissions of sulfur dioxide, mercury, and other air pollutants; and reduced energy costs for businesses and the poor—produced more immediate and tangible improvements *in those states* than the greenhouse gas emission reductions that accompanied these benefits.[46] Recent laws requiring greater use of renewable energy and energy efficiency, in fact, can be fairly characterized as economic devel-

---

43. Rio Declaration, *supra* note 33, prin. 15.
44. Framework Convention, *supra* note 5, art. 3.3.
45. 2014 IPCC Mitigation Report, *supra* note 3, at 292-93, 296-97.
46. John Dernbach and the Widener University Law School Seminar on Global Warming, *Moving the Climate Debate From Models to Proposed Legislation: Lessons From State Experience*, 30 ELR 10933 (Nov. 2000).

opment laws for those industries; their economic development benefits are a major reason they were adopted.[47] The effect of renewable energy portfolio standards and feed-in-tariffs for renewable energy has been to build the renewable energy industry in jurisdictions where these laws have been adopted.[48] Similarly, the IPCC has found "significant co-benefits for human health, ecosystem impacts, and sufficiency of resources and resilience of the energy system" in mitigation scenarios that are consistent with keeping temperatures under 2°C.[49]

B.   A More Attractive Approach Than Conventional Development

Sustainable development is more fair and equitable than conventional development. It also can produce more benefits and fewer costs. It is thus an essential framework for making decisions to keep the temperature increase "well below 2°C."

Sustainable development is based on a critique of conventional development as not only environmentally damaging, but also unfair and inequitable.[50] Conventional development works by producing economic and, to a lesser degree, social benefits for certain individuals or companies.[51] At the same time, it occurs at the expense of the environment as well as people who depend on that environment. These people tend not to be the same as those benefited. The adversely affected people could exist in the present generation, or in future generations, or both. That is exactly how conventional fossil-fuel based energy development is working now and, as explained earlier, will only makes things worse if business as usual continues. Sustainable development—low-carbon or zero-carbon development—gives us our best chance (not a certainty) of keeping the global average temperature increase under 2°C; would produce obvious benefits; and should not make people less well off than they were originally. Articulating the equitable or moral basis for sustainable development approaches to climate change also enhances the likelihood that nations and communities will agree to and implement these approaches.[52]

---

47.   John C. Dernbach, *Creating the Law of Environmentally Sustainable Economic Development*, 28 PACE ENVTL. L. REV. 614 (2011).

48.   Jonas Meckling et al., *Winning Coalitions for Climate Policy*, 349 SCIENCE 1170 (Sept. 11, 2015).

49.   2014 IPCC MITIGATION REPORT, *supra* note 3, at 17.

50.   OUR COMMON FUTURE, *supra* note 37, at 28-37 (explaining how conventional development has contributed to poverty and environmental degradation).

51.   *Id.*

52.   2014 IPCC MITIGATION REPORT, *supra* note 3, at 290-91.

In addition, sustainable development should produce more benefits than conventional development, with fewer costs. In fact, one of the most important features of sustainable development is that it sidesteps the binary "development *or* environment" thought structure that constrains conventional development decisionmaking. By providing a third choice—"development *and* environment"—sustainable development changes the decisionmaking structure and opens up a policy space that is capable of producing more benefits and fewer costs.

Sustainable development thus reframes the policy debate about how to decarbonize the global economy. As Nicholas Stern explains, the "prevailing assumption" is that decarbonization involves "higher cost substitutes" and "burden sharing" among countries.[53] However, in the last decade or two, there have been substantial improvements in energy efficiency technology and management systems, and renewable energy "has advanced far quicker and a greater scale" than anyone anticipated.[54] In addition, the policy space of "development and environment" is now being filled by a variety of new or modified laws that foster renewable energy; energy efficiency and conservation in buildings, transportation, and industry; and distributed energy, among other things.[55] There is also a "better understanding of the potential attractiveness of alternative, low-carbon paths for more durable and better-quality growth, development, and poverty reduction."[56] Instead of the prevailing gloomy assumption about decarbonization, then, the question should be "how to reduce emissions in ways that provide very widespread benefits to people over time."[57]

III.   Deep Decarbonization Scenarios

Two major international reports outline approaches to decarbonization. They provide a way of understanding what it would mean to make genuine progress toward keeping the atmospheric temperature increase from greenhouse gas emissions below 2°C. One describes basic elements, and the other includes both basic elements and technically feasible country-specific outcomes. Nevertheless, they do not provide country-specific *legal* pathways to those outcomes.

---

53.   STERN, *supra* note 30, at 298.
54.   *Id.* at 86.
55.   *See, e.g.*, JOHN C. DERNBACH ET AL., ACTING AS IF TOMORROW MATTERS: ACCELERATING THE TRANSITION TO SUSTAINABILITY (Envtl. L. Inst. 2012).
56.   STERN, *supra* note 30, at 298.
57.   *Id.*

One of these reports, *Decarbonizing Development: Three Steps to a Zero-Carbon Future*, was issued by the World Bank in 2015.[58] The report focuses on carbon dioxide, and not other greenhouse gases, because carbon dioxide is the most important greenhouse gas and because it can stay in the atmosphere for hundreds of years.[59] It includes not only actions to reduce carbon dioxide emissions but also to remove carbon dioxide from the atmosphere; "achieving the 2°C target will necessitate negative emissions . . . in the second part of this century."[60]

A key to effective action, the report says, is "early action."[61] Early action is prudent, cost-effective, and cheaper, and avoids technological lock-in (e.g., construction of fossil-fuel-based power plants that will likely be in service for 40 or more years).[62] It is also more likely to work. The more time passes before carbon dioxide emissions peak and then decline, the steeper the annual reductions must be—from 4-5% (peaking date of 2015) to 8% (peaking date of 2025).[63] Excluding situations where economic collapse has occurred, there is only one example of a country that achieved annual greenhouse gas reductions of more than 4%.[64]

According to the report, "three broad principles must guide countries' low-carbon efforts."[65] First, "every country needs to define a long-term target—say, for 2050—that is consistent with decarbonization and to build short-term, sector-specific plans that contribute to that target and are adapted to the country's wealth, endowments, and capacity."[66] Countries should also "favor measures with high emission-reduction potential" even if these measures are more costly and will take longer to implement than other measures.[67]

Second, every country needs to get "prices right" for carbon, not just as good climate policy, but also as "good economic and fiscal policy."[68] The core problem is that the price of carbon-based energy does not reflect its

---

58. Marianne Fay et al., International Bank for Reconstruction and Development/The World Bank, Decarbonizing Development: Three Steps to a Zero-Carbon Future (2015), *available at* http://www.worldbank.org/content/dam/Worldbank/document/Climate/dd/decarbonizing-development-report.pdf.
59. *Id.* at 25.
60. *Id.* at 26.
61. *Id.* at 39.
62. *Id.*
63. *Id.* at 40.
64. *Id.* (citing France when it was developing nuclear power).
65. *Id.* at 2.
66. *Id.* at 2.
67. *Id.*
68. *Id.* at 79.

many social, environmental, and economic costs.[69] Getting the prices right includes elimination of fossil fuel subsidies.[70] However, because prices alone don't necessarily induce desired behavior or achieve specified emissions reductions, they must be supplemented with other measures, including "targeted investment subsidies, performance standards and mandates, or communication campaigns that trigger the required changes. . . ."[71]

Finally, countries must put together policy packages that are not only attractive to most voters, but also "avoid impacts that appear unfair or that are concentrated in a region, sector, or community."[72] Policies thus must be designed to protect the poor and vulnerable.[73] In addition, for pragmatic reasons, governments must find ways to address adversely affected economic sectors by providing compensation, helping sectors that would otherwise lose to become part of the solution, and enacting measures to address competitiveness.[74]

The other major report is based on the Deep Decarbonization Pathways Project of the Sustainable Development Solutions Network and the Institute for Sustainable Development and International Relations.[75] The project was undertaken "to understand and show how individual countries can transition to a low-carbon economy" based on the limit of 2°C.[76] The project focuses on carbon dioxide "emissions from the burning of fossil fuels and industrial processes,"[77] not on all greenhouse gas emissions. In addition, it assumes a century-long effort divided in two parts, 2011-2050 and 2051-2100; the bulk of the emissions reduction will occur in the first period, and the rest will occur in the second period as emissions reach zero.[78] Working from the overall IPCC budget for greenhouse gases, and analyzing various IPCC scenarios for future emissions, the project's authors conclude that annual global carbon dioxide emissions from fossil fuel combustion and industrial processes would need to be reduced to "close to" 11 gigatons by 2050 to have a "likely" chance of keeping emissions within the 2-degree limit.[79] In 2011, emissions

---

69. National Research Council, Hidden Costs of Energy: Unpriced Consequences of Energy Production and Use (2010).
70. Decarbonizing Development, *supra* note 58, at 79.
71. *Id.* at 3.
72. *Id.*
73. *Id.* at 139-51.
74. *Id.* at 153-64.
75. Pathways to Deep Decarbonization, *supra* note 25.
76. *Id.* at iii.
77. *Id.* at 7-8.
78. *Id.* at 8.
79. *Id.* at viii.

from the same sources totaled 34 gigatons.[80] The required reduction is thus almost 68%.

The first stage of the project was completed in 2014.[81] It consists of "preliminary findings on technically feasible pathways to deep decarbonization" for 15 countries representing 70% of global greenhouse gas emissions—Australia, Brazil, Canada, China, France, Germany, India, Indonesia, Japan, Mexico, Russia, South Africa, South Korea, the United Kingdom, and the United States.[82] Research teams in each of these countries used a "backcasting" approach that assumes the 2°C goal based on the IPCC carbon budget has been met, and then describes the changes that were needed to achieve that goal.[83] They used 1.6 tons of carbon dioxide emissions per capita by 2050 as a benchmark, which is much lower than the current global average of 5.2 tons.[84] Because per capita emissions tend to be higher in developed countries than developing countries, the needed emissions reductions in developed countries are greater. The research teams, which worked independently of their governments, appear to have been comprised primarily of technology, energy, and economic analysts; the U.S. research team drew from a consulting firm, Energy and Environmental Economics (E3), and two government laboratories, Lawrence Berkeley National Laboratory and Pacific Northwest National Laboratory.[85]

Significantly, the two reports reach similar conclusions about the overall approach that each country should take to decarbonization. Both make clear the need to use sustainable development to create economic, social, environmental, and other benefits.[86] As the table on page 34 shows, energy efficiency, decarbonizing the electricity sector, and switching to low-carbon or zero-carbon fuels are common elements in both. The World Bank adds carbon sinks, which remove carbon dioxide from the atmosphere.

---

80. *Id.*
81. The second stage, which was to be completed in 2015, "will refine the analysis of the technical decarbonization potential, exploring options for even deeper decarbonization." *Id.* at iii. *See also infra* note 107 and accompanying text.
82. PATHWAYS TO DEEP DECARBONIZATION, *supra* note 25, at iii-iv.
83. *Id.* at x. For an explanation of the use of backcasting in achieving sustainability, see Philip Vergragt & Jaco Quist, *Backcasting for Sustainability: Introduction to the Special Issue*, 78 TECHNOLOGICAL FORECASTING & SOCIAL CHANGE 747 (2011).
84. PATHWAYS TO DEEP DECARBONIZATION, *supra* note 25, at viii, 24-26. For current per capita emission levels in the United States, China, and the European Union, see *infra* note 92 and accompanying text.
85. JAMES H. WILLIAMS ET AL., ENERGY AND ENVIRONMENTAL ECONOMICS (E3), LAWRENCE BERKELEY NATIONAL LABORATORY, & PACIFIC NORTHWEST NATIONAL LABORATORY, PATHWAYS TO DEEP DECARBONIZATION IN THE UNITED STATES (2014), *available at* http://unsdsn.org/wp-content/uploads/2014/09/US-Deep-Decarbonization-Report.pdf.
86. PATHWAYS TO DEEP DECARBONIZATION, *supra* note 25, at vii; DECARBONIZING DEVELOPMENT, *supra* note 58, at 55.

Key Elements of National Decarbonization Strategies

World Bank	Deep Decarbonization Project
• Decarbonized electricity production. • Electrification (to include reliance on that clean electricity), and where that is not possible, a switch to cleaner fuels. • Improved efficiency and reduced waste in all sectors. • Preservation and increase of carbon sinks such as forests and other vegetation and soils.[a]	• Energy efficiency and conservation across all sectors of the economy, including power generation, transportation, buildings, industry, and urban design. • Low-carbon electricity from replacement of fossil fuel-based generation with renewable energy or the use of carbon capture and storage at fossil fuel-based generating facilities. • Switching from more carbon-intensive fuels to less carbon-intensive fuels in all economic sectors.[b]

a.   DECARBONIZING DEVELOPMENT, *supra* note 58, at 27-28.
b.   PATHWAYS TO DEEP DECARBONIZATION, *supra* note 25, at xii.

Unlike the World Bank report, however, the Deep Decarbonization project also describes country-specific pathways to decarbonization. The United States and China are perhaps the two countries whose decarbonization pathways matter the most. In 2013, the world's two largest emitters of carbon dioxide from fossil fuel combustion and industrial processes were China and the United States.[87] China replaced the United States as the world's largest emitter of carbon dioxide in 2006.[88] Remarkably, China's total carbon dioxide emissions in 2013, only seven years later, were nearly double those of the United States (29% of the global total compared to 15%).[89] U.S. per capita carbon dioxide emissions were 16.6 tons, compared to 7.4 tons for China (and 7.3 tons per capita for the European Union).[90] In that same year, China's population was more than four times that of the United States (1.357 billion compared to 316 million).[91]

The United States and China decarbonization pathways are illustrative of what the researchers learned. For the United States, the most important finding "is that it is technically feasible for the U.S. to reduce [carbon dioxide] emissions from fossil fuel combustion" by 85% from 1990 levels

87.   JOS G.J. OLIVIER ET AL., PBL NETHERLANDS ENVIRONMENTAL ASSESSMENT AGENCY & EUROPEAN COMMISSION JOINT RESEARCH CENTRE, TRENDS IN GLOBAL CO$_2$ EMISSIONS: 2014 REPORT 4 (2014), *available at* http://edgar.jrc.ec.europa.eu/news_docs/jrc-2014-trends-in-global-co2-emissions-2014-report-93171.pdf.

88.   JOS G.J. OLIVIER ET AL., PBL NETHERLANDS ENVIRONMENTAL ASSESSMENT AGENCY & EUROPEAN COMMISSION JOINT RESEARCH CENTRE, TRENDS IN GLOBAL CO$_2$ EMISSIONS: 2012 REPORT 28 (2012), *available at* http://edgar.jrc.ec.europa.eu/CO2REPORT2012.pdf.

89.   TRENDS IN GLOBAL CO$_2$ EMISSIONS: 2014 REPORT, *supra* note 87, at 4.

90.   *Id.* at 24.

91.   POPULATION REFERENCE BUREAU, 2013 WORLD POPULATION DATA SHEET 2 (2013), *available at* http://www.prb.org/pdf13/2013-population-data-sheet_eng.pdf.

by 2050, which is "an order of magnitude decrease in per capita emissions compared to 2010."[92] If the U.S. did that, it could reduce its overall greenhouse gas emissions by 80% below 1990 levels by 2050.[93] Moreover, the United States could meet that longer term objective by meeting a shorter term objective it has already established, the report said.[94] The shorter term objective, stated by the United States in 2015, is "to achieve an economy-wide target of reducing its greenhouse gas emissions by 26%-28% below its 2005 level in 2025."[95]

Enormous changes would be required in the U.S. energy system to make those reductions happen. Because it is difficult to decarbonize gas and liquid fuels, the researchers said, meeting the 2050 objective would require almost complete decarbonization of electricity and, among other things, switching a "large share" of end uses that require gasoline and liquid fuels over to electricity (such as electric cars).[96] It would also be necessary to produce fuel from electricity itself, they said, citing the production of hydrogen from hydrolysis as an example.[97] That would double electricity generation but reduce its carbon intensity to 3% to 10% of current levels, requiring a vast increase in either renewable energy (as much as "2,500 gigawatts (GW) of wind and solar generation (30 times present capacity))" or carbon capture and sequestration.[98] The average fuel economy for light duty vehicles such as cars would need to be over 100 miles per gallon, and these vehicles would need to be fueled almost entirely by electricity and hydrogen.[99] The overall cost of this effort would be roughly 1% of GDP, the researchers say.[100]

Unlike the United States, which has significant emissions of carbon dioxide from electricity generation, industry, transportation, and buildings,[101] the great bulk of Chinese carbon dioxide emissions are from electricity generation and industry, with most of the electricity used by industry.[102] Indeed, half of the energy use in the industrial sector is from a handful of energy-

---

92. Pathways to Deep Decarbonization, *supra* note 25, at 204.
93. Pathways to Deep Decarbonization in the United States, *supra* note 85, at xiii.
94. *Id.* at xv.
95. United States, Cover Note, INDC [Intended Nationally Determined Contribution], and Accompanying Information (2015), *available at* http://www4.unfccc.int/submissions/INDC/Published%20Documents/United%20States%20of%20America/1/U.S.%20Cover%20Note%20INDC%20and%20Accompanying%20Information.pdf.
96. Pathways to Deep Decarbonization in the United States, *supra* note 85, at xiii.
97. *Id.*
98. *Id.*
99. *Id.*
100. *Id.* at xii.
101. Pathways to Deep Decarbonization, *supra* note 25, at 203.
102. *Id.* at 85.

intensive industries (including iron and steel as well as cement).[103] China's stated greenhouse gas emission goals are also quite different from those of the United States. China's objectives are to "achieve the peaking of carbon dioxide emissions around 2030" and make "best efforts" to peak earlier, to "lower carbon dioxide emissions per unit of GDP by 60% to 65% from the 2005 level" by 2030, and to "increase the share of non-fossil fuels in primary energy consumption to around 20%."[104]

In the report's "illustrative" decarbonization pathway, China's energy-related carbon dioxide emissions decrease by 34% between 2010 and 2050.[105] This reduction is achieved through large-scale use of nuclear power (25% of electricity generation by 2050), wind and solar energy (35%), and hydro-electricity (18%). While fossil fuel plants provide the remaining electricity, many are either natural gas plants that back up renewable energy or are based on highly efficient coal burning technologies coupled with carbon capture and sequestration.[106] For industry, final energy consumption grows only 28%, mostly because of energy efficiency improvements through technologi-cal innovation and carbon sequestration.[107] Carbon dioxide emissions from transportation and buildings grow to 49% of total emissions, but energy efficiency, rail transportation, and decarbonized electricity keep emissions much lower than they would otherwise be.[108]

These, of course, represent dramatic changes from our current situation. As previously explained, this first stage of the Deep Decarbonization project analyzes only the technical feasibility of achieving these outcomes. The second stage of the project, which was not yet published as this chapter was com-pleted, is to systemically analyze costs and benefits, finance requirements, and "domestic and global policy frameworks" for achieving these outcomes, and explain in greater detail how deep decarbonization and sustainable develop-ment can be met at the same time.[109] As helpful as this second stage of work is likely to be in explaining possible pathways, it will still be necessary to translate those pathways into effective laws that are capable of being adopted.

---

103. *Id.* at 84.
104. People's Republic of China, Enhanced Actions on Climate Change: China's Intended Nationally Determined Contributions (June 20, 2015), *available at* http://www4.unfccc.int/submissions/INDC/ Published%20Documents/China/1/China's%20INDC%20-%20on%2030%20June%202015.pdf. China also intends, by 2030, to "increase the forest stock volume by around 4.5 billion cubic meters on [from?] the 2005 level." *Id.*
105. PATHWAYS TO DEEP DECARBONIZATION, *supra* note 25, at 87.
106. *Id.* at 88.
107. *Id.* "If CCS is deployed appropriately on a commercialized scale after 2030 in key industry sectors, it is expected to sequester 28% of total CO_2 emissions in the industry sector in 2050. . . ." *Id.*
108. *Id.* at 87-89.
109. *Id.* at x.

IV. Translating Decarbonization Scenarios Into Law

Decarbonization is highly unlikely to happen at the national level unless it is translated into a supportive legal structure. At least two elements are needed to translate such decarbonization scenarios into law. The U.S. scenario is illustrative.

A. Incorporation of Backcasting Into Law and Policymaking

Most legal and policy approaches to reducing greenhouse gas emissions move from the present toward some point in the future and are bounded by the technical and economic feasibility of achieving a particular result. For example, the Energy Policy and Conservation Act of 1975 directs the U.S. Department of Transportation (DOT) to adopt corporate average fuel economy (CAFE) standards for automobiles.[110] Each standard is to be based on "maximum feasible fuel economy" that the Secretary of Transportation determines can be achieved for a particular year.[111] Under the Clean Air Act, standards for emissions of air pollutants for new motor vehicles "shall take effect after such period as the [EPA] Administrator finds necessary to permit the development and application of the requisite technology, giving appropriate consideration to the cost of compliance within such period."[112]

In 2012, exercising their authority under both acts, EPA and DOT issued combined fuel economy standards/greenhouse gas emission limits for passenger cars, light-duty trucks and medium-duty passenger vehicles for model years 2017-2025.[113] The final standards are projected to result in an average industry fleetwide level of 163 grams/mile of carbon dioxide in model year 2025, which is equivalent to 54.5 miles per gallon if achieved exclusively through fuel economy improvements.[114] The 54.5 miles per gallon requirement, in turn, is built on previous fuel economy standards that, taken together, have moved fuel economy standards in steps toward higher and higher levels. According to EPA, this regulation will have significant greenhouse gas reduction and economic benefits.[115] From today's perspective, in which average U.S. fuel economy is in the neighborhood of 25 miles per

110. 42 U.S.C. §§32901-19.
111. *Id.* §32902(a).
112. 42 U.S.C. §7521(a)(2).
113. 77 Fed. Reg. 62624 (Oct. 15, 2012) (codified at 40 C.F.R. Parts 85, 86, and 600).
114. 77 Fed. Reg. at 62627.
115. U.S. Environmental Protection Agency, *Transportation and Climate—Regulations & Standards: Light-Duty*, http://www.epa.gov/oms/climate/regs-light-duty.htm (last visited Sept. 10, 2015) (estimating that it will reduce greenhouse gas emissions by two billion metric tons and provide "net benefits up to $451 billion.").

gallon,[116] an average fleetwide fuel efficiency level of 54.5 miles per gallon for new vehicles is a fairly impressive achievement.

Backcasting, by contrast, looks at a desired future state and asks what it would take to achieve that future state.[117] Under the deep decarbonization future described earlier for the United States, the average fuel economy for light duty vehicles in 2050 would be more than 100 miles per gallon. In addition, those vehicles would be fueled not by gasoline or diesel fuel but by electricity or hydrogen.[118] Moreover, those vehicles would need to be powered by an electricity generation system that is both twice the size of today's system and based almost entirely on renewable energy and, where fossil fuels are still used, carbon sequestration.[119]

Assuming that the United States can achieve 54.5 miles per gallon as a fleetwide average for *new* vehicles by 2025, how does it achieve a fleetwide average of more than 100 miles per gallon for *all* vehicles by 2050? As the deep decarbonization report for the U.S. explained, "[t]his would require the deployment of roughly 300 million alternative fuel vehicles by 2050."[120] Backcasting would oblige policymakers to consider that question and develop credible and workable laws and policies that answer it, at the same time as they develop shorter-term laws and policies. It seems likely that the United States will require a much higher level of ambition regarding motor vehicles' fuel efficiency between 2025 and 2050 to achieve the outcome described in the deep decarbonization report. It also seems possible that a more ambitious 2025 standard or goal would have better positioned the United States to achieve the required reductions.[121]

Similarly, EPA's Clean Power Plan, finalized in August 2015, would reduce greenhouse gases from electric generating facilities by 32% from 2005 levels by 2030.[122] As ambitious as that goal is, the pathway from that result in 2030 to the Deep Decarbonization Project's virtually decarbonized and expanded electrical generation system in 2050 is even more ambitious.

---

116. MICHAEL SIVAK & BRANDON SCHOETTLE, UNIVERSITY OF MICHIGAN TRANSPORTATION RESEARCH INSTITUTE, BENEFITS OF RECENT IMPROVEMENTS IN VEHICLE FUEL ECONOMY 1-2 (2014).

117. *See supra* note 83 and accompanying text.

118. PATHWAYS TO DEEP DECARBONIZATION IN THE UNITED STATES, *supra* note 85, at xiii.

119. *Id.*

120. *Id.*

121. *Cf.* Howard A. Latin, *Climate Change Mitigation and Decarbonization*, 25 VILL. ENVTL. L.J. 1, 82 (2014) ("[T]he fundamental climate change policy choice for America is between a decarbonization strategy that will be 'difficult to accomplish' and the conventional multi-decade emissions-reduction approaches that are 'certain to fail.'").

122. U.S. Environmental Protection Agency, Carbon Pollution Emission Guidelines for Existing Stationary Sources: Electric Utility Generating Units (2015), *available at* http://www2.epa.gov/sites/production/files/2015-08/documents/cpp-final-rule.pdf.

The value of backcasting as a reality check on the ambitiousness of plans to reduce greenhouse gas emissions also applies at the international level. The objective of keeping the global average temperature increase from greenhouse gas emissions under 2°C, within the emissions reduction timetables set by the IPCC (40% to 70% reduction by 2050; zero or negative emissions by 2100), provides a framework for backcasting. In the run-up to the December 2015 Paris Conference of the Parties to the Convention on Climate Change, countries submitted their Intended Nationally Determined Contributions (INDCs).[123] The INDCs reflect the level of emissions reduction that each country intends to achieve. The objectives stated earlier for both the United States and China are the INDCs that each country submitted under the Convention.[124] The question is whether the sum of each national INDC will actually put the world on track to keep the increase in world temperatures under 2°C. In the summer of 2015, the International Energy Agency released a report stating that the answer is no:

> With INDCs submitted so far, and the planned energy policies in countries that have yet to submit, the world's estimated remaining carbon budget consistent with a 50% chance of keeping the rise in temperature below 2°C is consumed by around 2040—eight months later than is projected in the absence of INDCs.[125]

The Paris Agreement acknowledges this "emissions gap"—between what has been submitted and what needs to be done—and creates a process for addressing it. Every five years beginning in 2015, every country is to submit nationally determined contributions that "represent a progression beyond the Party's then current nationally determined contribution and reflect its highest possible ambition."[126] Every five years beginning in 2023, the Conference of the Parties is to "take stock of the implementation of this Agreement to assess the collective progress towards achieving" its purpose.[127] These requirements should encourage or prod governments to be more ambitious over time, without being prescriptive about what they should do.

One way to meld forward-looking emission limits with backcasting is for each nation to prepare nonbinding deep decarbonization plans that extend into the future past 2020, 2025, or 2030, toward 2050 and even 2100.

---

123. United Nations Framework Convention on Climate Change, Intended Nationally Determined Contributions (INDCs), http://unfccc.int/focus/indc_portal/items/8766.php (last visited Sept. 19, 2015) (explaining INDCs and containing links to national INDC submissions).
124. *See supra* notes 95 (United States) and 104 (China) and accompanying text.
125. INTERNATIONAL ENERGY AGENCY, ENERGY AND CLIMATE CHANGE, *supra* note 18, at 2.
126. Paris Agreement, *supra* note 9, art. 4.3.
127. *Id.* arts. 14.1 & 14.2.

Unlike the deep decarbonization plans prepared as part of this project, they would be prepared by the governments themselves. Such plans would enable governments to see farther into the future than 2025 or 2030 (the end dates of the United States and China INDCs), and give governments a sense of whether the nationally determined contributions they submit every five years are ambitious enough to enable achievement of deep decarbonization.[128]

B.   Use of Legal Scenarios

Scenarios are a commonplace part of the discussion concerning climate change and sustainability. "A scenario is essentially a story about the future."[129] Scenarios are not predictions; they are narrative descriptions of possible futures if events unfold in a certain way.[130] They involve four elements—a description of the current state of things, an explanation of "driving forces" that propel the system, a description of other forces that can change the trajectory of the system, and "sideswipes, major surprises that can alter an otherwise straightforward outcome."[131] The IPCC reports and Deep Decarbonization reports use scenarios extensively. Scenarios add value by making it possible to understand possible futures, in somewhat concrete terms, if events unfold in a certain way. However, in those reports, the scenarios tend to focus on science, policy, and technology.

The use of legal scenarios—either stand-alone legal scenarios or multidisciplinary scenarios with a distinct legal component—would likely help decide how to achieve deep decarbonization at the national and subnational levels. Laws are one of the "driving forces" that propel action in any country and could, if changed, propel a country in a different direction. Legal scenarios could illuminate the ways in which different kinds of laws could affect emissions reductions most effectively and fairly. They could also show different legal pathways and illustrate how to design laws to maximize economic, social, and environmental benefits.

One of the signal contributions of the Deep Decarbonization scenarios for individual countries is that they particularize the 2°C goal to the circumstances of individual countries. However, they do not take the additional step of describing the particular laws or types of laws that would be needed to get to those outcomes. What legal framework, for example, would be needed

---

128. Pathways to Deep Decarbonization, *supra* note 25, at xiv.
129. Gilberto C. Gallopín & Paul Raskin, *Windows on the Future: Global Scenarios and Sustainability*, Env't, Apr. 1998, at 7, 8.
130. *Id.*
131. *Id.*

to get from 54.5 miles per gallon for new vehicles in the United States in 2025 to 300 million alternative fuel vehicles by 2050? Legal scenarios about different laws or combinations of laws would make it possible for decision-makers and the public to visualize what the choices are.

Many possible legal and policy approaches to decarbonization are available, including government supported research and development, carbon taxation, regulation, public information, and land use and transportation law changes. They can be used singly or in combination, and they can be sequenced in different ways over time. Legal scenarios could illuminate trade offs among and between different approaches and identify ways in which various tools could be mutually reinforcing or mutually antagonistic. Scenarios could also make clear what approaches are indispensable—or at least highly valuable—in keeping the temperature increase well below 2°C. It appears, for example, that laws and policies that foster clean energy development help build a counterweight to the fossil fuel industry and thus make it more politically possible to adopt laws setting a price on carbon. Nearly two-thirds of the countries and subnational jurisdictions that had adopted a carbon pricing scheme by 2013 had previously adopted renewable energy portfolio standards or feed-in tariffs for renewable energy.[132] Carbon pricing, as previously indicated, is likely an essential element of any deep decarbonization strategy.

Legal scenarios could also be of use in assessing the role of negative emissions in any decarbonization strategy. In contrast to emissions reductions, which are about preventing additional carbon dioxide from entering the atmosphere, negative emissions occur when carbon dioxide already in the atmosphere is removed. Negative emissions can be increased by enhancing the capacity of carbon sinks such as soil and trees to absorb carbon dioxide; they could also be achieved through a variety of technologies.[133] Overall carbon dioxide concentrations in the atmosphere are already very high. Concentrations of greenhouse gases are at levels that have not been seen for at least 800,000 years.[134] That fact suggests the value of removing carbon dioxide from the atmosphere for precautionary reasons. In addition, the 2°C goal will require a remarkable and in many ways unprecedented level of international cooperation to achieve, and there is a significant likelihood of lag-

---

132. Meckling et al., *supra* note 48.
133. *See, e.g.*, BEN CALDECOTT ET AL., UNIVERSITY OF OXFORD SMITH SCHOOL OF ENTERPRISE AND THE ENVIRONMENT, STRANDED CARBON ASSETS AND NEGATIVE EMISSIONS TECHNOLOGIES (2015), *available at* http://www.smithschool.ox.ac.uk/research-programmes/stranded-assets/Stranded%20.Carbon%20 Assets%20and%20NETs %20-%2006.02.15.pdf.
134. 2013 IPCC PHYSICAL SCIENCE REPORT, *supra* note 1, at 11.

gards. Negative emissions provide a way of obtaining protection from the effects of laggards.

Still, a considerable effort will need to be made to develop technologies for negative emissions. Although the Deep Decarbonization project includes carbon capture and sequestration from fossil fuel plants, it does not address the use of biomass to produce energy followed by the capture and sequestration of resulting carbon, because that technology is regarded as too uncertain at present.[135] To be sure, law and policy at the national level, coupled with international cooperation efforts, can help foster the development of such technologies. But what kinds of other laws and policies are needed—in industry, agriculture, forestry, electricity generation, and other sectors—to produce negative emissions? What are the most cost-effective, equitable, and permanent ways of accomplishing that result, and with the most benefits? The development of legal scenarios—based on different tools and combinations of tools—could assist in answering those questions.

The sustainable development frame, which would maximize the social, economic, environmental, and security benefits of legal measures taken to decarbonize the economy, also indicates the value of legal scenarios. Reductions in greenhouse gas emissions do not produce local benefits; the co-benefits of those measures do, and designing legal measures that maximize these co-benefits is a key element in getting these measures adopted. National laws that allow subnational governments such as states and municipalities to particularize implementation to local circumstances, for example, may lead to greater co-benefits than more uniform laws.[136] Similarly, what role could a properly motivated public play in individual efforts to reduce greenhouse gas emissions? If such efforts had a greater impact, perhaps other and less attractive measures would be unnecessary.[137] Similarly, what are the best measures to protect the poor and manage the impact of the transition on the fossil-fuel industry? By helping answer these and other questions, legal scenarios based on sustainable development could identify the most attractive and politically achievable legal pathways for keeping the temperature increase well below 2°C.

---

135. PATHWAYS TO DEEP DECARBONIZATION, *supra* note 25, at 8-9. For an overview of one proposal, see Graciela Chichilnisky & Peter Eisenberger, *Carbon Negative Power Plants*, CRYOGAS INT'L, May 2011, at 36, *available at* http://www.chichilnisky.com/wp-content/uploads/2011/04/Carbon-Negative-Power-Plants.pdf.

136. John C. Dernbach et al., *Making the States Full Partners in a National Climate Change Effort: A Necessary Element for Sustainable Economic Development*, 40 ELR 10597 (June 2010).

137. Thomas Dietz et al., *Household Actions Can Provide a Behavioral Wedge to Rapidly Reduce US Carbon Emissions*, 106 PROC. NAT'L ACAD. SCI. 18452 (2009).

V.   Conclusion

An essential part of the decarbonization challenge is proposing, analyzing, and comparing various legal pathways to that result in each individual country. Those legal pathways should be capable of reducing greenhouse gas emissions at a speed and scale needed to give the world its best change of keeping the global average temperature increase below 2°C while also producing as many economic, social, environmental, and security benefits as possible. In the face of a daunting challenge, there exists a real possibility that law and lawyers can help improve human quality of life throughout the world by facilitating zero-carbon development.

Chapter 3
Thinking Ecosystems, Providing Water: The Water Infrastructure Imperative

Keith H. Hirokawa & Jonathan Rosenbloom

As climate change impacts become more pronounced, already strained infrastructure necessary to ensure the provision of critical services will be put under additional stress. In the context of urban water supplies, climate change guarantees instability in the acquisition, transmission, provision, and disposal of water. Such challenges facing water-related services, including the provision of potable water and control of floods, pose immediate and long-term threats to health, safety, and welfare, and importantly, accompany failures in a wide array of essential public services. Nevertheless, notwithstanding widespread agreement regarding the risks, the potential for grave danger, and the high costs to improve water supplies and associated infrastructure, we have seen surprisingly little effective long-term water planning to ensure continued water-related services in the era of climate change.

Most significantly, planning for future provision of water-related services continues to focus on conventional "gray infrastructure" in which the manufactured, engineered, built environment is viewed as the primary, if not sole, means to provide essential services. Often working against natural processes, gray infrastructure—such as diversion systems, pipes, tunnels, culverts, detention basins, berms, tiling systems, and cost-intensive water treatment

Authors' Note: The authors would like to thank the attendees at the Environmental Law Collaborative (2014), and give special thanks to Stephen Miller, Robin Craig, and Jessie Owley for organizing and compiling the written documents for this book. Being a part of the Collaborative has been among the most gratifying experiences we have had in legal academia.

facilities—is the traditional method used to provide potable water and/or to prevent damage from unwanted water.[1]

In this chapter, we look to emerging systems often called "green infrastructure" as short and long-term cost effective methods for providing services in the face of climate change impacts. Green infrastructure—such as wetlands, urban forests, bio-filtration, ponds, rain gardens and other natural-based treatments—leverages ecosystem services and capitalizes on vegetation, soils, and natural processes to provide potable water, prevent damage from flooding, lower costs, and create healthier, vibrant communities.

While we focus predominantly on threats to water systems stemming from climate change, we do so recognizing that urban water infrastructure in many locations is already greatly stressed and overtaxed by population growth, migration, and age of a neglected infrastructure. The challenges facing water-based services are amplified not only because they are related to essential human services, but also because the existing infrastructure is both vast and vulnerable. For example, each year trillions of gallons of water are lost through hundreds of thousands of miles of pipe used to transport water. Updating this infrastructure is estimated to cost hundreds of billions, if not trillions, of dollars.

In its Final Report, the Intergovernmental Panel on Climate Change (IPCC), Working Group II acknowledged the infrastructure challenges rising from climate changing conditions and the significant risks they pose to crucial services, stating:

> Climate Change will have profound impacts on a broad spectrum of infrastructure systems (water and energy supply, sanitation and drainage, transport and telecommunication), services (including health care and emergency services), the built environment and ecosystem services. These interact with other social, economic, and environmental stressors exacerbating and compounding risks to individual and household well-being (medium confidence based on high agreement, medium evidence).[2]

For purposes of this chapter, Working Group II's statement contains two critical observations. First, it is significant that Working Group II chose to

---

1.   Tiling is a sophisticated underground drainage system, designed to get water off agricultural land as quickly as possible. An example of the widespread use of tiling can be seen in the Midwest where about 48%, 48%, and 42% of Illinois', Ohio's, and Indiana's cropland, respectively, is tiled. ZACHARY SUGG, ASSESSING U.S. FARM DRAINAGE: CAN GIS LEAD TO BETTER ESTIMATES OF SUBSURFACE DRAINAGE EXTENT 6 (World Resources Institute Aug. 2007), *available at* http://pdf.wri.org/assessing_farm_drainage.pdf.

2.   INTERGOVERNMENTAL PANEL ON CLIMATE CHANGE, CLIMATE CHANGE 2014: IMPACTS, ADAPTATION, AND VULNERABILITY 538 (2014), *available at* https://www.ipcc.ch/report/ar5/wg2/ [hereinafter 2014 IPCC ADAPTATION REPORT].

associate climate change with stress to critical infrastructure. Second, it is equally significant that this stress will make it increasingly more difficult and expensive to provide public services. When aggregated, these two observations suggest a simple imperative: sound responses to climate change must concern securing infrastructure and ensuring the continued provision of public services.

Because many critical public services fall within the purview of local governance, communities will face the burden of providing an effective and efficient water infrastructure system. Recent water-based challenges involving the quantity and quality of water illustrate some of the service disruptions local communities face. For example, the 2015 floods in South Carolina brought *too much* water, over-taxing public service systems, resulting in local governments' losing capacity in water treatment plants, water main breaks, boil water alerts, and thousands of citizens scrambling to find potable water.[3] Meanwhile severe, extreme, and exceptional droughts throughout the West in 2015 involved *too little* water, making it difficult to provide the requisite water to citizens.[4] In addition to quantity-based challenges, many communities are also struggling with ensuring the proper quality of potable water. The 2014 algae blooms in Lake Erie that left thousands without potable water illustrate the type of quality-based challenges cities face.[5]

As local governments address these and other water infrastructure challenges, it is essential to consider "green infrastructure" and ecosystem services in particular. For purposes of this chapter, the divergence between gray and green infrastructure emphasizes the importance of ecosystem services. The term "ecosystem services" refers to the "measurable benefits that people receive from ecosystems. Ecosystems produce goods and services as a result of ecosystem process, function, and structure."[6] The study of ecosystem services combines ecology and economics in a way that focuses on ecosystem processes and ecosystem functionality. This approach identifies and appreci-

---

3.   Sean Breslin, *Flooding in Columbia, South Carolina, Leads to Drinking Water Shortages; Residents Urged to Boil All Water*, WEATHER.COM (Oct. 5, 2015), http://www.weather.com/news/news/columbia-south-carolina-water-shortage.

4.   Nat'l Drought Mitigation Center, *U.S. Drought Monitor* (Sept. 28, 2015), http://droughtmonitor.unl.edu/.

5.   Michael Wines, *Behind Toledo's Water Crisis, a Long-Troubled Lake Erie*, N.Y. TIMES (Aug. 4, 2014), http://www.nytimes.com/2014/08/05/us/lifting-ban-toledo-says-its-water-is-safe-to-drink-again.html?_r=0.

6.   *A New View of Our Economy: Nature's Value in the Snoqualmie Watershed*, EARTH ECON. 15 (June 2010), *available at* http://www.eartheconomics.org/FileLibrary/file/Reports/Puget%20Sound%20and%20Watersheds/Earth_Economics_Report_on_the_Snoqualmie_Watershed_compressed.pdf [hereinafter EARTH ECON.].

ates the manner in which ecosystems produce goods of value, the manner in which ecosystems provide services that are essential to human well-being, and the economic worth that can be attributed to functioning ecosystems as the value of the services they provide.

Although not directly addressed in this chapter, the comparison of gray and green infrastructure also highlights different perspectives on how to fund public infrastructure. Where traditional, gray infrastructure relied predominantly on municipal bonds (and fees or assessments to make bond payments), green infrastructure makes available previously unrecognized economic benefits embedded in ecosystem services. For instance, green infrastructure programs produce water and energy efficiencies, often by cap-italizing on existing natural services such as climate control (shade), storm surge (stormwater capture by root systems), and pollution control services (air and water filtering) provided by urban forests. Capturing this value can help fund green infrastructure projects. Research around funding green infrastructure is continuing to develop, but it remains a critical part of mak-ing ecosystem services a reality.[7]

With an eye on developing appropriate principles for implementing Working Groups II's directive on infrastructure, this chapter explores the threats to urban water infrastructure and solutions to abate those threats based on green infrastructure. This move from gray to green infrastruc-ture addresses the water challenge by recognizing the need to migrate away from the counterproductive assumption that nature is harmful and must be resisted, and toward the assumption that nature is helpful and must be embraced. If infrastructure and the built environment are to be sustain-able and resilient in the face of climate changes—if infrastructure will have the capacity to meet the social, economic, and environmental necessities of our time and over time—an understanding of ecological services must be addressed at the local level with local land use planning tools for infrastruc-ture and the built environment.

The first section below describes the current state of water infrastructure in the United States and its susceptibility to climate change impacts. The second section introduces ecosystem services as a method to address some of those impacts. The final section concludes with three core areas in which cit-ies can begin to recognize and embrace opportunities in ecosystem services to implement green infrastructure projects as a means to avoid catastrophic loss as we enter a period of climate change.

---

7.   For more information on funding local adaptation projects connected with climate change, see gener-
        ally Jonathan Rosenbloom, *Funding Adaptation*, 47 J. MARSHALL L. REV. 657 (2014).

I. Water Infrastructure and Infrastructure Accounting

We cannot ignore the anticipated problems concerning adequate water quality and quantity. Failure of a water supply, sewage disposal, or stormwater system will result in significant, unrecoverable losses. As such, it is critical to identify the challenges currently facing cities and design ways to make water infrastructure more sustainable and resilient.

To accomplish this task, it is important to recognize that water infrastructure does much more than merely provide potable water. Traditional water management is framed as an acquisition-to-disposal system: the capture of water from the surface, ground, and air; treatment of water for potable supplies; transportation of water from capture to user; wastewater disposal to prevent disease; and mitigation of unwanted water, such as from storm surges and flooding. Historically, water systems provide these services through an intentional coordination of constructed artificial and, more recently, natural systems in the form of "gray infrastructure." These systems are designed to capture, convey, store, and treat water through complex arrangements in the built environment.

In general, the success of a water system depends upon its ability to perform the tasks associated with water. Interruptions in water provision such as breaks in water lines, emergency substitution, water quality advisories resulting from contamination, excessive and uncontrolled flooding, suggest failures. The strength of the water supply system is assessed by capacity and security—generally, miles of pipe, anticipated life span of the built infrastructure, and the ability of the system to accommodate changes in population and environmental standards.

In most typical communities in the United States, engineered solutions consisting of gray infrastructure for water services are the norm. For instance, roads are "crowned" in their center to direct the flow of water to the edges of roadways, where concrete accelerates the removal of runoff water to curbs, which capture and deliver runoff towards storm drains. Then, pipes and ditches, berms and dams, even improved riverbeds (with concrete) keep water from intruding into the ground, basements, and residential and commercial areas. They also eliminate risks to vehicle traffic by preventing ponding on road surfaces, transport water away from the built environment, and deliver water to sophisticated filtering facilities, which guarantee (in many cases) the delivery of clean, fresh water to many homes, businesses, and fields.

And, as sure as water goes in, we have designed the system for removal of waste and wastewater from human structures. The U.S. Environmental

Protection Agency (EPA) summarized conventional infrastructure planning as the following:

> To date, the focus of traditional stormwater management programs has been concentrated largely on structural engineering solutions to manage the hydraulic consequences of the increased runoff that results from development. Because of this emphasis, stormwater management has been considered primarily an engineering endeavor. Economic analyses regarding the selection of solutions that are not entirely based on pipes and ponds have not been a significant factor in management decisions. Where costs have been considered, the focus has been primarily on determining capital costs for conventional infrastructure, as well as operation and maintenance costs in dollars per square foot or dollars per pound of pollutant removed.[8]

Maintaining the current system of gray infrastructure is a gargantuan and costly task. At present, there are approximately 52,000 community water systems and 21,400 not-for-profit non-community water systems.[9] Each system consists of miles and miles of infrastructure. For example, the provision of water in and around Chicago servicing five million people has *hundreds of thousands* of miles of pipes.[10]

Many water infrastructure systems across the United States are currently strained by two forces: age of the system and added burdens levied by climate change. As to the age and deterioration of the system:

> [T]he task of providing an adequate supply of clean water and sufficient wastewater and storm water treatment capacity in the U.S. is more challenging now than ever before. Some of the country's water, wastewater and storm water systems were constructed over 100 years ago. Most were built during the last 50 years with the spread of suburbanization, largely unrestrained by concerns for sustainability. Many of these facilities are at the end of their useful life and need to be either renewed or replaced. Meanwhile, changes in federal clean water and drinking water programs require upgrades in plants, technology and practices that require various forms of investment. In addition, periods of economic distress, taxpayer or ratepayer revolt, rapid increases or decreases in service population, and instability in municipal bond markets have left many

---

8.   U.S. ENVTL. PROTECTION AGENCY, REDUCING STORMWATER COSTS THROUGH LOW IMPACT DEVELOP-MENT (LID) STRATEGIES AND PRACTICES 6 (Dec. 2007), *available at* http://water.epa.gov/polwaste/green/upload/2008_01_02_NPS_lid_costs07uments_reducingstormwatercosts-2.pdf.
9.   U.S. ENVL. PROT. AGENCY, DRINKING WATER INFRASTRUCTURE NEEDS AND ASSESSMENT, FOURTH REPORT TO CONGRESS I (EPA 816-R-09-001) (Feb. 2009). *See also* AM. WATER WORKS ASS'N, BURIED NO LONGER: CONFRONTING AMERICA'S WATER INFRASTRUCTURE CHALLENGE 3 (2011).
10.   David Schaper, *As Infrastructure Crumbles, Trillions of Gallons of Water Lost*, NPR.ORG (Oct. 29, 2014), http://www.npr.org/2014/10/29/359875321/as-infrastructure-crumbles-trillions-of-gallons-of-water-lost?utm_medium=RSS&utm_campaign=news.

communities struggling to fund the maintenance and replacement of their water infrastructure. . . .[11]

As the infrastructure ages, it deteriorates. A 2015 report estimated that 2.1 trillion gallons of water are lost yearly to leaky pipes. That number amounts to almost six billion gallons of lost water per day. Chicago is estimated to lose 22 billion gallons of water per year, enough to service 700,000 people.[12] Importantly, water loss at this scale suggests economic hardships in addition to environmental and social impacts. The water lost through leakage has often already been treated for water quality purposes. Once the water is lost, the water authority is unable to recover its investment as the water does not reach the paying customer.

In addition to its diminishing status, existing water infrastructure is burdened by the consequences of climate change. Climate change makes an already difficult and costly situation more complex and unpredictable, adding risk that will threaten the physical constitution of water infrastructure. Floods, landslides, avalanches, mudslides, forest fires from hotter, drier summers, and loss of snow pack will disrupt water flow expectations.[13] Storms will impact infrastructure as a result of their frequency, intensity, and predictability. Sea-level rise will have a direct effect on the location of population and infrastructure. Changing precipitation patterns, especially combined with temperature changes, will make it difficult to plan for disease control, water availability and quality, and pest control.

These climate change impacts can be expected to have associated costs. When local communities aim to resist climate impacts by widening pipes, building more dams, dikes, and berms, building more treatment capacity, and converting salt water in yet-to-be-built in a cost effective way desalination plants, there is an associated cost. And that cost is daunting. With respect to water supply, EPA observes that:

> Without global GHG mitigation, damages associated with the supply and demand of water across the U.S. are estimated to range from approximately $7.7-190 billion in 2100. The spread of this range indicates that the effect of climate change on water supply and demand is highly sensitive to projected

---

11. Ray Bolger et al., *Sustainable Water Systems: Step One—Redefining the Nation's Infrastructure Challenge*, Aspen Inst. 9 (May 2009), *available at* http://www.aspeninstitute.org/sites/default/files/content/docs/pubs/water_infra_final.pdf.
12. Schaper, *supra* note 10.
13. The U.S. Geological Survey reports that although a century ago, there were over 150 glaciers in the peaks and ridgelines of Glacier National Park, there are currently 25 glaciers larger than 25 acres remaining. Retreat of Glaciers in Glacier National Park, http://nrmsc.usgs.gov/research/glacier_retreat.htm.

changes in runoff and evaporation, both of which vary greatly across future climate projections and by U.S. region.[14]

Similarly,

In 2009, the National Association of Clean Water Agencies (NACWA) estimated the cost of adapting water utilities to climate change in the U.S. to be between $448 billion and $944 billion. The report states that NACWA based its estimates on the IPCC's 2007 report and expects changes upon a review of the now released IPCC 2013 report, which shows significantly more severe climate changing impacts. NACWA's report is nonetheless telling, as it provides a uniquely comprehensive estimate of the costs to adapt a single local government service.[15]

According to one estimate, the average cost of drinking water[16] infrastructure replacement will range from $550-$2,300 per household to $6,300 per household for smaller systems, but up to $10,000 per household if treatment plants and pumps need replacement.[17] In the meantime, the useful life of water infrastructure has declined: the average life expectancy for gray infrastructure has decreased from 120 years (for systems features

---

14.   U.S. ENVTL. PROT. AGENCY, CLIMATE CHANGE IN THE UNITED STATES: BENEFITS OF GLOBAL ACTION 56 (2015).

15.   Rosenbloom, *supra* note 7, at 669.

16.   Wastewater infrastructure suffers similar liability. EPA reported as follows in 2008:

> The needs for Wastewater Treatment, Pipe Repairs, and New Pipes are $187.9 billion, an increase of $28.6 billion (18 percent) since 2004. Of this increase, $16.3 billion is for Advanced Wastewater Treatment (Category II) needs, $7.0 billion is for Secondary Wastewater Treatment (Category I) needs, and $4.8 billion is for Pipe Repair (Category III) needs.

> These needs increases are mainly for improvements to rehabilitate aging infrastructure, to meet more protective water quality standards, and to respond to and prepare for population growth. New York ($17.0 billion), California ($16.3 billion), Florida ($9.4 billion), and New Jersey ($6.3 billion) reported almost half (47 percent) of the Secondary Treatment (Category I) and Advanced Treatment (Category II) needs. Similarly, nearly half (47 percent) of the Pipe Repair (Category III) and New Pipe (Category IV) needs were reported by California ($7.9 billion), Florida ($6.5 billion), New York ($5.0 billion), Ohio ($4.4 billion), Texas ($4.2 billion), Puerto Rico ($3.7 billion), North Carolina ($3.7 billion), and Massachusetts ($3.6 billion).

U.S. ENVTL. PROT. AGENCY, CLEAN WATERSHEDS NEEDS SURVEY, 2008 REPORT TO CONGRESS vi (EPA 832-R-10-002) (2008).

17.   EPA notes that "[t]he nations' drinking water utilities need $334.8 billion in infrastructure investments over the next 20 years for thousands of miles of pipe, as well as thousands of treatment plants, storage tanks, and other key assets to ensure the public health and economic well-being of our cities, towns, and communities." U.S. Envtl. Prot. Agency, *Drinking Water Infrastructure Needs Survey and Assessment, Fourth Report to Congress*, at i, EPA 816-R-09-001 (Feb. 2009); *see also* Richard A. Krop et al., *Local Government Investment in Municipal Water And Sewer Infrastructure: Adding Value to The National Economy*, The U.S. Conference of Mayors (Aug. 14, 2008):

> The $334.8 billion represents the need associated with thousands of miles of pipe, thousands of treatment plant and source projects, and billions of gallons of storage. Investments in water systems not only provide assurances of continued delivery of safe drinking water to our homes, schools, and places of business, they are key to local economies across our nation.

installed in the late 1800s) down to 75 years for post-WWII infrastructure. The staggered life expectancies of water infrastructure components makes financing infrastructure more complicated, including equitably allocating scarce resources to the replacement where and when systems come to the end of their useful life.[18]

In all, the cost of sustaining the built infrastructure to ensure the provision of potable water in the climate change era will be profound.[19] Given that water is an imperative, communities must struggle with these infrastructure questions, costs, and risks. No local government may opt out or race to the bottom of water. Hence, the question arises of whether it is time to adjust infrastructure thinking to leverage ecosystem services.

II.   Recognizing Ecosystem Services as a Preparedness Necessity

Having established the dire need for effective water infrastructure planning and the gargantuan cost associated with ensuring the provision water-related services, this chapter now addresses the benefits of integrating ecological economics into infrastructure planning. In the past, this integration was absent from infrastructure planning. Nevertheless, against the challenges set forth in Part I, local governments need better options to develop water infrastructure that demonstrates "the ability of a system and its component parts to

---

18.   The costs of built infrastructure maintenance and replacement have associated benefits that do not have a corresponding counterpart in maintenance of natural capital. As stated in a recent report by the U.S. Conference of Mayors:

>   The estimates exhibit a wide range, but the consensus is that public infrastructure investment yields positive returns, and investment in water and sewer infrastructure has greater returns than most other types of public infrastructure.
>   • A recent study estimates that one dollar of water and sewer infrastructure investment increases private output (Gross Domestic Product, GDP) in the long-term by $6.35.
>   • With respect to annual general revenue and spending on operating and maintaining water and sewer systems, the US Department of Commerce's Bureau of Economic Analysis estimates that for each additional dollar of revenue (or the economic value of the output) of the water and sewer industry, the increase in revenue (economic output) that occurs in all industries is $2.62 in that year.
>   • The same analysis estimates that adding 1 job in water and sewer creates 3.68 jobs in the national economy to support that job.

>   THE U.S. CONFERENCE OF MAYORS, LOCAL GOVERNMENT INVESTMENT IN MUNICIPAL WATER AND SEWER INFRASTRUCTURE: ADDING VALUE TO THE NATIONAL ECONOMY I (Aug. 14, 2008).

19.   DAVID MONSMA ET AL., SUSTAINABLE WATER SYSTEMS: REDEFINING THE NATION'S INFRASTRUCTURE CHALLENGE 10 (The Aspen Institute 2009) ("Greatly adding to these challenges are the far-reaching impacts of climate change, which, through changing precipitation patterns, more intense storms, and warmer temperatures that increase snowpack melt and add to droughts, pose a number of new and uncertain challenges for our water supply and management.").

anticipate, absorb, accommodate, or recover from the effects of a potentially hazardous event in a timely and efficient manner."[20]

When we observe the long-term costs and ecological destruction associated with gray infrastructure,[21] consideration of ecologically based solutions to infrastructure needs presents an opportunity. Of course, from the engineering perspective, ecological solutions to infrastructure challenges may seem like a foreign language because they challenge the idea that *built* infrastructure should determine the direction of infrastructure solutions. Nevertheless, ecosystem concepts may provide an advantage over a gray infrastructure approach because ecosystem planning requires an accounting of needs that are local, contextual, and environmentally situated.[22] In comparison, gray infrastructure planning is typically based on more universal criteria that relate to manufactured elements such as roads and dams, to the exclusion of local ecological assets and needs.

By appreciating ecosystem functionality, ecosystem services analyses reveal aspects of ecosystems that are important to human well-being, even though such features are otherwise invisible in the market.[23] As noted by the

---

20. Intergovernmental Panel on Climate Change, Managing the Risks of Extreme Events and Disasters to Advance Climate Change Adaptation 561 (2012).

21.

> Incorporation of conventional stormwater treatment, end-of-pipe solutions, into development has resulted in improvements to how stormwater runoff is released from a development. Primarily these improvements are in the form of reduced localized flooding directly downstream of the development but this improvement is often negated over time due to lack of maintenance of the facilities. Research has shown that ponds at the end of a developed site will never adequately achieve the goal of maintaining pre-developed runoff conditions. Severe changes in the landscape upstream of the pond just cannot adequately be addressed by the pond. The lack of ability to meet this difficult goal is apparent in the ever increasing requirements for sizing conventional stormwater ponds and may eventually be recognized as an unachievable goal through conventional stormwater treatments.

Pierce County Low Impact Development Study 38-39 (Apr. 11, 2001), *available at* http://www.co.pierce.wa.us/archives/150/LID%20Report%20final%20complete.pdf.

22.

> Green infrastructure design and performance is generally more context-specific then gray infrastructure. Because these types of controls must be designed and built to suit the soil, terrain and hydrologic conditions of each individual site. As a result, however, they can be designed and implemented to address local concerns and values.

American Rivers et al., Banking on Green: A Look at How Green Infrastructure Can Save Municipalities Money and Provide Economic Benefits Community-Wide 9 (Apr. 2012), *available at* http://www.americanrivers.org/assets/pdfs/reports-and-publications/banking-on-green-report.pdf.

23. James Salzman et al., *Protecting Ecosystem Services: Science, Economics, and Law*, 20 Stan. Envtl. L.J. 309, 312 (2001) ("[These] services themselves have no market value for the simple reason that no markets exist in which they can be exchanged."). *See also* Ruth Mathews, *Instream Flow Protection and Restoration: Setting a New Compass Point*, 36 Envtl. L. 1311, 1314 (2006):

> Often invisible, ecosystem services and their value to society are frequently ignored when determining the allocation of water to instream flows. If included, ecosystem services would further underline the importance of dedicating water to instream flows beyond just the

National Research Council, "The value of capital is defined by flows of useful services. Defining ecosystems as natural capital that yields useful services is the first step toward quantifying the value of ecosystems."[24] Ecosystem services analysis identifies the manner in which ecosystems produce goods (such as marketable products, including food, medicines, building materials and other goods), regulate climatic and ecosystem conditions (such as climate and air and water quality), provide important spiritual and cultural services (such as recreational, aesthetic, and spiritual opportunities), and support other processes and physical structure (such as soil formation, geological structure, and nutrient cycling).[25]

Ecosystem services thinking demands a break from commodity-based valuation. By focusing attention on the market values of goods that can be taken from ecosystems, without also accounting for the methods of sustaining the production of those goods or the loss of production in the future, we have expedited the decline of functionality throughout the natural system. Both consumption and the corresponding inattention to ecosystem functions that occurs in the commodification of nature have limited the ability of ecosystems to regenerate and sustain themselves, requiring the production of substitutes.

The ecosystem services approach suggests that water infrastructure planning should associate—instead of separate—infrastructure services with ecosystem services. An ecosystem services approach to infrastructure planning will require us to contextualize the costs of built infrastructure in relation to the costs of losing natural capital in the construction process and the benefits of including natural capital in infrastructure planning. As shown in the examples below, by incorporating ecosystem services into the planning process, we benefit from a collaboration of ecology and economics: an understanding of how natural processes and functions produce services that have real, measurable economic worth.[26] Because ecosystem service value is based on the worth of natural capital to human needs, an ecosystem services accounting is always measuring the value of ecosystems to human

---

minimum flow. Degradation of river, floodplain, and estuarine ecosystems through alteration of the flow regime results in lost opportunities for individuals and society, opportunities inherent in healthy ecosystems. Therefore, ecosystem services must be considered in the determination of instream flows if society is going to have access to the full benefits available from these ecosystems.

24. COMM. ON MO. RIVER ECOSYSTEM SCI., NAT'L RESEARCH COUNCIL, The Missouri River Ecosystem: Exploring the Prospects for Recovery 101 (2002).

25. See Stephen Farber et al., *Linking Ecology and Economics for Ecosystem Management*, 56 BIOSCIENCE 121, 123 tbl. 1, 124 (2006).

26. See EARTH ECON., *supra* note 6, at 54.

well-being, where humans are the beneficiaries of this form of wealth.[27] As a result, green infrastructure approaches tend to outperform in costs pertaining to built capital, repair and maintenance, mitigation of external impacts, and structural replacement.

Moreover, the change in thinking toward ecosystem services is a monumental move toward resiliency. Consider two realizations that come with ecosystem services thinking: (1) we have typically displaced and interrupted ecosystems to build infrastructure systems and the built environment,[28] and (2) built infrastructure has a relatively short lifespan. A resilient water infrastructure system leverages the role that natural systems play in producing clean and sufficient water (rivers, lakes, streams, groundwater aquifers, floodplains, floodways, wetlands, and the watersheds) and integrates those processes in formulating the means to capture, treat, store, and deliver water to places it is needed. Attentiveness to environmental quality in general will tend to promote resiliency in at least three ways: strengthen ecosystems and their resiliency to change; reduce the risks of pollution resulting from climate events: and reduce the negative impacts of adaptation measures implemented to protect the built, human environment.[29]

For purposes of this chapter, a final important characteristic of ecosystem services and water infrastructure is the relative importance of local governments. Elsewhere, we have argued that local governments are critical participants for the effective design and execution of climate change preparedness.[30] Although it is not the intention to reargue the point here, it is worth mentioning the advantages that local governments offer in this

---

27. *See* Kai M.A. Chan et al., *Conservation Planning for Ecosystem Services*, 4 PLoS Biology 2138, 2138-39 (2006), *available at* http://www.ncbi.nlm.nih.gov/pmc/articles/PMC1629036/. *See also* EARTH ECON., *supra* note 6, at 18-21 ("Ecosystems are assets, a form of wealth.").

28. Built infrastructure typically displaces and eliminates natural areas and ecosystems, interrupting or interfering with habitat, hydrology and other ecosystem feature. In some cases, the elimination of natural systems is intended to facilitate a value or amenity that is entirely different than the displaced ecosystem. In this case, we discuss trade offs. As a simple matter of space, every built infrastructure choice entails a replacement of some natural feature or amenity with a built one. Yet, trade offs often prioritize the provision of built infrastructure. For example, we fill coastal wetlands to capture the market value of a view and more convenient access to water. In the process, we may lose the ability of the land to mitigate storm surges. In others, however, infrastructure replaces an ecosystem process with built infrastructure that provides essentially the same service. This notion that the loss of ecosystem features is an unaccounted cost is a critical question for climate change preparedness.

29. *See* Jonathan Verschuuren, *Climate Change Adaptation and Environmental and Pollution Control Law*, *in* RESEARCH HANDBOOK ON CLIMATE ADAPTATION LAW 383 (Jonathan Verschuuren ed., 2013).

30. *See, e.g.*, Keith H. Hirokawa & Jonathan Rosenbloom, *The Cost of Federalism: Ecology, Community, and the Pragmatism of Land Use*, *in* THE LAW AND POLICY OF ENVIRONMENTAL FEDERALISM: A COMPARATIVE ANALYSIS (Kalyani Robbins & Erin Ryan eds., 2015); Keith H. Hirokawa & Jonathan Rosenbloom, *Land Use Planning in a Climate Change Context*, *in* RESEARCH HANDBOOK ON CLIMATE ADAPTATION LAW (Jonathan Verschuuren ed., 2013). *See also generally* Keith H. Hirokawa, *Sustaining Ecosystem Services Through Local Environmental Law*, 28 PACE ENVTL. L. REV. 760 (2011).

regard and how these advantages are emphasized in light of ecosystem services valuation. First, the benefits stemming from ecosystem services are partially felt locally, both as to matter of scale and gratification. Communities—much more than state or federal governments—identify specifically with local ecosystem processes, features, and their benefits. Second, the loss of such services is disproportionately appreciated across levels of government. The loss of productive soils can be crushing to an agricultural community, the loss of trees or logging rights can crush a logging community, and the depletion of fisheries can wreak havoc on coastal communities. Because such losses are felt so acutely at the local level, their value is most accurately identified at the local level. Third, water infrastructure has traditionally and historically been a matter for local concern and responsibility. At least, these points demand careful consideration of the role that local governments might play in climate change preparedness. In all likelihood, these points suggest we look to local innovation to understand how infrastructure needs can be met effectively by integrating ecosystem concepts into infrastructure planning.

III. Greening the Gray: Climate Preparedness Through Ecosystem Services Implementation

In this final part, we begin what we hope is a sustained dialog about where and how ecosystem services can be implemented at the local level to help provide water-based services. The areas of focus and the examples below are meant to illustrate the benefits of ecosystem services planning. They also showcase opportunities where cities and communities are investing in ecosystem functionality to ensure that ecosystems performing at a fraction of the cost of built infrastructure while illustrating that implementing ecosystem services at the local level can occur in many ways, from broad-based approaches (such as "low impact development" practices described in Section A) to specific ordinances (such as mitigation of urban forest losses set forth in Section B). In addition, ecosystem services may apply to diverse and core local legal instruments, including comprehensive plans, zoning and building codes, and water distribution regulations.

A. Low Impact Development

One example of green infrastructure for reducing stormwater impacts has been "low impact development" (LID) practices. LID generally refers to conservation-based land use strategies that minimize impervious surfaces and emphasize the use of natural features and native vegetation as stormwater control tools. Common implementation programs include reduction of lot sizes and parking lot sizes while maintaining overall density (and preserving open space), rooftop capture of stormwater, downspout disconnection, adjusting curb design to capture instead of transport stormwater in vegetated swales, replacing impervious surfaces with permeable surfaces, and increasing vegetation on development sites. Common targets for these practices are parking lots, roads and driveways, street curbs, rooftops and residential and commercial developments. In recent decades, many communities and municipalities have implemented LID practices to control stormwater flows and improve water quality, especially in communities suffering the challenges of combined sewer overflows (CSO).

A study commissioned by Pierce County, Washington, illustrates some potential LID practices in local residential subdivisions. The consultant was directed to evaluate the costs and benefits of implementing green infrastructure solutions to the stormwater impacts caused by new development. The report analyzed a typical lot size, but on atypical developments that incorporated LID practices. The report described the following:

> [T]he LID design attempts to reduce the severity of the changes in the landscape thereby reducing the change in the hydrology from the predeveloped state. Mitigation for changes in the landscape are completed as close to the source of runoff as possible with nonstructural [best management practices] such as swales, bioretention areas, and open spaces. If designed correctly and allowed to function without encroachment from incompatible uses these stormwater treatments should function much more like natural systems thereby meeting the goal of maintaining the predeveloped hydrology of the site.[31]

The report identified significant benefits from the use of green infrastructure techniques and provided support for the notion that green infrastructure can facilitate stormwater infiltration at volumes closer to natural and background levels of stormwater control. These designs also incorporate air and water filtration through the protection of vegetation and wetlands, reductions to habitat impacts, and reduced peak flows through groundwater infiltration. Interestingly, the report also identified "non-quantified benefits," which included a reduction in automobile traffic as a result of the creation of

---

31.   PIERCE COUNTY, PIERCE COUNTY LOW IMPACT DEVELOPMENT STUDY 38-39 (Apr. 11, 2001), *available at* http://www.co.pierce.wa.us/archives/150/LID%20Report%20final%20complete.pdf.

a more walkable neighborhood, as well as environmental literacy benefits by including residents in the water quality process.[32]

The approach set forth in the Pierce County Report exemplifies the initiatives taken by local governments across the nation to infuse infrastructure planning with ecosystem concepts. New York City, for example, has committed roughly $2.4 billion to green infrastructure practices over the next 18 years to integrate green roofs and streets, bioswales, and other natural systems to manage stormwater. This approach is intended to reduce the amount of "contaminant-latent water" flowing into the waterways. The city of Philadelphia has committed $1.2 billion to green infrastructure over the next 25 years to manage stormwater, including the conversion of 9,600 impervious acres into permeable surfaces. Washington, D.C., has proposed nearly $60 million in green infrastructure along its Rock Creek waterway and another $30 million along the Potomac River. These projects will capture pollutants and retain stormwater to prevent flooding, while providing green space and recreational opportunities. Portland, Oregon, has launched a campaign to promote rooftop rainwater capture, downspout disconnection, curb cuts to feed runoff water into bioswales, and permeable road surfaces to complement Oregon's smart growth system.

These examples of LID practices implement an ecosystem services approach by using natural processes to control and mitigate stormwater flows. As a component of the local land use regulatory process, LID practices integrate resiliency by improving the natural environment and the dependency on gray, temporary solutions.

B.   Urban Forests as Water Infrastructure

In addition to LID practices, cities are looking to forests to help ensure the provision of water-based services. From the forestry perspective, urban forests are relevant to an ecosystem services analysis because urban trees are engaged where people live, work, and play. From the infrastructure perspective, urban forests are relevant because of the critical and essential services they provide.[33] The shade offered by urban trees results in lower climate control costs. Trees capture air pollutants, provide shelter and food for urban critters, and even contribute community assets such as neighborhood attractiveness and

---

32. *Id.* at 39.
33. Trees in urban areas "soothe eyes and spirits, they shade, they form special places for recreation or relaxation, they provide habitat for birds and other wildlife, they purify the air, and they increase the market value of real estate." Henry W. Lawrence, *The Neoclassical Origins of Modern Urban Forests*, 37 FOREST & CONSERVATION HIST. 26, 35 (1993).

property values. For our purposes here, urban forests also provide substantial stormwater control services by retaining soils and by capturing and filtering stormwater, resulting in cleaner water and reducing flood flows. Urban forests illustrate the importance of ecosystem function and transform our understanding of nature "from amenity to living technology."[34]

Some local governments protect these values by requiring tree removal applications, imposing stringent tree replacement requirements, and mandating the planting of native species.[35] Other cities incorporate urban forest resources throughout their land use planning scheme because of the significant economic benefits they accrue as infrastructure. For instance, the city of Vancouver, Washington, has noted in its comprehensive plan that, "unlike traditional grey infrastructure capital improvements, such as transportation and water systems, which begin to depreciate as soon as they are installed, green infrastructure accrues value and provides greater services as time passes."[36] As part of its comprehensive plan, the city of Vancouver has been active in protecting its urban forest resources for some time. Currently, urban forestry is included as part of the city's compliance with state stormwater control requirements. To protect the benefits of urban trees, the city of Vancouver has created an urban forestry commission,[37] adopted regulations to protect street trees,[38] and regulated clearing in priority habitat areas to maintain "habitat function and value."[39] In its tree conservation ordinance, Vancouver also regulates the destruction or removal of "any tree" without an approved tree plan.[40] Development applicants under this program are

34. E. Gregory McPherson, *Accounting for Benefits and Costs of Urban Greenspace*, 22 Landscape & Urb. Plan. 41, 41 (1992).
35. For instance, the Township of Jackson, New Jersey, has declared that its trees are "important cultural, ecological, scenic and economic resources" and regulates land uses to preserve tree canopy, biomass production, air filtering and oxygen production. Jackson, N.J., Admin. Code §100:A (2003). Applications must be accompanied by a reforestation plan and may be denied where the proposed activity indicates "any negative effect upon ground and surface water quality, specimen trees, soil erosion, dust, reusability of land, and impact on adjacent properties." *Id.*; *see also* New Jersey Shore Builders Association. v. Township of Jackson, 970 A.2d 992 (N.J. 2009) (in which the New Jersey Supreme Court upheld the Jackson Ordinance).
36. City of Vancouver, Vancouver Urban Forestry Management Plan 7 (Dec. 2007), *available at* http://www.cityofvancouver.us/parksrecreation/parks_trails/urban_forestry/pdf/UFMP_final-web. pdf. *See also* Vancouver Watersheds Alliance, Report of 2014 Activities by the Vancouver Watersheds Alliance Supporting Vancouver's NPDES Phase II Permit (2014), *available at* http://www.cityofvancouver.us/sites/default/files/fileattachments/public_works/page/1125/5c_vwa2014annualreport.pdf.
37. The purpose of the Urban Forestry Commission for "managing, conserving and enhancing the existing trees located in the parks and public areas owned by the city of Vancouver and in public right-of-way, and thereby enhancing the appearance of the city and protecting an important environmental and economic resource. . . ." Vancouver, Wash. Mun. Code 12.02.010 (2009).
38. Vancouver, Wash. Mun. Code 12.04 (2006).
39. Vancouver, Wash. Mun. Code 20.740.110 (2009).
40. Vancouver, Wash. Mun. Code 20.770.020.A (2004).

required to preserve any tree that could be protected by selection of a "feasible and prudent location alternatives on-site" for the project.[41] Development applicants must also demonstrate meeting the minimum 30 tree units per acre for most projects.[42]

Vancouver estimates that its tree canopy captures enough stormwater to save $12.9 million in avoided construction costs for stormwater retention structures and $78.3 million in air pollutant removal services. Vancouver estimates an annual net benefit per tree of $1 to $8 for small trees, $19 to $25 for medium-sized trees, and $48 to $53 for large trees. Vancouver has stated:

> Improving aesthetics of our community has tangible economic benefits. Systems of open space and bike trails give a community a reputation for being a good place to live and visit. Increased recreational and community activity attracts new businesses and stimulates tourism. Well-maintained trees improve residential "curb appeal" and increase potential buyers' willingness to pay a 3-7% premium for property. Trees in retail settings increase shoppers' willingness to pay for goods and services by 12%.[43]

Tree protection programs similar to Vancouver's stand apart from conventional water infrastructure wisdom. Without pipes and dams to measure, urban forestry programs break free of preferences for the built environment. Yet, tree protection programs typically provide added societal benefits and critical functions needed in water infrastructure at a substantially decreased cost and with a longer lifespan.

C. City Creation and Infrastructure Planning

A third example of innovative, ecosystem-based infrastructure planning is illustrated in the city of Damascus, Oregon. When Damascus was drawn into the Portland Urban Growth Boundary in 2002, public infrastructure

---

41. VANCOUVER, WASH. MUN. CODE 20.770.070.B.1 (2004).

42. VANCOUVER, WASH. MUN. CODE 20.770.080 (2007).

43. CITY OF VANCOUVER, *supra* note 36, at 9. In the Vancouver Municipal Code, the city declares that trees are protecting and valuable for the following functions: 1. Increasing the air quality with the absorption of air pollutants, assimilation of carbon dioxide and generation of oxygen, and with the reduction of excessive noise and mental and physical damage related to noise pollution; 2. Minimizing the adverse impacts of land disturbing activities and impervious surfaces on runoff, soil erosion, land instability, sedimentation and pollution of waterways, thus, minimizing the public and private costs for stormwater control/treatment and utility maintenance; 3. Cost-effective protection against severe weather conditions with cooling effects in the summer months and insulating effects in winter; 4. Providing habitat, cover, food supply and corridors for a diversity of fish and wildlife; and 5. Economic support of local property values and contribution to the region's natural beauty and enhancing the aesthetic character of the community. VANCOUVER, WASH. MUN. CODE 20.770.010 (2004).

served only 10% of its area.[44] Damascus subsequently incorporated and took on significant infrastructure responsibilities.[45] The cost for constructing built infrastructure and public services was estimated at $3 to $4 billion.[46] In the process of developing a comprehensive land use plan and an ecosystem services master plan,[47] the city prioritized ecosystem services as a component of its utility infrastructure and stormwater management "to forestall increased costs to the citizens of Damascus. These increased costs take the form of built infrastructure to replace the service (as in stormwater management), increased regulatory compliance hurdles (as in Clean Water Act and Endangered Species Act compliance), and loss of quality of life."[48] The city prepared a public facilities plan that mapped the existing ecosystem services to develop "relative level of service (LOS)" that incorporated the location and quality of the ecosystem services.[49] With input from service providers and the public, Damascus developed an Integrated Water Resource Management Plan (IWRMP) "to establish an integrated, cost-effective, and sustainable approach for providing water, wastewater, reclaimed water, and stormwater services to new and existing development in the city."[50]

The city of Damascus has not completed its infrastructure, and in likelihood, the road ahead will be complicated. In the summer of 2015, the city was presented with an infrastructure white paper that detailed an accounting of the needs and assets required to maintain an effective water infrastructure. The white paper referred to the city's ecosystem services obligations in its capital facilities plan.[51] It relied on the capital facilities plan map previously produced that located gray infrastructure based in part on minimizing interruption of ecosystem services. On the other hand, the city has not yet adopted the LID concepts that were intended to govern new development and integrate ecosystem services ideas. Even worse, the white paper does not illustrate the importance of ecosystem services in the accounting for infra-

---

44. Anita Yap et al., *Ecosystem Services & City Planning: The City of Damascus Develops a Model Approach to Public Facilities Planning*, Or. Insider 1, 4 (Aug. 2009), on file with the authors.
45. *Id.* at 1.
46. *Id.*
47. *Id.* at 3, 9.
48. Work Session, City of Damascus City Council, Ecosystem Services—Executive Summary From the Tier II Ecosystem Services Report ES-1 (2010), on file with the authors.
49. *Id.*
50. CH2MHILL, Damascus Integrated Water Resources Management Plan ES-1 (2011), *available at* http://ci.damascus.or.us/References/Misc/Draft_Damascus_IWRMP_07062011.pdf.
51. The white paper notes, "In addition to the traditional public facilities, the plan also took into consideration ecosystem services, which are the unique and irreplaceable service provided by the existing natural resources such as air and water quality, stormwater management, erosion control, and fish and wildlife habitat." *Infrastructure White Paper*, City of Damascus 3-4 (June 22, 2015), http://www.damascusoregon.gov/AgendaCenter/ViewFile/Agenda/06252015-397.

structure needs. Rather, the white paper provides a needs assessment for new pipes and culverts, roads, and treatment facilities.[52]

The example of Damascus is interesting from a resiliency planning standpoint because of the breadth of the challenge: because Damascus' water infrastructure was, in a sense, starting "from scratch," it was not bound to conventional formulae and engineering preferences. Under these circumstances, the idea of accounting for ecosystem services and ecosystem vulnerabilities as a launching point for infrastructure planning is a great experiment. In the climate change era, many, if not most, cities will undergo transformation and will bear the burden of reinvention as climatic changes are more extreme and vulnerabilities become more pronounced. Cities will have opportunities to rebuild.

IV. Conclusion

The objective of this chapter is to promote fluency in ecosystem service vocabulary so that we are able to recognize infrastructure opportunities that exist in the natural environment. Ecosystem services will improve water infrastructure planning because it is contextual, builds in resilience and provides services at a lower cost than the built environment. Such an approach will have continuing importance as we address the challenges of the climate change era.

That water infrastructure is addressed by the IPCC as a climate change planning mandate is no small thing: without an effective infrastructure, individuals may be unable to obtain basic needs and the consequences will be catastrophic. Of course, clean, dependable water is often difficult to guarantee. As such, the IPCC statement acknowledges the immense cost of infrastructure maintenance and replacement into the next century, as well as the "profound" importance that civil society effectively plan for scarcity and challenges to the provision of basic human needs.

Confronting the challenges of climate change requires a more accurate accounting of infrastructure needs and resources. Our water infrastructure must be designed with resiliency in mind to meet the challenge. Some opportunities are relatively unobjectionable and proven: protecting wetland functions along riparian areas provides protection from floods during storm events, increases resiliency in coastal and riparian communities, filters water, and provides biomass and habitats; and retaining trees at building sites provides shade, reducing energy costs to cool buildings, captures stormwater,

---

52. *Id.* at 6-11.

and facilitates community building. Other ecosystem investments may be more controversial: ecosystem restoration often disrupts historical land uses, such as agricultural uses benefitting from diking floodplains; and conservation decisions in times of water shortage may disrupt industrial and agricultural needs, such as shutting off irrigation pumps to maintain minimum river flows.

The cities discussed above have realized that the built or gray infrastructure that comprises the water system is designed to deliver services that are already provided by natural systems, including water and sewer, storm and flood protection, temperature control and climate stabilization, waste cycling and assimilation, and other natural services. As an additional benefit, natural systems provide these services effectively and efficiently, while also securing other foundational goods and services including oxygen, water, land, recreational opportunities, aesthetic value, and spiritual attachment and energy. Although ecosystem services planning does not benefit from a long history, it is essential that water managers incorporate ecosystem services concepts into the decisionmaking process. The result of an integration will be to capture the benefits of functioning ecosystems, while protecting the valuable assets of natural capital. Ecosystem services thinking connects ecosystem function with basic human needs—not merely as a means to protect the environment, but as a means to assure human well-being.

In large part, the shift to a more resilient infrastructure will be a project of environmental literacy. Ecosystem services may be accounted for as opportunities when the services provided by ecosystems are understood. Unfortunately, communities often must suffer ecosystem loss and disruption to grasp the value of the loss of ecosystem functionality. As such, resiliency may also demand that local governments experiment with a wide variety of literacy projects, such as participating in and facilitating markets in ecosystem services to raise awareness and establish the economic worth of ecosystem processes. Infrastructure, which historically has comprised the local government's obligation to insure the delivery of services for human needs, is a good place to start.

Chapter 4
Flexible Conservation
in Uncertain Times
Jessica Owley & David Takacs

We know, beyond question, that the climate is warming: the Intergovernmental Panel on Climate Change (IPCC) labels the evidence as "unequivocal."[1] Climate change will impact all human communities. It will also impact nonhuman communities. According to the IPCC:

- A large fraction of both terrestrial and freshwater species faces increased extinction risk under projected climate change during and beyond the 21st century, especially as climate change interacts with other stressors, such as habitat modification, over-exploitation, pollution, and invasive species (*high confidence*).

- Extinction risk is increased under all . . . scenarios,[2] with risk increasing with both magnitude and rate of climate change. Many species will be unable to track suitable climates under mid-and high-range rates of climate change . . . during the 21st century (*medium confidence*).

- Lower rates of change . . . will pose fewer problems. . . . Some species will adapt to new climates. Those that cannot adapt sufficiently fast will decrease in abundance or go extinct in part or all of their ranges. Management actions, such as maintenance of genetic diversity, assisted species migration and dispersal, manipulation of disturbance regimes (e.g., fires, floods), and reduction of other stressors, can reduce, but not

Authors' Note: The authors would like to thank Stephen Miller and Robin Craig for their careful editing and dedication to this project. Valuable research assistance was provided by Mike Enright and Meron Amare. Professors Owley and Takacs are particularly indebted to their excellent co-authors.

1. INTERGOVERNMENTAL PANEL ON CLIMATE CHANGE, CLIMATE CHANGE 2013: THE PHYSICAL SCIENCE BASIS, 4 (2014) [hereinafter 2013 IPCC PHYSICAL SCIENCE REPORT].
2. The IPCC provides high and low estimates for the amount of greenhouse gases we will allow to be emitted. Obviously, the higher the amount, the worse the effects of climate change, and the more severe the impacts on species.

eliminate, risks of impacts to terrestrial and freshwater ecosystems due to climate change, as well as increase the inherent capacity of ecosystems and their species to adapt to a changing climate (*high confidence*).[3]

Climate change is already affecting biodiversity and ecosystems, shrinking or shifting species ranges, and leading to asynchronicities between predator and prey or plant and pollinator relationships.[4] Such effects are unsurprising because most climatic impacts result in significant changes to the landscape. For example, we will see increased droughts and other natural disasters.[5] Additionally, the IPCC predicts decreasing snow cover[6] and rising sea levels[7] with "very high confidence." Indeed, sea level rise is expected to proceed at an unprecedented rate because of the contributing effects from the increased ocean warming causing thermal expansion and the loss of glaciers and ice sheets; ocean warming alone will result in major disruptions in heat-sensitive coral reefs and Arctic ecosystems.[8]

Climate change will thus alter the composition of our landscapes and the natural communities that comprise them. While it is easy to get wrapped up in the *predicted* dire consequences of climate change, the reality is that landscape changes and species shifts are already occurring on every continent.[9] For example, IPCC Working Group II's Summary for Policymakers notes that "[m]any terrestrial, freshwater, and marine species have shifted their geographic ranges, seasonal activities, migration patterns, abundances, and species interactions in response to ongoing climate change (*high confidence*),"[10] and "[s]ome unique and threatened systems, including ecosystems and cultures, are already at risk from climate change (*high confidence*)."[11] The evidence of already-occurring climate change impacts is strongest for what the

---

3.   Intergovernmental Panel on Climate Change, Climate Change 2014: Impacts, Adaptation, and Vulnerability 14-15 (2014) [hereinafter 2014 IPCC Adaptation Report].

4.   *See, e.g.*, Suzanne Goldenberg, *Extreme Arctic Sea Ice Melt Forces Thousands of Walruses Ashore in Alaska*, Guardian, Aug. 27, 2015; Nicholas St. Fleur, *Climate Change Is Shrinking Where Bumblebees Range, Research Finds*, N.Y. Times, July 9, 2015; Press Association, *UK Acorn Crop "Being Hit by Climate Change,"* Guardian, Apr. 17, 2015; Sue Meyer, *U.S. Fish & Wildlife Service: Polar Bear Unlikely to Survive a Warming Climate*, Nossaman LLP Endangered Species L. & Pol'y (July 7, 2015), http://www.endangeredspecieslawandpolicy.com/2015/07/articles/fish-wildlife-service/u-s-fish-wildlife-service-polar-bear-unlikely-to-survive-a-warming-climate/?utm_source=Nossaman+LLP+-+Endangered+Species+Law+and+Policy&utm_medium=email&utm_campaign=e8717dfc32-RSS_EMAIL_CAMPAIGN&utm_term=0_f2072431ce-e8717dfc32-70691469.

5.   2013 IPCC Physical Science Report, *supra* note 1, at 7, 12 (Table SPM.1) (with medium confidence).

6.   *Id.* at 9.

7.   *Id.* at 11.

8.   *See id.* at 25; 2014 IPCC Adaptation Report, *supra* note 3, at 12.

9.   2014 IPCC Adaptation Report, *supra* note 3, at 4.

10. *Id.*

11. *Id.* at 12, Assessment Box SPM.1.

IPCC terms "natural" systems (as opposed to human systems),[12] meaning that we can already see changes in species distributions, habitat degradation, and loss of ecosystem functions. The IPCC acknowledges that we risk losing terrestrial, coastal, and marine ecosystems, leading to a loss of the "goods, functions, and services" those ecosystems provide.[13]

The quotations with which this chapter begins emphasize that we stand to lose a considerable number of the species with which we share the planet. As governments promulgate more and more laws to protect biodiversity, there is a simultaneous cataclysm of species extinctions, with rates of decimation between 1,000-10,000 times the "normal" (i.e., without human interference) level.[14] The number of wild animals has been halved in the last 40 years.[15] One in three amphibian species, one in four mammal species, and one in eight birds face a high risk of extinction.[16] The situation will probably get worse, because the human population is expected to grow from 7 to 9 billion by 2050, and likely to 11 billion by 2100.[17]

Thus, we find ourselves in the midst of an extinction crisis, with some experts calling our age the "Anthropocene" era in recognition of the fact that humans dominate and degrade the planet's life cycles and processes.[18] As we lose biodiversity and convert more of the planet's land to human uses, we undercut our own life support systems. As our demands on the planet are growing, we are destroying the Earth's ecological systems that support human life. According to a recent estimate, ecosystem services provide humans with US$125-145 trillion of "free" services each year.[19] We ignore this source of human prosperity at our own peril: notably, between 1997 and 2001, humans lost US$4.3-$20.2 trillion per year as a result of land degra-

---

12. *Id.* at 4.
13. *Id.* at 13, n.viii.
14. INTERNATIONAL UNION FOR THE CONSERVATION OF NATURE (IUCN), SPECIES EXTINCTION—THE FACTS, https://cmsdata.iucn.org/downloads/species_extinction_05_2007.pdf (last visited Sept. 3, 2015).
15. Damian Carrington, *Earth Has Lost Half Its Wildlife in the Last 40 Years, Says WWF*, GUARDIAN, Sept. 30, 2014.
16. IUCN, *supra* note 14.
17. Damian Carrington, *World Population to Hit 11bn in 2100—With 70% Chance of Continuous Rise*, GUARDIAN, Sept. 18, 2014.
18. Paul Crutzen & Eugene F. Stoermer, *The Anthropocene*, GLOBAL CHANGE NEWSL. 41 (2000). For a review of human domination, see the opening paragraph of Tim Caro et al., *Conservation in the Anthropocene*, 26 CONSERVATION BIOLOGY 185, 185 (2011). In 2016, the International Commission on Stratigraphy's Subcommission on Quaternary Stratigraphy may decide to designate a new geologic era bearing the name "Anthropocene." SUBCOMMISSION ON QUATERNARY STRATIGRAPHY, WORKING GROUP ON THE "ANTHROPOCENE," http://quaternary.stratigraphy.org/workinggroups/anthropocene/ (last updated May 5, 2015).
19. Robert Costanza et al., *Changes in the Global Value of Ecosystem Services*, 26 GLOBAL ENVTL. CHANGE 152, 156 tbl. 3 (2014).

dation.[20] If we are to continue to depend on functioning ecosystems, based on a healthy complement of nonhuman species, we need a new toolkit for conservation informed by a new ethic of stewardship.

While we face varying levels of certainty with respect to the exact impacts of climate change, it is clear that we are entering into an era of uncertainty, a "no-analog future," where the only thing we can depend on is change.[21] In this context of thinking about a changing world, this chapter examines how we can accommodate change while, and through, protecting biodiversity and ecosystem services, particularly through land conservation. In many cases, this accommodation will mean using flexible tools that have mechanisms to incorporate change. Specifically, we need to develop multiple flexible response tools that can be tailored to different locations and include mechanisms for evolution and learning. Bolstering our toolbox for adaptive land conservation will help us figure out how we can accommodate change while protecting key ecosystem functions and preserving biodiversity.

This chapter explores some mechanisms that could find a place in our adaptation/mitigation toolbox. We suggest some ideas, programs, and property tools that could incorporate changing landscapes while still providing environmental benefits. Some of the programs are well established and we embrace them; some have been in use but we suggest changes; and some ideas are not fully developed but hopefully will serve as inspiration or conversation starters. We acknowledge that the list is by no means comprehensive but simply an array of possibilities. Because of the complexity of climate change as well as the political and social landscapes, these tools will not all be equally attractive in all areas. Additionally, the tools could be misused and lead to maladaptation or unanticipated, unintended consequences. Therefore, we conclude this chapter with a discussion of concerns related to these tools—an offering that could also serve as a checklist of considerations when forming implementation plans. Thus, we conclude not with a magic pill but with a variety of vitamins that haven't yet received FDA approval. We think they will be good for you, but, as with all such medications, taken in the wrong quantities or in ill-advised combinations, they may be harmful to your health. Be sure to consult with your local climate scientists, biologists, policymakers, and neighbors before taking them.

---

20. *Id.*
21. J.B. Ruhl, *Climate Change and the Endangered Species Act: Building Bridges to the No-Analog Future,* 88 B.U. L. Rev. 1, 23 (2008).

I.   Creating Flexible Response Tools

Climate change measures proceed on two fronts: mitigation and adaptation. Climate change *mitigation* means taking steps to reduce the harm that will be caused by climate change by reducing the amount of greenhouse gases (GHGs) we emit into the atmosphere or by taking greenhouse gases out of the atmosphere. We can use less energy, switch from high-GHG-emitting fossil fuels to low-GHG-emitting renewable energy sources, change agricultural practices and business practices to modes with fewer emissions, and undertake carbon sequestration activities like planting trees or finding ways to capture the gases we emit before they reach the atmosphere (e.g., burying them in the ground). Climate adaptation addresses the changes that we know will occur. Instead of fighting change, adaptation programs ask how we can respond to the change—because we must. For example, in addressing sea level rise, mitigation programs seek to limit how high the level will be, while adaptation programs address how a community will deal with the new sea level (e.g., by building sea walls, elevating homes, or building new water filtration systems).

While some climate change efforts fall squarely into either the mitigation or adaptation camp, some—like land conservation—help on both fronts. Indeed, some of the initiatives we discuss below to curb deforestation and other destruction of natural habitat blur the bounds between mitigation of and adaptation to climate change. Restoring degraded land or saving land from clearing or degradation that would otherwise occur *mitigates* climate change when biomass retains carbon that would otherwise be released. Through the alchemy of photosynthesis, terrestrial ecosystems absorb about a quarter of human carbon dioxide (CO_2) emissions; deforestation disrupts this vital ecosystem service and currently accounts for somewhere between 11% and 28% of GHG emissions.[22] So, as climate change and human needs degrade natural ecosystems—as plants are felled, burned, or eaten, as tundra melts, as peat bogs desiccate—climate change worsens, further imperiling species and ecosystems. However, healthy forests and other preserved habitats simultaneously help communities *adapt* to climate change. They provide resilience against future climate change shocks through sustaining ecosys-

---

22.   U.N. Dev. Programme, Human Development Report 2007/2008: Fighting Climate Change: Human Solidarity in a Divided World 2007 1, 40-41 (2007), http:// hdr.undp.org/sites/default/ files/reports/268/hdr_20072008_en_complete.pdf; American Clean Energy and Security Act, H.R. 2454, 111th Cong. §752(2) (2009); Gleb Raygorodetsky, *Can REDD Ever Become Green?*, Our World (Aug. 1, 2012), http://ourworld.unu.edu/en/can-redd-ever-become-green/; Intergovernmental Panel on Climate Change, Climate Change 2014: Synthesis Report 46 (2014) [hereinafter 2014 IPCC Synthesis Report].

tem services—well-functioning ecosystems increase rainfall, buffer against floods, purify drinking water, prevent erosion, and harbor crop pollinators and other species crucial for human survival.[23] We take these free ecosystem services for granted—until the ecosystem no longer provides them for free.[24] Well-maintained watersheds, wetlands, and forests improve water quality and quantity by acting as natural filters to purify water; regulate flows in both wet seasons (including flood buffering) and dry seasons; prevent erosion and thus reduce sediment load; and enhance biodiversity both in streams, and, through careful protection of buffers, in adjacent lands.[25] Land conservation sometimes fits under the aegis of "restoring natural capital," i.e., "any activity that integrates investment in and replenishment of natural capital stocks to improve the flows of ecosystem goods and services, while enhancing all aspects of human wellbeing"[26]

Experts disagree on how much land we have available for flexible conservation. While some experts project that as the human population grows to 9 billion in 2050, we will convert another 200 million to 1 billion hectares of land to human use,[27] others assert that breakthroughs in agricultural technology can yield big gains for conservation. Corn production has quintupled in the United States without increasing the amount of land farmed.[28] Abandoned marginal agricultural land has returned 30-60 million hectares to nature in Eastern Europe and the former Soviet Union.[29] Partly because of

---

23. Strategic Integrated Project 19, "Ecological Infrastructure for Water Security." Final Draft for Submission to the Presidential Infrastructure Coordinating Commission, Revision 6.1, 31 Oct. 2014 at 14 [hereinafter SIP 19]; United Nations Environment Programme, Green Infrastructure: Guide for Water Management (2014) http://www.unepdhi.org/-/media/microsite_unepdhi/publications/documents/unep/web-unep-dhigroup-green-infrastructure-guide-en-20140814.pdf at 5, 14-16 [hereinafter UNEP, Green Infrastructure]; Barton H. Thompson Jr., *Markets for Nature*, 25 Wm. & Mary Envtl. L. & Pol'y Rev. 261, 295 (2000); United Nations Environment Programme World Conservation Monitoring Ctr., Reducing Emissions From Deforestation: A Key Opportunity for Attaining Multiple Benefits 9-10 (2007), http://www.unep-wcmc.org/medialibrary/2010/09/27/fa100d32/REDD_Multiple_benefits.pdf; *see* Johannes Ebeling, *Risks and Criticisms of Forestry-Based Climate Change Mitigation and Carbon Trading*, in Climate Change and Forests: Emerging Policy and Market Opportunities 43, 53 (Charlotte Streck et al. eds., 2008).

24. SIP 19, *supra* note 23, at 14.

25. *Id.*; UNEP, Green Infrastructure, *supra* note 23, at 5, 14-16; Thompson, *supra* note 23, at 295.

26. Carsten Nesshover et al., The Economics of Ecosystems and Biodiversity for National and International Policy Makers 5 (2009) (citing J. Aronson et al., *Restoring Natural Capital: Definitions and Rationale*, in Restoring Natural Capital: Science, Business and Practice 3-8 (J. Aronson et al. eds., 2007)); *see also* The Natural Capital Project, About the Natural Capital Project, http://www.naturalcapitalproject.org/about.html (last visited Aug. 18, 2015).

27. Carrington, *supra* note 17; Martine Marona et al., *Faustian Bargains? Restoration Realities in the Context of Biodiversity Offset Policies*, 155 Biological Conservation 141, 141 (2012).

28. Jesse H. Ausubel, *The Return of Nature: How Technology Liberates the Environment*, Breakthrough (Spring 2015), http://thebreakthrough.org/index.php/journal/issue-5/the-return-of-nature.

29. Florian Schierhorn et al., *Post-Soviet Cropland Abandonment and Carbon Sequestration in European Russia, Ukraine, and Belarus*, 27 Global Biogeochemical Cycles 1175 (2013).

decreased demand, partly because of improved management, and partly as a result of enforcement of endangered species laws, logged areas in the United States decreased from 17.8 to 14.7 hectares between 1976 and 2001.[30] One-third of the world's food is thrown away; cutting that shocking waste means less land for agriculture, and, one hopes, more land for nature.[31]

A.   Adaptive Management and Resilience

The only thing certain about the no-analog future is unpredictable change. Because we face uncertainties in the responses to different adaptation and mitigation measures, we should consider multiple scenarios when we are planning because we don't know which one we will be living under. Thus, scenario planning and creative thinking are necessary hallmarks of a successful climate change program. Two guiding principles—adaptive management and resilience—help frame this discussion.

Principles of adaptive management emerged from conservation biology, which itself first emerged as a recognized discipline in the 1970s.[32] The field uses biological principles to further conservation, while incorporating concepts from many other fields, including economics, sociology, natural resource management, and law. Over the years, conservation biologists and like-minded experts have investigated how to decide what we should protect if biodiversity and ecosystem health are our goals, as well as provided guidelines for how to protect what we've decided to protect. Climate change has the ability to accelerate the pace of change and make the change more significant—or permanent, if it leads to species extinction or ecosystem collapse. Conservation biologists generally agree that successful climate change measures need to incorporate both learning (increasing our understanding of climate change and its impacts) and flexible adaptive tools.[33] That is, the best tools will facilitate changing our approach as we learn and understand more both about climate change and the ecosystems and species we are seeking to protect. As the IPCC explains, "[r]esponding to climate-related risks involves decision making in a changing world, with continuing uncertainty

---

30. Ausubel, *supra* note 28.
31. Food and Agriculture Organization (FAO), Food Wastage Footprint: Impacts on Natural Resources 6 (2013), *available at* http://www.fao.org/docrep/018/i3347e/i3347e.pdf.
32. For a history of the discipline's founding, see David Takacs, The Idea of Biodiversity (1996).
33. Barbara Cosens et al., *Identifying Legal, Ecological and Governance Obstacles, and Opportunities for Adapting to Climate Change*, 6 Sustainability 2338, 2345-46 (2014); Russell M. Wise et al., *Reconceptualising Adaptation to Climate Change as Part of Pathways of Change and Response*, 28 Global Envtl. Change 325, 330 (2014); Byron K. Williams, *Adaptive Management of Natural Resources—Framework and Issues*, 92 J. Envtl. Mgmt. 1346, 1347 (2011).

about the severity and timing of climate-change impacts and with limits to the effectiveness of adaptation."[34]

Conservationists often talk about the concept of adaptive management, which means making decisions regarding natural resource use and management in a context that promotes flexibility and incorporation of new information. Over time, natural resource managers take what they have learned (either by their experiences or through the availability of new studies) to update their plans and processes. Adaptive management requires an iterative approach and a continuous use of monitoring both the resource and the available science. Importantly, adaptive management doesn't require adherence to any one method or project but encourages "organizations and policies [to] change appropriately to achieve specific environmental and social objectives."[35] As J.B. Ruhl explains, incorporating adaptive management principles from conservation biology into policy instruments means "regulators use models of natural resource systems to develop performance measurements and initial policy choices," while building an "implementation framework a process for continuous monitoring, evaluation, and adjustment of decisions and practices" into the regulatory framework.[36]

We must be cautious in our use of adaptive management. Projects or organizations may adopt an adaptive management framework but fall short of real adaptive management implementation because they lack mechanisms (e.g., budget or personnel or simply the legal requirement to monitor and adjust) to revisit and improve the project.[37] Adaptive management must mean more than just having a mechanism that responds to change; it should have components that gather new information and systematically revisit goals and processes. Additionally, adaptive management cannot be an excuse to simply delay decisions. Too often we have seen conservation programs that fail to develop a full plan for conservation because they push the harder decisions into a management plan that comes later, if at all.[38] Thus, while we embrace the idea of adaptive management and encourage its practice, it must be an authentic use of the tool to achieve the best results.

34. 2014 IPCC ADAPTATION REPORT, *supra* note 3, at 9 (with high confidence).

35. Ruhl, *supra* note 21, at n.200.

36. *Id.*

37. Kai N. Lee, *Appraising Adaptive Management, in* BIOLOGICAL DIVERSITY: BALANCING INTERESTS THROUGH ADAPTIVE COLLABORATIVE MANAGEMENT 3 (Louise E. Buck & Charles C. Geisler eds., 2001); *see also* Barry L. Johnson, *Adaptive Management—Scientifically Sound, Socially Challenged?*, 3 ECOLOGY & SOC'Y 10 (1999) (part of a special feature on adaptive management).

38. ADENA R. RISSMAN ET AL., PRIVATE LAND CONSERVATION AND CLIMATE CHANGE: RETHINKING STRATEGIES AND TOOLS. A REPORT TO THE LAND CONSERVATION COMMUNITY (forthcoming 2016).

We have to be flexible—adaptive—in how we manage natural systems so those systems maintain maximum resiliency when faced with the coming chaos of climate change. The ecological concept of resiliency (or resilience thinking) also a helps us think about protecting species and habitats in a changing world. Resilience is the capacity of an ecosystem to respond to perturbation or change. High resiliency is a function of both an ability to resist impacts and an ability to recover quickly from disturbances.[39] A resilient system is not one that continues to look the same but one that responds and reorganizes while retaining function. Healthy functioning systems are not wedded to a specific external appearance. Working towards resiliency means assessing what the thresholds of a system are—how far we can push it before its function is impaired—and how close we are to those thresholds. Thinking of adaptation in resiliency terms goes beyond assessing whether humans will be able to respond to the coming climatic changes and considers our capacity to manage resistance and influence resilience. Resilience thinking acknowledges that change is inevitable and encourages theorizing of ways to best withstand or respond to the change.[40] Considering where species will move or how habitats will shift means we must contemplate many moving parts in an uncertain context.[41] Climate change reinforces the fact that ecological and human systems are constantly undergoing change: management mechanisms must be flexible with clear goals that evolve as the climate and landscape evolve.

B.   Ensuring Performance

Once we have programs in place, we might also be concerned about enforcing those programs over the long term. Often, a lot of time and energy goes into establishing programs without putting money or attention on stewarding or enforcing the projects over time. For example, studies of wetland mitigation projects revealed many failures.[42] Research tracking habitat mitigation

---

39. Brian Walker & David Salt, Resilience Thinking 1-2, 164 (2006).
40. See Melinda Harm Benson & Robin Kundis Craig, The End of Sustainability, 27 Soc'y & Nat. Resources 777, 777-82 (2014).
41. Jessica Owley, Sustainability Thinking for the Climate Change Generation, in Rethinking Sustainability to Meet the Climate Change Challenge 5 (Jessica Owley & Keith Hirokawa eds., 2015) ("While embracing concepts like adaptive management and resiliency, however, we must be cautious. Embedded in both ideas is the notion of some ideal state that we want to achieve. Often land managers, conservationists, and decisionmakers envision a current or former state as the ideal state.").
42. Rebecca L. Kihslinger, Success of Wetland Mitigation Projects, 30 Nat'l Wetlands Newsl. 14 (2008), available at http://www.wetlandsnewsletter.org/pdf/30.02/kihslinger.pdf (reviewing studies of compensatory mitigation projects).

revealed that that we don't even have good systems right now for learning about land protection restrictions and agreements.[43]

If we are looking for "flexible conservation in uncertain times," perhaps we can still have specificity with flexibility. While it might be tempting to specify concrete *actions* a party must do to fulfill conservation imperatives, concrete actions are useless if they lead to no concrete improvement in species conservation, or that stop being effective when climate change changes ecological conditions. Outcome-based performance standards—in the words of the U.S. Fish and Wildlife Service, "measurable attributes used to determine if the management plan meets the agreed upon goals and objectives"[44]— require conservation actors to shift interventions along with shifting climate and give regulators clear guidelines by which to assess conservation success.

A clear, ongoing system of measuring, monitoring, reporting, and verification with clear rights and responsibilities for those performing conservation and those monitoring the efforts will be essential to any flexible conservation scheme in light of our ongoing climate change-addled future.[45] As the World Resource Institute notes, "You can't manage what you can't measure."[46] Once the baseline stock of an ecological entity (e.g., the number of individuals of a given species, the amount of hectares of a habitat type) is *measured*, and a baseline scenario is established, funders or regulators can ascertain whether the conservation implementers are performing to the specifications of the performance standards. To *monitor* is to assess the changes in species composition, ecosystem health, or any other variable over time, to measure progress and allow adjustments.[47] To *report* means making public what has been measured and monitored, thus allowing others to gauge progress and learn from what a party is doing.[48] To *verify* is for some party to check the

---

43. Jessica Owley, *Keeping Track of Conservation*, 42 ECOLOGY L.Q. 79 (2015) (describing struggles with learning about mitigation programs under the Endangered Species Act).

44. U.S. FISH & WILDLIFE SERVICE, GREATER SAGE-GROUSE RANGE-WIDE MITIGATION FRAMEWORK 30 (2014), *available at* http://www.fws.gov/greatersagegrouse/documents/Landowners/USFWS_GRSG%20RangeWide_Mitigation_Framework20140903.pdf.

45. For a comprehensive coverage of measuring, monitoring, reporting, and verifying in the context of REDD+, see generally David Takacs, *Forest Carbon (REDD+), Repairing International Trust, and Reciprocal Contractual Sovereignty*, 37 VT. L. REV. 653 (2013).

46. Remi Moncel & Kelly Levin, *Transparency and Accountability (MRV) in the Durban Climate Deal*, WORLD RESOURCES INSTITUTE BLOG (Feb. 13, 2012), http://insights.wri.org/news/2012/02/transparency-and-accountability-mrv-durban-climate-deal.

47. TANJA HAVEMANN ET AL., THE TERRESTRIAL CARBON GROUP PROJECT, POLICY BRIEF 5: MEASURING AND MONITORING TERRESTRIAL CARBON AS PART OF "REDD+" MRV SYSTEMS 2 (2009), *available at* www.goes.msu.edu/sumernet/docs/TCG_Policy_Brief_MRV.pdf.

48. JAKE SCHMIDT, NRDC, TRACKING CARBON WITH TRANSPARENCY 1 (2010), *available at* http://www.nrdc.org/globalwarming/files/trackingcarbon-fs.pdf; CLARE BREIDENICH & DANIEL BODANSKY, MEASUREMENT, REPORTING AND VERIFICATION IN A POST-2012 CLIMATE AGREEMENT 29 (2009), *available at* http://www.c2es.org/docUploads/mrv-report.pdf.

accuracy of information that has been measured, monitored, and reported is accurate.[49] Each of these elements is crucial for flexible conservation, allowing disparate experts to participate in course corrections and to learn from others as we implement flexible land conservation in a no-analog future.

II.   Techniques and Concepts

Given the urgency of climate change and the uncertainty of which of our proposed solutions will be successful in a given context, we generally advocate for an all-of-the-above approach to climate change (Quick! Everyone do everything they can!). In a no-analog future, we may need innovation laboratories to discern what can work and under what particular conditions. Conservationists generally agree that certain habitat features are desirable. We want to protect species refugia, corridors, and migration pathways.[50] We want to assemble larger parcels and think about connecting them together.[51] Nevertheless, we note that proceeding in such a fashion can lead to piecemeal protection: everyone doing what they can in isolation may not be the most strategic way to maximize conservation outcomes. Conservation planners need some kind of coordinated holistic planning approach on how these individual actions complement each other to sustain human and non-human communities.

As discussed in Part I, many techniques and legal concepts already exist that do or could promote land conservation—particularly land conservation that can help to preserve biodiversity as the climate changes. This part discusses each of these techniques and concepts in turn. Notably, moreover, many of the techniques we discuss here may also promote socioeconomic climate change adaptation through new sources of income by providing, for example, direct payments for preserving forests, by teaching new conservation-related income-generating skills,[52] or by providing for more secure,

---

49.   Jorgen Wettestad, *Monitoring and Verification, in* THE OXFORD HANDBOOK OF INTERNATIONAL ENVIRONMENTAL LAW 974, 975 (Bodansky et al. eds., 2007).

50.   *See, e.g.*, James R. Sedell et al., *Role of Refugia in Recovery From Disturbances: Modern Fragmented and Disconnected River Systems,* 14 ENVTL. MGMT. 711 (1990); Francis Gilbert et al., *Corridors Maintain Species Richness in the Fragmented Landscapes of a Microecosystem,* 265 PROCEEDINGS B OF THE ROYAL SOCIETY 577 (1998); Frank R. Moore et al., *Habitat Requirements During Migration: Important Link in Conservation, in* ECOLOGY AND MANAGEMENT OF NEOTROPICAL MIGRATORY BIRDS, 121 (Thomas E. Martin & Deborah E. Finch eds., 1995).

51.   California Department of Fish and Wildlife, *Conservation and Mitigation Banking,* https://www.wildlife.ca.gov/Conservation/Planning/Banking (last visited Oct. 11, 2015); U.S. FISH & WILDLIFE SERVICE, GUIDANCE FOR THE ESTABLISHMENT, USE, AND OPERATION OF CONSERVATION BANKS 4, 6 (2003).

52.   Jared E. Knicley, *Debt, Nature, and Indigenous Rights: Twenty-Five Years of Debt-for-Nature Evolution,* 36 HARV. ENVTL. L. REV. 79, 81 (2012); *see also* ARANNAYK FOUNDATION, http://www.arannayk.

formal land title.[53] Managing REDD+, biodiversity offsetting, or debt-for-nature swaps, or securing community-based natural resources management may further institutional adaptation as community leaders, landowners, and government officials develop and manage projects and hone skills and institutions to negotiate effectively with project developers, funders, and government functionaries.[54] We explain each tool in turn below.

A.   Public Trust Doctrine

The public trust doctrine is a legal idea dating to the Holy Roman Empire in A.D. 529, when the Emperor Justinian added these words to the body of law by which he ruled: "By the law of nature these things are common to all mankind, the air, running water, the sea and consequently the shores of the sea."[55] This idea has spread throughout the planet because it encapsulates a fundamental idea: some resources are so vital for human flourishing that the sovereign must steward those resources for the public benefit.[56] Private parties must never be allowed to gain permanent control over these resources.

While the public trust doctrine, as this notion came to be known, began its peripatetic life applied to water, it is now applies much more widely in various locales.[57] Some activists in the United States and elsewhere have been advocating for an expanded use of the public trust doctrine, both in reaching

org/curproject_biram.php (last visited Sept. 3, 2015); Richard Tipper, *Helping Indigenous Farmers to Participate in the International Market for Carbon Services: The Case of Scolel Té*, in SELLING FOREST ENVIRONMENTAL SERVICES: MARKET-BASED MECHANISMS FOR CONSERVATION AND DEVELOPMENT 223, 232 (Stefano Pagiola et al. eds., 2002); Margaret Skutsch et al., *Alternative Models for Carbon Payments to Communities Under REDD+: A Comparison Using the Polis Model of Actor Inducements*, 14 ENVTL. SCI. & POL'Y 140, 143 (2011); Promode Kant, *REDD Should Create Jobs, Not Merely Bring Compensation* 3 (Inst. of Green Econ., Working Paper No. 13, 2010), *available at* http://www.igrec.in/REDD_should_create_Jobs_Not_merely_bring_ compensation.pdf.

53. DAVID TAKACS, CONSERVATION INTERNATIONAL, FOREST CARBON + PROPERTY RIGHTS 25-26, 37, 38 51, 62 (2009) [hereinafter TAKACS, FOREST CARBON + PROPERTY RIGHTS]; Ashwini Chhatre et al., *Social Safeguards and Co-Benefits in REDD+: A Review of the Adjacent Possible*, 4 CURRENT OPINION ENVTL. SUSTAINABILITY 654, 655 (2012); 2008 FOREST GROUP, KATOOMBA GROUP & UNEP, PAYMENTS FOR ECOSYSTEM SERVICES: GETTING STARTED 10 (2008), *available at* http://www.katoombagroup.org/documents/publications/GettingStarted.pdf; William D. Sunderlin et al., *Rights & Resources Initiative, From Exclusion to Ownership? Challenges and Opportunities*, in ADVANCING FOREST TENURE REFORM 29-30 (2008).

54. Chhatre et al., *supra* note 53, at 657; Patricia Nelson, *An African Dimension to the Clean Development Mechanism: Finding a Path to Sustainable Development in the Energy Sector*, 32 DENV. J. INT'L L. & POL'Y 615, 623 (2004); Alfred Ofosu-Ahenkorah, *CDM Participation and Credit Pricing, in* AFRICA, IN EQUAL EXCHANGE: DETERMINING A FAIR PRICE FOR CARBON 127, 133 (Glenn Hodes & Sami Kamel eds., 2007).

55. David Takacs, *The Public Trust Doctrine, Environmental Human Rights, and the Future of Private Property*, 16 N.Y.U. ENVTL. L.J. 711, 771 (2008).

56. Joseph L. Sax, *The Public Trust Doctrine in Natural Resource Law: Effective Judicial Intervention*, 68 MICH. L. REV. 471, 484 (1970); Takacs, *supra* note 55, at 713-15.

57. Takacs, *supra* note 55, at 79.

beyond the traditional geographical (beyond the low tide line as discussed below) and topical limits (beyond water) and in extending the purposes for which public resources can be protected and managed. While the classic public trust doctrine was confined to protecting waterways subject to the ebb and flow of tides to enable public rights of navigation and fishing, today's public trust doctrine encompasses many categories of waterways and land adjacent to waterways for purposes that now include recreation and environmental protection. For example, in one of India's seminal cases reinstituting the public trust doctrine, the Supreme Court held that a public market and park are public trust resources that may not be given away to a private developer for a shopping center.[58] In South Africa, the 1998 National Environmental Management Act invokes the public trust in an expansive way: "[t]he environment is held in public trust for the people, the beneficial use of environmental resources must serve the public interest and the environment must be protected as the people's common heritage."[59] A California appeals court has declared that "it has long been recognized that wildlife are protected by the public trust doctrine" as "they are natural resources of inestimable value to the community as a whole."[60]

Protection of public resources is vital as climate change reshapes the landscape, and expanded recognition and application of the public trust doctrine could serve as an important tool for both mitigation and adaptation. Unfortunately, public officials and courts in the United States (and elsewhere) have been slow to acknowledge the important role this doctrine could play. As one California court pointed out, "public agencies do not always strike an appropriate balance between protecting trust resources and accommodating other legitimate public interests."[61] Indeed, governments may completely ignore the protection of the trust resources. The suggestion that members of the public have no right to object if the agencies entrusted with preservation of wildlife or other resources fail to discharge their responsibilities is contrary to the holding in pivotal California Supreme Court case *National Audubon Society*[62] and to the entire tenor of the cases recognizing the public trust doctrine elsewhere.

The public thus has the right to demand that government agencies steward resources wisely; such wisdom includes attending to the changing needs of

58. M.I. Builders Pvt. Ltd. v. Radhey Shyam Sahu (1999), S.C.C. 464 (India).
59. National Environmental Management Act of 1998, Ch. 1, §2(4)(o), *available at* https://www.environ-ment.gov.za/sites/default/files/legislations/nema_amendment_act107.pdf (last visited Sept. 8, 2015).
60. Center for Biological Diversity v. FPL Group, Inc, 83 Cal. Rptr. 3d 588, 597, 599 (Cal. App. 1st Dist. 2008).
61. *Id.* at 602.
62. National Audubon Soc'y v. Super. Court., 658 P.2d 709, 732 (1983).

biodiversity as climates change and human needs change accordingly.[63] The public trust doctrine demands that as trust resources evolve, conservation evolves with it. We should continue to acknowledge the rights of citizens to claim sound stewardship of their evolving public trust resources, and courts should recognize that public trust doctrine logically applies to other natural resources including a wide variety of ecosystems and habitat based on the ecosystem services that they can provide the public.[64]

B.   Payments for Ecosystem Services

While we can employ the public trust doctrine to press governments to steward resources, we can also employ market forces to pay private citizens to cooperatively protect those resources. IPCC's Working Group II suggests that "existing and emerging economic instruments" might provide a route to adaptation.[65] The Working Group's Summary for Policymakers specifically identifies payments for environmental services and subsidies as possible adaptation tools, but cautions that if not used carefully these economic tools "can provide disincentives, cause market failure and decrease equity."[66] Payments for ecosystem services (PES) is central tenet of many of the economic instruments used in climate change measures. Landowners are remunerated for managing their land to produce or maintain ecosystem services.[67] Ecosystem services are "components of nature, directly enjoyed, consumed, or used to create human wellbeing,"[68] and the concept acknowledges that natural ecosystems perform critical life-supporting services upon which the wellbeing of all society depends.[69] The main ecosystem services are categorized as provisioning, regulating, supportive, and cultural services.[70] Provisioning services include food, water, fiber, and fuel; these have quantifiable market

---

63. Robin Kundis Craig, *A Comparative Guide to the Western States' Public Trust Doctrines: Public Values, Private Rights, and the Evolution Toward an Ecological Public Trust*, 37 Ecology L.Q. 53, 80 (2010).

64. A current focus of public trust doctrine advocates is asserting that the doctrine applies to climate stability and air quality as embodied in the atmospheric trust litigation. Mary Christina Wood, *The Planet on the Docket: Atmospheric Trust Litigation to Protect Earth's Climate System and Habitability*, 9 Fla. A&M L. Rev. 1 (2015).

65. 2014 IPCC Adaptation Report, *supra* note 3, at 26.

66. *Id.*

67. Evan Mercer et al., *Taking Stock: Payments for Forest Ecosystem Services in the United States*, Forrest Trends: Ecosystem Marketplace 1 (2011), *available at* www.forest-trends.org/documents/files/doc_2673.pdf.

68. James Boyd & Spencer Banzhaf, Resources for the Future, What Are Ecosystem Services?: The Need for Standardized Environmental Accounting Units 8 (2006), *available at* http://www.rff.org/rff/Documents/RFF-DP-06-02.pdf.

69. *Id.*

70. Pushpam Kumar et al., *Behavioral Foundation of Response Policies Management: What Can We Learn From Payments for Ecosystem Services (PES)*, 10 Ecosystem Services 128, 129 (2014).

values.[71] Regulating services include flood control, and soil erosion prevention, while supporting services include nutrient cycling and soil formation. Cultural services include recreational use and spiritual values, the values of which are uncertain.[72]

The type, quality, and quantity of services provided by an ecosystem are affected by our resource decisions.[73] When the benefits of an ecosystem service accrue mainly to those who make management decisions (e.g., as in production of crops or livestock), private markets are likely to work relatively well.[74] However, when the benefits of an ecosystem service flow primarily to others, such as with water purification or climate stabilization, public interests and the interests of the resource manager may be misaligned.[75] This difference in private and social benefits, or the problem of externalities, results in a classic market failure: individuals will tend to provide too little of the ecosystem service.[76] PES can serve as "an effective mechanism to translate external, nonmarket values of ecosystem services into financial incentives" for individuals to provide conservation and socioeconomic development.[77]

After identifying important services or amenities provided by ecosystems, we could pay landowners to undertake pro-conservation management practices, such as habitat restoration or practices to reduce soil runoff. Such payment plans can enable private organizations or governments to influence landowner behavior without acquiring a formal property interest in the land or needing extensive regulatory programs. The parties to the contract, moreover, can modify the nature of the requirements or the level of payments as a changing climate changes local and global needs. It's usually easier to modify contracts than statutes!

This mechanism also enables private organizations to promote land conservation where they believe government entities aren't adapting quickly enough to prevailing local conditions. Thus, conservation organizations might pay landowners to engage in specific management practices to promote climate change adaptation or even pay landowners to allow the conservation organizations to undertake those management practices. For example, the U.S, Department of Agriculture pays farmers to undertake conservation efforts on

---

71. *Id.*
72. *Id.*
73. Jack B. Kelsey et al., *Designing Payments for Ecosystem Services: Lessons From Previous Experience With Incentive Based Mechanisms*, 105 PNAS 9465, 9465 (2008).
74. *Id.*
75. *Id.*
76. *Id.*
77. Hua Zheng et al., *Benefits, Costs, and Livelihood Implications of a Regional Payment for Ecosystem Service Program*, 110 PNAS 16681, 16681 (2014).

their land.[78] Farmers can receive an annual "rental" payment in exchange for maintaining certain vegetative cover. This program focuses on soil conservation and encourages native grasses and other plantings that reduce soil erosion while supporting healthy ecosystems.[79] Prevention of erosion has many benefits, including watershed protection and providing riparian habitat for birds and other species.

Payments for ecosystem services allow those who benefit from ecosystem services to direct and redirect funding to where it is most needed as the needs of human and ecological communities evolve as the climate changes. Costa Rica is the paradigmatic success story—"an icon"[80]—in implementing innovative programs to pay property owners for conserving ecosystem services. Costa Rica's Payment for Environmental Services program (PES, or PSA, *Pagos por Servicios Ambientales*) was introduced in 1996 in Forestry Law No. 7575, which describes the terms by which property owners with forests, tree plantations, or agroforestry systems are compensated for mitigating GHG emissions, providing hydrological services, conserving biodiversity, and preserving scenic beauty for ecotourism.[81] Since 1997, the program has funded conservation of about 1 million hectares of forests, and forest cover in the nation has grown from 20% in 1987 to over 50% in 2013.[82] Although the program has faced some criticisms—e.g., payments were not directed to priority conservation areas and didn't consider additionality, i.e., the government paid for areas that would have been conserved anyway—the government has continuously made improvements to target both priority conservation areas and to channel more funds to indigenous communities and women-owned properties.[83]

C.   Conservation Easements

While PES is rooted in contract law, conservation easements emerged from traditional property law. For centuries, common law countries have enabled restrictions on private land through servitudes, often in the categories of easements and covenants. The traditional servitudes enable private

---

78. USDA, Natural Resources Conservation Service, Conservation Reserve Program, http://www.nrcs.usda.gov/wps/portal/nrcs/detail/national/programs/?cid=stelprdb1041269 (last visited Aug. 18, 2015).
79. *Id.*
80. Ina Porras et al., Learning From 20 Years of Payments for Ecosystem Services in Costa Rica, IIED 2 (2013), *available at* http://pubs.iied.org/pdfs/16514IIED.pdf?.
81. Takacs, Forest Carbon + Property Rights, *supra* note 53, at 40.
82. Porras et al., *supra* note 80, at 8.
83. *Id.* at 10-11, 53; Takacs, Forest Carbon + Property Rights, *supra* note 53, at 44.

(or public) parties to limit land use.[84] They could also sometimes be used to achieve environmental protection goals, but common law impediments that restricted who could enter into the agreement, what the agreement could be for, how long it could last, and whether it could be transferred made conservationists hesitant to use them.[85] To get around these problems, states enacted conservation easement statutes that enabled government agencies and nonprofit organizations to hold perpetual restrictions on land.[86] Conservation easements prohibit landowners from acting in otherwise permissible ways with the goal of yielding a conservation benefit. For example, in many conservation easements, the landowner agrees to limit development on her land, and the conservation easement holder is the entity that can enforce the agreement. In exchange for agreeing to this limitation, the landowner usually receives tax breaks, cash payments, or permits to develop elsewhere.

Most conservation easements are perpetual, and their stipulations allow for little or no change. The current landowner and conservation easement holder determine the specifics of the agreement temporally (by naming the length of the conservation easement's term), spatially (by drawing the conservation easement boundaries), and ecologically (by establishing the exact restrictions on the land). These conservation easements run with the land. In other words, when an owner sells her property, the new owner must also abide by the terms of the agreement. While some conservation easements may use management plans and rely on adaptive management procedures to respond to changing conditions, many conservation easements state that the property is to be preserved in its "natural state."[87] A baseline document (required by the IRS for donated conservation easements)[88] makes it likely

---

84. Federico Cheever, *Public Good and Private Magic in the Law of Land Trusts and Conservation Easements: A Happy Present and a Troubled Future*, 73 Denv. U. L. Rev. 1077, 1081 (1996) (contrasting conservation easements with traditional easements). *See generally* Gerald Korngold, Private Land Use Agreements: Easements, Real Covenants, and Equitable Servitudes (2d ed. 2004).
85. Jessica Owley, *The Emergence of Exacted Conservation Easements*, 84 Neb. L. Rev. 1043, 1075-82 (2006).
86. Mary Ann King & Sally K. Fairfax, *Public Accountability and Conservation Easements: Learning From the Uniform Conservation Easement Act Debates*, 46 Nat. Resources J. 65, 71-72 (2006) (describing the Uniform Conservation Easement Act and other state enabling acts).
87. *See, e.g.*, San Juan Preservation Trust, *Conservation Easement*, http://sjpt.org/what-you-can-do/conserve-your-land-2/conservation-options/conservation-easements/ (last visited Oct. 7, 2015) (describing conservation easements to protect land in its "natural state"); Southwest Michigan Land Conservancy, *Why Protect Your Land*, http://www.swmlc.org/content/why-protect-your-land (last visited Oct. 7, 2015) (describing conservation easements as protecting land "in its natural state forever").
88. Elizabeth Byers & Karin Marchetti Ponte, The Conservation Easement Handbook 100-15 (2005) (describing conservation easement baseline requirements and offering guidelines for completing a baseline report).

that the natural state will be assessed by comparison to the conditions of the property on the day the conservation easement was recorded.[89]

Conservation easements are a useful tool for climate change in both mitigation and adaptation programs. The ability to tailor the agreements to the landscape and to ensure long-term protection of natural resources is invaluable. Indeed, many of the other conservation tools we discuss often work alongside conservation easements. However, the classic perpetual static conservation easement will not always be the ideal tool to meet conservation goals. Some modifications of the classic tool can yield benefits as well. For example, non-perpetual conservation easements may be appropriate in many circumstances. These could take different forms: term conservation easements that expire on a specified date or perhaps renewable conservation easements in which the holder retains an option to terminate the agreement if it no longer makes sense for protection of the land's conservation values.[90] Some suggest that removing perpetuity from conservation easements without clear guidelines for modification is unlikely to reduce the vulnerability of conserved lands to climate change.[91] However, land trusts may find term conservation easements an attractive path because they allow the holder or the community to change its mind about which lands to conserve and what the restrictions on those lands should be. Other land trusts are looking at their holdings and wishing some of the agreements weren't perpetual, expressing the concern that they haven't protected the right lands and are now stuck with stewardship obligations over lands they no longer view as desirable for meeting their conservation goals.[92] There may also be a hybrid approach where the conservation easement remains in place but there are requirements to periodically revisit and reassess the terms of the agreement.[93] This arrangement would allow incorporation of principles of adaptive management.

Conservation easements have largely been couched in terms of negative restrictions. That is, they tell landowners what they can't do. They rarely require affirmative obligations by the landowners.[94] When they do, those

---

89. For a discussion and critique of baselines, see generally J.B. Ruhl & James Salzman, *Gaming the Past: The Theory and Practice of Historic Baselines in the Administrative State*, 64 Vanderbilt L. Rev. 1 (2011).

90. Nancy A. McLaughlin, *Conservation Easements: Perpetuity and Beyond*, 34 Ecology L.Q. 673, 708 (2007); Jessica Owley, *Changing Property in a Changing World: A Call for the End of Perpetual Conservation Easements*, 30 Stan. Envtl L.J. 121, 163 (2011).

91. Adena R. Rissman, *Evaluating Conservation Effectiveness and Adaptation in Dynamic Landscapes*, 74 L. & Contemp. Probs. 145, 166-67 (2011).

92. Confidential interviews with land trust employees.

93. See Owley, *supra* note 90, at 163.

94. Alexander R. Arpad, Comment, *Private Transactions, Public Benefits, and Perpetual Control Over the Use of Real Property: Interpreting Conservation Easements as Charitable Trusts*, 37 Real Prop. Prob. & Tr. J. 91, 112-21 (2002) (explaining that the affirmative aspect of conservation easements is often ignored).

obligations tend to be minimal, like keeping certain areas landscaped or, in rare circumstances, requirements to control invasive species or engage in pest management.[95] Conservation easements also rarely enable the holder to undertake conservation activities on the land. While some conservation easements have provisions for public access or periodic visits to the land, it may be more desirable to enable holders to restore degraded habitat, relocate species to or from the land, or remove invasive flora and fauna. Most land trusts, the private land conservation organizations that hold conservation easements, are not well equipped currently to undertake active land management. They often have few employees, most of whom are not trained in ecology, conservation biology, or restoration.[96] Changing the framework of conservation easements to make them more active sites of conservation work will involve engaging new players in the effort. Where the holders are government agencies, such expertise may already be available on staff or in other units. Either way, we may see contracting out for active conservation expertise and labor. The climate change-addled future may see a blossoming of new economic livelihoods from restoring the planet.

Some tools inspired by conservation easements are only now entering into use or being proposed. One example is the use of real estate options. Where it appears possible that a specific parcel will become an important building block in a landscape protection system, options may become attractive.[97] An option is the right to buy a conservation easement or full title ownership to a property at a future point for a specified price. Options can keep future alternatives open without requiring the investment needed for immediate purchase. They can enable planning for an uncertain future, identifying multiple potential sites for species or ecosystem migration and asserting control over larger land area without the level of investment needed for purchase of full title or conservation easements.

Annuity or endowment conservation easements[98] occur when a conservation organization wants to protect a parcel of land but is not sure whether the land will retain its conservation value in the future. Rather than paying the

---

95. Jessica Owley & Adena Rissman, *Trends in Private Land Conservation: Increasing Complexity, Shifting Conservation Purposes and Allowable Private Land Uses*, 51 LAND USE POL'Y 76-84 (2016).

96. *See* Jessica Owley, *Conservation Easements at the Climate Change Crossroads*, 74 L. & CONTEMP. PROBS. 199, 223 (2011) (describing both the potential need for and the problems with active land management by conservation easement holders). *See also* Rissman, *supra* note 91 (describing role land trust could play in adaptive management while acknowledging the short comings of such organizations).

97. Federico Cheever & Jessica Owley, *Enhancing Conservation Options: An Argument for Statutory Recognition of Options to Purchase Conservation Easements (OPCEs)*, 40 HARV. ENVTL. L. REV. __ (forthcoming 2016).

98. ADENA R. RISSMAN ET AL., PRIVATE LAND CONSERVATION & CLIMATE CHANGE: RETHINKING STRATEGIES & TOOLS (forthcoming 2016).

landowner up-front for the conservation easement, the conservation organization invests what it would otherwise pay for a perpetual conservation easement in an annuity. As the annuity accrues interest or increases in value, the holder transfers those funds to the landowner for as long as the organization wishes to retain the conservation easement. If the holder decides to terminate the conservation easement, it stops making payments. So long as the conservation organization makes the payments, however, the conservation easement can last in perpetuity.[99]

Recognizing that the land important for conservation can change over time in response to changes in sea level, habitat, and the like, it may be desirable to design conservation easements (or a succession of them) that "move" in response to climate conditions. An inspiration for this is a rolling easement along a shoreline that shifts as the high water mark shifts.[100] The public trust doctrine discussed above recognizes a public right of use and access to coastal areas.[101] The line demarcating public ownership varies, but whether set at low tide, high tide, or the vegetation line (for some examples), it is a line that will be changing with sea level rise and other complications resulting from climate change. In the United States, the law generally recognizes that as the line changes, the property that we consider part of the public trust (and thus either owned by the state or imbued with a public trust easement protecting access and use of the area) shifts. While it is not yet clear how this concept would work with changing property owners (or with the constraints on donated conservation easements), rolling conservation easements limiting development and land use would be more closely tied to ecological boundaries than property lines. In particular, sea level rise projections predict submergence, coastal flooding, and coastal erosion with very high confidence,[102] suggesting that there may be a place for tools like rolling conservation easements and shifting rules regarding protected areas.[103]

Even within the context of the traditional rolling coastal easement that demarcates the line between public access and use and private prop-

---

99. Not all state conservation easement statutes will accommodate this structure currently (particularly states that require perpetuity) but many will and experimentation with this tool should begin.

100. Jesse J. Richardson Jr., *Conservation Easements and Adaptive Management*, 3 SEA GRANT L. & POL'Y J. 31, 50-51 (2010).

101. Richard J. Lazarus, *Changing Conceptions of Property and Sovereignty in Natural Resources Law: Questioning the Public Trust Doctrine*, 71 IOWA L. REV. 631, 636 (1986).

102. 2014 IPCC ADAPTATION REPORT, *supra* note 3, at 17.

103. Coastal adaptation could be expensive. Low-lying countries and small island states face different circumstances and rolling easements will make little sense where there isn't much room to which to roll, but in larger countries with coastal areas, recognizing protection and public use of coastal areas should acknowledge a flux in that coastal area.

erty, there may be opportunities for developing better conservation tools. The rules governing the boundaries of public trust property (or a public trust easement) often vary depending on the rate of the shifts in the sea level. Usually, shifts in shoreline occur gradually over the course of years or decades. Many states therefore adopt an average of the mean high tide line to determine which lands are public trust lands and which are private (and therefore belong to adjoining property).[104] Where the change happens quickly, as with a storm surge, the property line doesn't generally change.[105] The reasoning for this rule is that it would be overly harsh to make such dramatic changes to private property lines. This reasoning is often not that persuasive, particularly where current IPCC reports and other studies continually improve our understanding of the likely levels of sea level rise and the increasing frequencies of storm surges and other coastal events. One approach may be not that the actual title and occupancy to the land needs to change hands but that we expand the public trust zone by having an expansive public easement over the private land in that area that lets those who need it have access to the shoreline and enables public entities to take measures to protect important resources and habitats. Indeed, states already have a lot of variation on their interpretation of these boundaries and judicial interpretation of the doctrine to encompass greater ecosystem protection in the context of climate change is not unrealistic.

Although not currently consistent with all state and federal laws regarding conservation easements, tradable or moveable conservation easements could provide an opportunity to shift conserved lands as the landscape changes. These may be more politically palatable than the idea of a rolling easement. With a predefined agreement between a landowner and conservation easement holder, tradable conservation easements could be terminated at any point so long as the proceeds of the termination are reinvested in another conservation easement that meets the same conservation values.[106] This strategy is already legally possible with preservation of property in fee simple (that is, holding full title to the parcel), if perhaps cumbersome. Adding this agility to conservation easements could provide greater flexibility when the value of particular land changes in the face of climate change.

---

104. Craig, *supra* note 63.

105. Joseph L. Sax, *The Accretion/Avulsion Puzzle: Its Past Revealed, Its Future Proposed*, 23 Tul. Envtl. L.J. 305, 343 (2009).

106. W. William Weeks, *A Tradable Conservation Easement for Vulnerable Conservation Objectives*, 74 L. & Contemp. Probs. 230, 235-37 (2011).

D.   Reducing Emissions From Deforestation and Forest Degradation: REDD+

As the Working Group III's Summary for Policymakers notes, "[p]olicies governing agricultural practices and forest conservation and management are more effective when involving both mitigation and adaptation. . . . When implemented sustainably, activities to reduce emission from deforestation and forest degradation (REDD+[107] is an example designed to be sustainable) are cost-effective policy options for mitigating climate change, with potential economic, social and other environmental and adaptation co-benefits. . . ."[108] In REDD+, a local community, individual landowner, private developer, or government entity reforests degraded land or preserves a forest that would otherwise be felled. The actor may then sell the stored carbon in that land or forest for a contracted period to entities that want to offset their GHG emissions or simply want to preserve forests.[109] REDD+ may happen on a project-by-project basis. Increasingly, however, it is operating on a broader scale: A nation, province, or state uses REDD+ funds to reduce deforestation or promote reforestation in a wide geographic area, resulting in greater stored carbon than would have occurred without the funding.[110]

REDD+ blurs the bounds between global mitigation and local adaptation. REDD+ mitigates climate change when trees retain carbon that deforestation would otherwise release, or if new growth absorbs extra carbon dioxide. Additionally, maintaining healthy forests helps communities adapt to climate change by sustaining ecosystem services—preventing erosion, increasing rainfall, buffering floods, cleansing drinking water, and harboring crop pollinators—and by preserving biodiversity crucial for human survival. REDD+ investments can promote socioeconomic climate change adaptation through new sources of income and by providing for more secure, formal land title.[111] REDD+ may also further institutional adaptation as com-

---

107. The "+" refers to going beyond preserving intact forests and reducing forest degradation, to removing extra carbon from the atmosphere by reforesting degraded land, storing extra GHGs in wetlands, peatlands, and farm lands, and improving forest management. *See* Takacs, *supra* note 45, at 658.

108. Intergovernmental Panel on Climate Change, Climate Change 2014: Mitigation of Climate Change 26 (2014) (internal citations omitted) [hereinafter 2014 IPCC Mitigation Report].

109. David Takacs, *Forest Carbon Projects and International Law: A Deep Equity Analysis*, 22 Geo. Int'l Envtl. L. Rev. 521, 532 (2010).

110. For overviews on how REDD+ works, see David Takacs, *Environmental Democracy and Forest Carbon*, 44 Envtl. L. 71 (2014) [hereinafter Takacs, *Environmental Democracy*]; Takacs, *supra* note 45.

111. Amy E. Duchelle et al., *Linking Forest Tenure Reform, Environmental Compliance, and Incentives: Lessons From REDD+ Initiatives in the Brazilian Amazon*, 55 World Dev. 53 (2014). *But see* Anne M. Larsen, *Forest Tenure Reform in the Age of Climate Change: Lessons for REDD+*, 21 Global Envtl. Change 540 (2011) (arguing that REDD and REDD+ programs have not been successful at protecting land tenure and securing benefits for local communities); Joanes O. Atela et al., *Are REDD Projects Pro-Poor*

munity leaders, landowners, and government officials develop and manage REDD+ projects and hone skills and institutions to negotiate effectively with project developers and government functionaries.[112]

Governments, international financial institutions, environmental and social justice nongovernmental organizations (NGOs), and private citizens have poured over US$5 billion into REDD+ thus far.[113] REDD+ financing may be one of the best friends tropical biodiversity has ever had, provided that safeguards to emphasize biodiversity protection are incorporated into REDD+ finance deals. The Climate, Community, and Biodiversity Alliance, a consortium of businesses, technical advising agencies, and environmental and social welfare NGOs, has issued the most widely used standards to ensure positive biodiversity and social welfare benefits for individual projects.[114] A formal verification process ensures that when a state, province, or nation that pledges to reduce deforestation over a larger area in exchange for REDD+ funding, it actually does so, and that the implementing entity adheres to the guidelines that ensure biodiversity and social welfare co-benefits.[115] Even more money should be flowing into REDD+ thanks to agreements on social and environmental safeguards, a regime of measuring, monitoring, reporting, and verifying REDD+ outcomes, and a system of REDD+ financing reached in advance of the UNFCCC Conference of Parties in Paris in December 2015.[116] The 2015 Paris Agreement itself reaffirms the role of REDD+ in mitigating climate change while calling for "results-based

in Their Spatial Targeting? Evidence From Kenya, 52 Applied Geography 14 (2014) (concluding that REDD projects in Kenya were more likely to benefit international companies and low vulnerability areas than to help poor communities).

112. *See* H. Carolyn Peach Brown et al., *Climate Change and Forest Communities: Prospects for Building Institutional Adaptive Capacity in the Congo Basin Forests*, 43 Ambio 759 (2014).

113. International Sustainability Unit, Emergency Finance for Tropical Forests: Two Years on: Is Interim REDD+ Finance Being Delivered as Needed? 7-10 (2011), http://www.pcfisu.org/wp-content/uploads/2011/11/Two-years-on_Is-interim-REDD+-Finance-being-delivered-as-needed.pdf; *see also* Forest Trends Initiative, Covering New Ground: State of the Forest Carbon Markets 2013 vii (2013), *available at* http://www.forest-trends.org/documents/files/SOFCM-full-report.pdf.

114. *See* Climate, Community, & Biodiversity Standards 40-46 (3d ed. 2013), *available at* https://s3.amazonaws.com/CCBA/Third_Edition/CCB_Standards_Third_Edition_December_2013.pdf.

115. REDD+ Social & Environmental Standards 16-17 (2d ed. 2012), *available at* http://www.redd-standards.org/images/site/Documents/REDDSESVtwo/REDDSES_Version_2_-_10_September_2012.pdf.

116. Climate Law & Policy, *Unpacking the Warsaw Framework for REDD+* (2014), http://reddcommunity.org/publications/briefing-note-unpacking-warsaw-framework-redd; Gustavo A. Silvez-Chavez, *Surprising Development at UN Climate Meetings: REDD+ Is Finished*, Forest Trends, June 10, 2015, http://forest-trends.org/blog/2015/06/10/surprising-development-at-un-climate-meetings-redd-is-finished/; Subsidiary Body for Scientific and Technological Advice, Methodological Guidance for Activities Relating to Reducing Emissions From Deforestation and Forest Degradation and the Role of Conservation, Sustainable Management of Forests, and Enhancement of Carbon Stocks in Developing Countries (2015).

payments" and "reaffirming the importance of incentivizing, as appropriate, non-carbon benefits associated" with REDD+.[117] REDD+ funding priorities may shift as climate change shifts the landscape and thus conservation needs arise in new or unexpected locales, but for now REDD+ seems certain to expand across multiple landscapes.

E.   Biodiversity Offsets

Biodiversity offsetting translates the logic of carbon offsetting—because greenhouse gases are fungible, let the market figure out where it makes best economic sense to mitigate their buildup in the atmosphere—into something more sweeping. In more than three dozen jurisdictions,[118] developers are allowed to destroy biodiversity—individual species, particular ecosystems—in one place in exchange for protecting biodiversity elsewhere. As in REDD+, success of biodiversity offsetting is all about wise, participatory planning to map where and why we want development and where and why we want nature. If done well, biodiversity offsetting allows experts to plan for maximum flexibility and resilience in face of climate change. If biodiversity offsetting works as its backers promise, then it's a win-win situation on a landscape level: jurisdictions encourage economic development where it is needed and can prioritize conservation where it makes the greatest ecological sense. For the regulated entity—the developer, the citizen wishing to build a home, even the government—offsets may reduce the costs of compliance with environmental laws and offer sensible flexibility for how to respond to laws protecting biodiversity.[119] For conservationists, offsets can help incentivize conservation on private land and can channel protection efforts to where they will do endangered species and ecosystems the most good.

To fulfill their promise, biodiversity offsets must both mitigate the original damage and enhance the chance for a species to survive. Let's put aside for the moment the question of whether it is ethically legitimate to harm one biological community (and perhaps harm the human communities that depend upon those biological communities) in exchange for biodiversity mitigation elsewhere.[120] In the name of preservation of an imperiled species or

117. Adoption of the Paris Agreement, U.N. Framework Convention on Climate Change, Conference of the Parties, Twenty-First Session, Paris, Dec. 12, 2015, FCCC/CP/2015/L.8.
118. Kerry Ten Kate & Michael Crowe, Biodiversity Offsets: Policy Options for Governments, Input paper for the IUCN Technical Study Group on Biodiversity Offsets i (2014).
119. Thompson, *supra* note 23, at 261.
120. For a conversation with multiple viewpoints, see Karl Mathiesen, *Is Biodiversity Offsetting a "License to Trash Nature,?"* Guardian, May 22, 2014, http://www.theguardian.com/environment/2013/nov/12/biodiversity-offsetting-license-trash-nature.

ecosystem, conservation biology may support offsetting. Conservation biologists often note that single large reserves are more ecologically sustainable, and may offer better long-term resilience, than several smaller reserves of the same surface area.[121]Larger reserves may lessen fragmentation where scraps of isolated habitat fail to provide area to support minimum viable population sizes or corridors to connect isolated populations, and thus provide more resilient species response to climate change.[122] Larger areas may support larger populations that are more likely survive disturbances and "edge effects" from surrounding habitats whose biota may invade and conquer the desired rare species.[123] Smaller preserves may allow species nowhere to go, creating islands of the doomed.[124] In sum, the U.S. Fish & Wildlife Service suggests, "larger reserves are more likely to ensure ecosystem functions, foster biodiversity, and provide opportunities for linking existing habitat."[125]

Mitigation banks are part of a market for ecosystem services and environmental amenities. The two most common types of mitigation banks are those for wetlands and those for endangered species habitat. Mitigation banks are created (often by for-profit private corporations but not necessarily) by setting aside areas of land to promote healthy wetlands or endangered species habitat. With wetlands, for example, often the bank buys existing or degraded wetlands and puts in place management plans to promote a healthy functioning wetland.[126] The governmental agencies overseeing the bank (in the case of wetlands in the United States, it is usually the U.S. Army Corps of Engineers) work with the bank to quantify the value of the wetlands. They rank the wetlands on a scale of how valuable/rich/healthy the wetland is.[127] The Corps then approves the bank to sell credits. The marketplace determines the price tag on those credits. Developers engaging in projects that harm or degrade wetlands then buy credits from the bank to compensate (or mitigate) for the environmental damage they are causing. Thus, wetlands mitigation banking turns wetlands into a fungible asset.

---

121. U.S. Fish & Wildlife Service, Conservation Banking: Incentives for Stewardship (2012), *available at* http://www.fws.gov/endangered/esa-library/pdf/conservation_banking.pdf [hereinafter USFWS, Conservation Banking].

122. *Id.*

123. For a good court explanation, see *Sierra Club v. Marita*, 46 F.3d 606, 618 (7th Cir. 1995).

124. USFWS, Guidance for the Establishment, Use, and Operation of Conservation Banks 4 (2003); U.S. Fish & Wildlife Service, *Building a Bank Takes More Than Just Snakes* (2011), http://www.fws.gov/sacramento/outreach/Featured-Stories/BuildingBanksSnakes/outreach_featured-stories_BuildingBanksSnakes.htm; *Marita*, 46 F.3d at 618.

125. USFWS, Conservation Banking, *supra* note 121.

126. USDA, Natural Resources Conservation Service, *Wetland Mitigation Banking*, http://www.nrcs.usda.gov/wps/portal/nrcs/main/national/water/wetlands/wmb/ (last visited Sept. 4, 2015).

127. WARPT: Wetlands-at-Risk Protection Tool, *Estimate Wetland Values*, http://www.wetlandprotection.org/estimate-wetland-values.html (last visited Sept. 4, 2015).

Government agencies may be responsible for biodiversity offsetting, as in when developers pay "in lieu" fees and officials use those fees to prioritize conservation in priority areas, such as Natural Community Conservation Plans or regional Habitat Conservation Plans in the United States (discussed below). Keeping offsetting in the hands of the government may make it more likely that democratically accountable institutions are balancing competing needs and prioritizing correctly. Biodiversity offsetting can provide money in the form of payments to help cash-strapped governments do what they might otherwise not be able to afford to do.[128] In Australia, for example, New South Wales (NSW) is newly prioritizing "biobanking," as it encourages "offsets on land that is strategically important for biodiversity in NSW, such as land adjacent to rivers, streams and wetlands and important mapped biodiversity corridors. Establishing offset sites in these areas may generate additional biodiversity credits, which can be sold by landowners."[129] A review of the potential of biodiversity offsetting in NSW notes that the government supplies only enough funds to manage 19% of species that are threatened.[130] Offsetting will potentially pour billions of dollars into biodiversity conservation.[131] Kiesecker et al. note that a single oil and gas field pumped US$24.5 million into a biodiversity mitigation fund in Wyoming, compared to US$4 million otherwise available for wildlife conservation.[132]

Some critics allege that biodiversity offsetting is just a sop for developers to circumvent existing, effective conservation laws.[133] Arguably, the existence of mitigation banks facilitates conversion of already-existing habitat. The ability to purchase credits can hamper pressure to minimize impacts or to find alternative mitigation opportunities. However, for the UK's leading biodiversity offset private company, "It is not a license to trash, it is the

---

128. For an example from Brazil, see Juan David Quintero & Aradhna Mathur, *Biodiversity Offsets and Infrastructure*, 25 CONSERVATION BIOLOGY 1121, 1122-23 (2011); Joshua Bishop, *Producing and Trading Habitat, or Land Development as a Source of Funding for Biodiversity Conservation*, IUCN World Conservation Union (May 10, 2003).

129. NSW GOVERNMENT, NSW BIODIVERSITY OFFSETS POLICY FOR MAJOR PROJECT 8 (2014), *available at* http://www.environment.nsw.gov.au/resources/biodiversity/140672biopolicy.pdf.

130. NEIL BYRON ET AL., INDEPENDENT BIODIVERSITY LEGISLATION REVIEW PANEL, A REVIEW OF BIODIVERSITY LEGISLATION IN NSW (2014), *available at* http://www.environment.nsw.gov.au/resources/biodiversity/BiodivLawReview.

131. Joseph M. Kiesecker et al., *Development by Design: Blending Landscape-Level Planning With the Mitigation Hierarchy*, 8 FRONTIERS ECOLOGY & ENV'T 261, 265 (2009).

132. *Id.*

133. Jessica Owley, *The Increasing Privatization of Environmental Permitting*, 46 AKRON L. REV. 1091, 1092 (2013) ("Many environmental laws appear to prohibit environmental degradation outright, but then contain provisions allowing for environmentally destructive activities after obtaining appropriate permits.); Bruce A. McKenney & Joseph M. Kiesecker, *Policy Development for Biodiversity Offsets: A Review of Offset Frameworks*, 45 ENVTL. MGMT. 165, 173 (2010); James Kanter, *Companies With Poor Track Records on Environmental Damage Try for Change*. N.Y. TIMES, Oct. 13, 2008.

complete opposite. When you put a value on biodiversity, you are putting a financial incentive for developers not to trash it."[134] In the continental United States, private parties own 73% of the land; one-half of all endangered and threatened species have at least 80% of their necessary habitat on private land.[135] Through biodiversity offsetting, endangered species become assets to a property owner to steward, not a liability to dread or even surreptitiously destroy.[136] Once a price is put on biodiversity, private landowners have an economic incentive to manage their land for conservation.[137] By one estimate, over US$1 billion/year is spent on biodiversity and ecosystem mitigation.[138] Thus, money provides jobs and boosts economic vitality in rural areas.

On the other hand, much of the money may go to private, for-profit biodiversity bankers as the offsetters. Offsetting creates a new class of "enviropreneurs"[139] who can participate in "free market" (although the market depends on formal statutes that require conservation in the first place!) solutions to environmental conservation. Such bankers may have particular restoration or conservation expertise and thus earn profit from sound stewardship, making conservation an economic asset rather than a liability. Under the U.S. Endangered Species Act, federal agencies can offset anticipated takes (i.e., destruction or harm) of listed species by investing in private biodiversity banks.[140] Private citizens can use banking offsets to help fulfill the requirements of the habitat conservation plan required when the U.S.

---

134. Tom Tew, CEO of the Environment Bank, *quoted in* Mathiesen, *supra* note 120.
135. MICHAEL BEAN ET AL., ENVIRONMENTAL DEFENSE, PRIVATE LANDS OPPORTUNITY: THE CASE FOR CONSERVATION INITIATIVES (2003), *available at* http://www.fws.gov/southeast/grants/pdf/2677_cci-report.pdf.
136. Bunn, Mark Lubell & Christine K. Johnson, *Reforms Could Boost Conservation Banking by Landowners*, 67 CAL. AGRIC. 86 (2013), *available at* http://californiaagriculture.ucanr.edu/landingpage.cfm?article=ca.v067n02p86&fulltext=yes.
137. Jessica Fox & Anamaria Nino-Murcia, *Status of Species Conservation Banking in the United States*, 19 CONSERVATION BIOLOGY 996, 997 (2005). The government of NSW, for example, cites this as a major impetus for a move to private biobanking. NEW SOUTH WALES GOVERNMENT, NSW BIODIVERSITY OFFSETS POLICY FOR MAJOR PROJECTS 8, 33 (2014), *available at* http://www.environment.nsw.gov.au/resources/biodiversity/140672biopolicy.pdf. The Australian Senate notes that biodiversity offsetting payments could also provide funds to help Aboriginal peoples manage communally owned land. AUSTRALIA SENATE REPORT ENVIRONMENT AND COMMUNICATIONS REFERENCES COMMITTEE, ENVIRONMENTAL OFFSETS 24 (2014).
138. KATE & CROWE, *supra* note 118, at 10.
139. Property and Environment Research Center, *PERC Enviropreneurs*, http://perc.org/programs/perc-enviropreneurs/enviropreneur-institute (last visited Sept. 8, 2015).
140. *See* 16 U.S.C. §1539; CALIFORNIA DEPARTMENT OF FISH AND WILDLIFE, CONSERVATION AND MITIGATION BANKING, http://www.dfg.ca.gov/habcon/conplan/mitbank/ (last visited Sept. 8, 2015); U.S. FISH & WILDLIFE SERVICE, GUIDANCE FOR THE ESTABLISHMENT, USE, AND OPERATION OF CONSERVATION BANKS 3-4 (2003); U.S. Fish & Wildlife Service, *For Landowners: Recovery Credits and Tax Deductions*, http://www.fws.gov/endangered/landowners/recovery-credits.html (last visited Sept. 8, 2015) [hereinafter USFWS, *For Landowners: Recovery Credits and Tax Deductions*].

Fish & Wildlife Service (USFWS) issues an incidental take permit allowing the property owner to "take" listed species. The USFWS has approved over 100 biodiversity banks in 11 states covering nearly 100,000 acres for more than 60 listed species.[141]

Some biodiversity banks we visited in central California and Victoria and Queensland, Australia,[142] were situated in prime habitat in ecologically prudent locations and saved land that otherwise would have been destroyed, or were well-restored prior agricultural land now hosting endangered species where otherwise such conservation would not have existed. Offsetting programs can also generate funding and support for other efforts. The Queensland Trust for Nature, for example, is using biodiversity offsetting not only to preserve crucial koala corridors, but also to raise funds for their other conservation efforts.[143] Biodiversity offset programs can sometimes be a model of corporate social responsibility: Paul Detmann, who is one of Victoria's prime biobankers, expresses his company's philosophy:

> Cassinia Environmental has a very long-term vision of reconnecting all of Australia's National Parks through a network of private land managed for conservation. We call this vision Biolinking Australia—and it's a goal we share with many other conservation organizations. . . . Biolinking Australia is both a company and a vision. We have a 100-year plan to see all Australia's significant natural assets connected through linkages—connecting private and public lands of environmental significance into a network of natural linkages. . . .[144]

Not all stories were as hopeful, though. Some of the U.S. wetland and habitat banks we visited had been severely degraded as a result of a lack of adequate caretaking and were secured with uncertain legal instruments. Moreover, democratically responsible governments may have a wider view of what both human and nonhuman communities need; if private offsetting is to be allowed, it should be under constant watchful government supervision.[145] If done right, offsetting may provide great benefits to biodiversity, now and as climate changes the landscape.

---

141. USFWS, *For Landowners: Recovery Credits and Tax Deductions, supra* note 140.
142. See the plans, vision, and business models of these organizations: Cassinia Environmental, http://www.cassinia.com (last visited Sept. 8, 2015); Queensland Trust for Nature, http://www.qtfn.org.au (last visited Sept. 8, 2015); Wildlands, http://www.wildlandsinc.com (last visited Sept. 8, 2015); Westervelt Ecological Services, http://www.wesmitigation.com (last visited Sept. 8, 2015).
143. Queensland Trust for Nature, http://www.qtfn.org.au (last visited Sept. 8, 2015); interview and site visit with CEO Ben O'Hara (Jan. 11, 2015).
144. Cassinia, *Biolinking Australia*, http://www.cassinia.com/#!biolinking/c1u8a (last visited Sept. 8, 2015).
145. Our interviews in California suggest this is often the case; failure to fulfill the terms of a given offsetting contract means the biodiversity banker will not receive future contracts.

Biodiversity offsetting programs can be part of larger landscape level protection efforts. As noted above, conservation biologists often advocate for large reserves for the protection of biodiversity.[146] At the same time, biodiversity advocates increasingly call for comprehensive conservation planning in the context of comprehensive development planning. Such planning will become even more urgent as climate change alters what both human and nonhuman communities require to survive. Resilient ecological communities support resilient human communities.[147] Rather than a project-by-project atomization of individual habitat conservation plans (where a given developer must mitigate her impacts on formally listed endangered species), such comprehensive plans would seek to identify and plan for "the full range of biological features, how they are currently distributed, and what minimum viability needs each biological target require to persist in the long term."[148] Successful programs must result from a public process, including government officials, environmental advocates, business interests, biologists, and representatives of the general public. Such participatory conservation planning, often incorporating private landowners as newly converted conservation allies, allows communities the space to plan sound development and conservation and the space to change their minds if climate change shapes the landscapes in unanticipated ways.

California has pioneered Natural Community Conservation Plans (NCCPs), which "review the landscape area by area and species by species, yielding a list of types of terrain that might be purchased for mitigation, such as creek side corridors, alkali wetlands and meadows, and serpentine rock types home to rare and specially adapted species."[149] In most NCCPs, developers pay the government fees that the government invests in biodiversity targets; these fees could just as easily be invested in privately run biodiversity banks. Supporters of offsetting point to the sound conservation planning and public buy-in for this kind of landscape-level planning, providing money for conservation that is less acrimonious and more likely to accommodate human and nonhuman needs.[150] Additionally, planning at this scale can enable protection of larger areas of land and put conservation programs in place before development projects even begin. This advanced

146. Lee Hannah & Lara Hansen, *Designing Landscapes and Seascapes for Change, in* CLIMATE CHANGE AND BIODIVERSITY 329 (Thomas E. Lovejoy & Lee Hannah eds., 2005).

147. KATE & CROWE, *supra* note 118, at 10; Kiesecker et al., *supra* note 131, at 262.

148. Joseph M. Kiesecker et al., *supra* note 131, at 262.

149. John Hart, *Planned Wilderness: A Big Deal for Bay Area Open Space*, BAY NATURE, Oct. 6, 2011, https://baynature.org/articles/planned-wilderness/.

150. DANIEL POLLAK, NATURAL COMMUNITY CONSERVATION PLANNING (NCCP) 21, 34, 41 (2001), *available at* https://nrm.dfg.ca.gov/FileHandler.ashx?DocumentID=6388&inline.

protection has the potential (but yet to be widely realized) advantage of enabling conservationists to evaluate the success of conservation projects before permitting development.

The U.S. Department of the Interior (DOI) supports streamlined approval for renewable energy projects in California's deserts, and thus "[m]itigation is being baked into an integrated, landscape-level management and planning exercise."[151] This program gives greater certainty to permit applicants and the public, and promotes "meaningful, landscape-level environmental needs— rather than small-bore and/or ad hoc mitigation efforts."[152] Incorporating biodiversity offsetting at an early stage means that parties can plan ahead so that both agencies and developers know what they have to do, and environmental advocates and conservation biologists can advise on where large new sources of cash can do the most good for biodiversity. According to the Bureau of Land Management (BLM), "a regional mitigation approach also shifts the BLM's mitigation focus from a permit-by-permit perspective to a proactive regional-scale mitigation planning perspective."[153]

One or more conservation organizations or governments could create a landscape-scale reserve in which the protections afforded to any particular area is dynamic and flexible over time. As conditions change and species and habitats move, the level and type of protection applicable to any portion of the reserve also would change. For example, one area of the reserve might initially be open to agriculture but then restored to native habitat at a later point if a species moves in that direction. In some cases, a sound strategy for land conservation is simply to create room for adaptation. The Environmental Defense Fund (EDF) has developed programs along these lines. For example, through the greater sage-grouse habitat exchange, landowners in the western United States are incentivized to engage in proactive measures "to grow habitat"[154] for sage grouse, including controlling the expansion of undesirable vegetation and invasive species, and restoring appropriate habitat

---

151. David J. Hayes, *Addressing the Environmental Impacts of Large Infrastructure Projects: Making "Mitigation" Matter*, 44 ELR 10016 (Jan. 2014). *See also* Amy Morris & Jessica Owley, *Mitigating the Impacts of the Renewable Energy Gold Rush*, 15 Minn. J. L. Sci. & Tech. 293 (2014) (detailing some of the concerns that occur when mitigation plans proceed on a case by case basis and focus on perpetual offsite mitigation).

152. Hayes, *supra* note 151, at 10017. *See also* Bureau of Land Management (BLM), Draft Regional Mitigation Strategies and Planning Manual (2014), *available at* http://www.blm.gov/pgdata/ etc/medialib/blm/wo/Information_Resources_Management/policy/im_attachments/2013.Par.57631. File.dat/IM2013-142_att1.pdf [hereinafter BLM, Mitigation Manual].

153. BLM, Mitigation Manual, *supra* note 152.

154. Environmental Defense Fund, *Greater Sage-Grouse Habitat Exchange*, http://www.edf.org/ecosystems/ greater-sage-grouse-habitat-exchange (last visited Sept. 8, 2015).

on degraded land.[155] Scientists evaluate the landowners' efforts and assign them a credit value. The landowners can then sell this credit to industries and developers looking to offset the impacts of their projects. Promoted as a win-win solution,[156] the program protects and increases habitat while providing an income stream for landowners. Developers also find the program desirable because it gives them a marketplace to buy credits and removes the onerous task of developing new mitigation projects for each new proposal. Although this EDF example concentrates on one type of species habitat, related programs could address broader goals. DOI is pursuing this philosophy on a grander scale as it seeks protections and new funding sources for the sage grouse[157] and lesser prairie chicken, whose habitats stand in the way of oil and gas development in the American West, and who have chosen to live largely in Republican congressional districts where support for endangered species protection at the property owners' expense is not robust.

F.   Debt-for-Nature Swaps

After gaining independence from colonizing northern nations, many southern governments, desperate to improve their citizens' quality of life, entered into loan agreements with the World Bank and other lending institutions and donor governments.[158] Many borrowing nations then found themselves unable to pay back their debts (totaling over US$1 trillion) without exploiting their natural resources via extractive industries such as mining and logging to earn hard currency.[159] It's precisely these resources—clean water, intact forests—citizens will require even more urgently as they adapt to an increasingly capricious climate.

In debt-for-nature swaps, lenders cancel or reduce debt in a developing nation if, instead, the nation invests the money (that otherwise would have flown from South to North) in actions to preserve nature within the country.[160] While critiqued for their threats to sovereignty, legitimation of "illegitimate" debt, and possible interference with the participation and

---

155. Environmental Defense Fund, *Central Valley Habitat Exchange*, http://www.edf.org/sites/default/files/CentralValley_HabEx_factsheet_05.pdf (last visited Sept. 8, 2015).

156. Kate & Crowe, *supra* note 8, at ii, 1.

157. U.S. Fish & Wildlife Service, Greater Sage-Grouse Range-Wide Mitigation Framework, Version 1.0, 3 Sept 2014. Listing of the Sage Grouse as an endangered species is currently warranted, according to USFWS; the agency is attempting to use offsetting as a means to avoid listing and the political headaches and legal battles such listing will incur. *Id.*

158. Knicley, *supra* note 52, at 81.

159. Amanda Lewis, *The Evolving Process of Swapping Debt for Nature*, 10 Colo. J. Int'l Envtl. L. & Pol'y 431, 432 (1999); Knicley, *supra* note 52, at 81.

160. For a comprehensive review and critique of such swaps, see Knicley, *supra* note 52.

property rights of indigenous or other local peoples,[161] when done carefully, debt-for-nature swaps can result in win-win-win results. When developing nations—and their sovereign indigenous groups—are full (and not coerced) participants, debt-for-nature swaps may enhance climate change mitigation and adaptation in the same way REDD+ can: through reducing greenhouse gas emissions from deforestation and degradation while, and through preserving local ecosystem services and the cultures dependent on those services.

For example, in one successful U.S.-funded (US$2 million) debt-for-nature swap in Bangladesh, local groups receive land rights and in turn reforested denuded hills and received training in alternative (to forest destruction) income generation, thus providing more land for conservation, greater buffering from erosion and flooding, and local institutional adaptation.[162] Debt-for-nature swaps could also be used to help developing nations fulfill their treaty obligations under the Convention on Biological Diversity and other multilateral environmental agreements whose obligations are good on paper, but are often difficult to fulfill for cash-strapped governments.[163] By allowing a nation to pay off its debts through investing in homegrown conservation solutions, debt-for-nature swaps could be reinvigorated as a means to facilitate climate change adaptation.

G.   Community-Based Natural Resource Management

There's only so much land that a given government can afford to set aside as public conservation lands and only so many private citizens willing to burden their properties with conservation easements. REDD+ and biodiversity offsetting are two ways to incentivize conservation for a no-analog climate change future. Some nations are also experimenting with directly incentivizing conservation by turning over management of biodiversity to local community groups, who may then profit directly from ecotourism. Wildlife, particularly in developing countries, requires cooperation from local people if it is to persist; limiting wildlife to formal protected areas shrinks the potential pool of lands where conservation can occur and limits migration corridors,[164] both of particular concern as climate change reshapes habitats and requires both greater genetic variability and larger areas where wildlife may be able to thrive in the future.

---

161. *Id.* at 81, 88; Timothy B. Hamlin, Comment, *Debt-for-Nature Swaps: A New Strategy for Protecting Environmental Interests in Developing Nations*, 16 Ecology L.Q. 1065, 1080 (1989).

162. Knicley, *supra* note 52, at 81.

163. *Id.*

164. Gregg Goldstein, *The Legal System and Wildlife Conservation: History and the Law's Effect on Indigenous People and Community Conservation in Tanzania*, 17 Geo. Int'l Envtl. L. Rev. 481, 483 (2005).

Much of the world's land is formally owned by national governments.[165] In some cases, those governments are finding it advantageous to devolve certain property rights to local community groups. For example, Namibia has established fifty local community conservancies; each conservancy is then legally enabled to manage biodiversity and benefit from visitors who wish to see (or even hunt, sustainably) the nation's spectacular wildlife.[166] Thus, even if the land is still legally owned by the national government, management and benefits accruing from tourism now rests in the hands of local communities. In one analysis, when they benefit directly from biodiversity, "many local people see wild animals, even troublesome animals such as elephants and rhino, as a key to an improved future."[167] In Namibia, one-half of the elephants live outside of officially protected areas, but the elephant populations have rebounded because community-based natural resource management has given extra incentive to communities to patrol against poaching.[168]

Community-based natural resource management not only maximizes the area in which biodiversity may thrive, it also maximizes corridors for flora and fauna to migrate as local ecological conditions change, stabilizes healthy local ecosystem services, and provides institutional adaptation as communities develop organizational structures to work together to manage their environmental resources.[169] For community-based natural resource management to work, communities must have clearly delineated property rights, management responsibilities, and economic incentives.[170] The programs are most successful where the natural resource decisions then made are supported by science and flexible enough to incorporate principles of adaptive management and resilience thinking.

Community-based natural resource management can meet other goals related to community development, as well. When conservation occurs only in areas set aside and designated for conservation, we create a dichotomy between areas where people live and work and areas dedicated to "nature." This approach focuses on isolating and protecting designated environmen-

---

165. *See, e.g.*, ANDY WHITE & ALEJANDRA MARTIN, FOREST TRENDS, WHO OWNS THE WORLD'S FORESTS? 5 (2002), *available at* http://www.cifor.org/publications/pdf_files/reports/tenurereport_whoowns.pdf (showing chart of government ownership in the world's major forest nations).

166. Karol Boudreaux, *A New Call of the Wild: Community-Based Natural Resource Management in Namibia*, 20 GEO. INT'L ENVTL. L. REV. 297, 308 (2008).

167. *Id.* at 300.

168. *Id.* at 309.

169. *Id.*; Katherine L. Babcock, Note, *Keeping It Local: Improving the Incentive Structure in Community-Based Natural Resource Management Programs*, 21 COLO. J. INT'L ENVTL. L. & POL'Y 201, 207-09 (2010).

170. Babcock, *supra* note 169, at 202-03. For a comprehensive overview of effective legal conditions for community based resource management, see Sean T. McAllister, *Community-Based Conservation: Restructuring Institutions to Involve Local Communities in a Meaningful Way*, 10 COLO. J. INT'L ENVTL. L. & POL'Y 195 (1999).

tal areas or amenities from human impact. Implicit is the assumption that human activity will negatively affect environmental resources and, therefore, human interaction with those resources should be eliminated, reduced, or controlled. Conservation, obviously, requires land devoted to activities other than intense human appropriation of primary production. Yet, that need not mean exclusion of all humans and their activities from the land.

III. A Coda on Equity

The IPCC notes that "[g]overning a transition toward an effective climate response and sustainable development pathway is a challenge involving rethinking our relation to nature, accounting for multiple generations and interests (including those based on endowments in natural resources), overlapping environmental issues, among actors with widely unequal capacities, resources, and political power, and divergent conceptions of justice."[171] REDD+ and biodiversity offsetting don't change existing societal patterns unless they're done in ways that are transformative: transferring large quantities of wealth from North to South, inventing nimble and flexible uses of land not subject to the strictures of private property or rigid governmental control, fomenting true environmental democracy as communities are empowered to formulate, manage, and reap economic and ecological benefits from REDD+ projects or biodiversity banks, and ensuring that projects are implemented with the broadest possible interpretation of international human rights law.[172]

Whether they function effectively in the short term or lead to genuine transformation in the long run, REDD+, biodiversity offsetting, or any other legal regime to preserve Earth's myriad species, ecosystems, and the humans that depend upon them must be implemented sustainably and in a deeply equitable way. For REDD+ or biodiversity offsetting to be sustainable, it must be: (1) effective—working for all stakeholders with minimal complication; (2) synergistic—maximizing benefits for climate, biodiversity, and local people; and (3) equitable—narrowing gaps between rich and poor.[173] "Deep equity," in turn, refers to the laws, policies, and values that promote sustainable pathways acting in synergy to maximize the health and potential of all individuals, communities, and ecosystems.[174] The equity is "deep" because

---

171. 2014 IPCC MITIGATION REPORT, *supra* note 108, at 283, 287.
172. David Takacs has written at length on these topics. *See* Social Science Research Network, *David Takacs Author Page*, http://ssrn.com/author=1393231 (last visited Sept. 8, 2015).
173. Takacs, *Environmental Democracy*, *supra* note 110, at 118.
174. Takacs, *supra* note 45, at 657.

values become rooted within each individual, requiring that we fundamentally re-envision our community structures and responsibilities and root these values and responsibilities in our legal systems. Our laws and policies would, in turn, support values and actions promoting even deeper equity.

With any climate change program, we need to assess the distribution of the benefits and harms. The impacts of climate change will be felt by everyone[175] but will not be evenly distributed.[176] The same is true when it comes to mitigation and adaptation measures. To some extent, everyone (all countries) will need to change behavior but there are some places that will end up doing more of the mitigation work or have to deal with more adaptation measures than elsewhere. Indeed, the IPCC acknowledges the disproportionate impacts of climate change. Working Group II makes the following statements in its Summary for Policymakers:

- "People who are socially, economically, culturally, politically, institutionally, or otherwise marginalized are especially vulnerable to climate change and also to some adaptation and mitigation responses (medium evidence, high agreement)."[177]

- "Risks are unevenly distributed and are generally greater for disadvantaged people and communities in countries at all levels of development (medium to high confidence)."[178]

- "Climate-related hazards exacerbate other stressors, often with negative outcomes for livelihoods, especially for people living in poverty (high confidence)."[179]

All attempts to implement flexible conservation in changing times that work across the North/South divide should take "common but differentiated responsibilities" (CBDR) seriously. CBDR is an emerging principle of customary international law and is a cornerstone of the UN Framework Convention on Climate Change and the Kyoto Protocol.[180] CBDR requires

---

175. 2014 IPCC ADAPTATION REPORT, *supra* note 3, at 4.

176. *See, e.g.*, 2013 IPCC PHYSICAL SCIENCE REPORT, *supra* note 1, at 20 ("Changes in the global water cycle in response to the warming over the 21st century will not be uniform.").

177. 2014 IPCC ADAPTATION REPORT, *supra* note 3, at 6 (continuing to explain that the heightened vulnerability "is the product of intersecting social processes that result in inequalities in socioeconomic status and income, as well as in exposure. Such social processes include . . . discrimination on the bases of gender, class, ethnicity, age, and (dis)ability.").

178. *Id.* at 12, Assessment Box SPM.1.

179. *Id.* at 6.

180. United Nations Framework Convention on Climate Change, art. 3(1), May 9, 1992, 1771 U.N.T.S. 107, 31 I.L.M. 849 (entered into force Mar. 21, 1994); Kyoto Protocol to the United Nations Framework Convention on Climate Change, Dec. 10, 1997, 37 I.L.M. 22 art. 10.

that all nations mitigate GHG emissions, contribute to adaptation, and take actions to conserve Earth's biological heritage, but it simultaneously requires more significant contributions from wealthier, developed nations.[181] CBDR legal principles found in the climate change conventions and other multilateral environmental agreements ground pragmatism in ethics. Pragmatically, developed nations have greater financial resources to mitigate GHG buildup, preserve biological resources, and help other nations adapt to climate change and preserve their own resources; rich nations got rich through industrial development whose excesses continue to pollute the global atmospheric commons and exploit biological resources. Poor nations and their citizens, on the other hand, have contributed less to climate change and will be hit hardest by its impacts.[182] Thus, the wealthy developed nations bear greater environmental responsibilities and should help poorer developing nations adapt to the effects of the GHG pollution that the North has caused en route to economic prosperity and preserve the resources that the North has exploited and continues to exploit.[183] While CBDR is a principle of international law, we believe that actors working within a nation should heed the underlying dicta that wealthier parties in a transaction owe some kind of ecological debt for whatever environmental consequences have resulted from accruing wealth, and their conservation actions should never exacerbate inequality.

How do we implement flexible conservation in an equitable way? Examples abound. Here's one: The South African "Working for Water" program has employed people to clear invasive species from more than 6 million acres in and around the nation's waterways.[184] Its founders note that these plants "pose a direct threat not only to South Africa's biological diversity, but also to water security, the ecological functioning of natural systems and the productive use of land."[185] Invasive plants suck up more water than native South African plants and thus leave less water for human use in a water-stressed nation. Officials estimate that invasive plants consume about 7% of total annual runoff and could eventually consume more than one-

---

181. Takacs, *supra* note 45, at 722-23.
182. ERIC A. POSNER & DAVID WEISBACH, CLIMATE CHANGE JUSTICE 11 (2010); RODA VERHEYEN, CLIMATE CHANGE DAMAGE AND INTERNATIONAL LAW: PREVENTION DUTIES AND STATE RESPONSIBILITY 34 (2005); Maxine Burkett, *Climate Reparations*, 10 MELBOURNE J. INT'L. L. 509, 513-14 (2009).
183. Anita M. Halvorssen, *Common, But Differentiated Commitments in the Future Climate Change Regime—Amending the Kyoto Protocol to Include Annex C and the Annex C Mitigation Fund*, 18 COLO. J. INT'L ENVTL. L. & POL'Y 247, 254 (2007); Lavanya Rajamani, *The Nature, Promise, and Limits of Differential Treatment in the Climate Regime*, 16 Y.B. INT'L ENVTL. L. 81, 93 (Ole Kristian Fauchald et al. eds., 2007).
184. SIP 19, *supra* note 23, at 55.
185. Republic of South Africa, Department of Water Affairs, *Welcome to the Working Water Webpage*, https://www.dwaf.gov.za/wfw/ (last visited Sept. 8, 2015).

half if left unmanaged.[186] Invasive plants slow stream velocity, increasing surface evaporation, which further decreases the amount of water available for human and nonhuman uses.[187] Obviously, invasive plants crowd out South Africa's unique, endemic flora and fauna, as well.[188] One study suggests that if 20% of the US$192 billion that developing countries invest in traditional infrastructure were replaced by green infrastructure, more than 100 million extra jobs would be created.[189] Working for Water employs tens of thousands of people, targeting women, youth, and disabled people[190] in a nation where high unemployment entrenches poverty and threatens stability of a fragile democracy.

However, even the Working for Water Program has not been designed through full local participation. When implementing flexible conservation, we must always keep in mind that most ecosystem services are local, and decisions we make can help or hurt people who most intimately depend on nearby functioning ecosystems. Thus, when making decisions about how environmental resources will (or won't) be developed, local people—those with intimate knowledge of land and resources, and who have the most to gain or lose from these decisions—should be full and active partners with developers, NGOs, government agencies, and whoever else is fomenting the conservation schemes. The legal norms of environmental democracy have arisen to ensure that conservation decisions are fair, well informed, and don't harm the human rights of local people. These norms comprise the right to participate in environmental decisionmaking; the right to access to information on environmental decisions; the right to redress and remedy when environmental rights are violated; and the right to Free Prior and Informed Consent (FPIC)—particularly for indigenous and forest-dependent peoples—when decisions are made that will affect vital resources and lands.[191] When those

---

186. SANBI (SOUTH AFRICAN NATIONAL BIODIVERSITY INSTITUTE), A FRAMEWORK FOR INVESTING IN ECOLOGICAL INFRASTRUCTURE IN SOUTH AFRICA 2 (2014).
187. United Nations Environment Programme, *Working for Water: A South African Sustainability Case*, http://www.unep.org/training/programmes/Instructor%20Version/Part_3/readings/WfW_case.pdf (last visited Sept. 8, 2015).
188. SIP 19, *supra* note 23, at 30.
189. UNITED NATIONS ENVIRONMENT PROGRAMME, GLOBAL GREEN NEW DEAL POLICY BRIEF (2009), *available at* http://www.unep.org/pdf/A_Global_Green_New_Deal_Policy_Brief.pdf.
190. Republic of South Africa, *supra* note 185.
191. Takacs, *Environmental Democracy, supra* note 110, at 79-89; United Nations Conference on Environment and Development, Rio de Janeiro, Brazil, June 3-14, 1992, Rio Declaration on Environment and Development, U.N. Doc. A/CONF.151/26/Rev.1 (Vol. I), Annex I (Aug. 12, 1992), http://www.un.org/documents/ga/conf151/aconf15126-1annex1.htm; UN-REDD PROGRAMME, LEGAL COMPANION TO THE UN-REDD PROGRAMME GUIDELINES ON FREE, PRIOR AND INFORMED CONSENT (FPIC): INTERNATIONAL LAW AND JURISPRUDENCE AFFIRMING THE REQUIREMENT OF FPIC 4 (2013), *available at* http://www.unredd.net/index.php?option=com_docman&task=doc_ download&gid=8792&Itemid=5.

who implement environmental conservation fail to respect environmental democracy norms, they may violate domestic and international law, and may consign a conservation project to failure, and worse, may violate the human rights and even destroy the lives of local citizens. Meaningful, informed participation is necessary if we are to have the most sustainable possible land and species conservation schemes. Such participation makes use of local people's wisdom about local resources; ensures their buy-in as equal partners; and furthers community adaptation through planning and managing projects.

IV.   Conclusion

The IPCC reports confirm that the world is and will be changing. As a result, species are struggling, habitats are moving, and ecosystems are shifting in unpredictable ways. Preserving species and ecosystems, in addition to being intrinsically good in a beautiful world, helps to mitigate climate change by preventing the carbon stored in plants and soil from being released and helps human communities adapt to the chaos of climate change by preserving the local ecosystem services that buffer their lives, and, in some cases, improving cash flows, individual skills, and community governance. Conservation of land and habitat has thus become critical as a basic biodiversity preservation measure that can promote all these other benefits, as well.

We have always lived in a changing world, but the pace of the change is accelerating. Past approaches to conservation will prove inadequate: we need to be creative. This chapter has explored some creative ideas—some already in use and some not—that go beyond regulatory mechanisms and even fee simple purchase of land. We should be embracing actions that provide flexibility while keeping in mind that "flexibility" is a double-edged sword. If it means "we'll figure it out eventually," we have few concrete measures by which to judge the success of our actions. Performance standards, with appropriate measuring, monitoring, reporting, and verification, that allow us to constantly adapt to changing conditions will be important.

Our list still comes with provisos.

We identify holistic planning as a vital component of conservation. Some of the strategies we discuss above are more conducive to holistic conservation planning than others. For example, mitigation banks may be more successful at targeting areas with desired characteristics, while conservation easements on their own are more likely to arise where individual landowners find them attractive for personal (meaning personal conservation goals, protecting cultural heritage, obtaining tax breaks and other public benefits) reasons. Habitat exchanges may work well with an entity overseeing the process and targeting specific landowners to garner engagement, but letting individual landowners drive the process may not be as successful in creating a coherent system.

Many of the approaches we discuss involve calculating the habitat or eco-system value of the land in isolation from the other roles that the parcels serve. Thinking about land as bits and pieces may be harmful. We lack a holistic view of the benefits that the land plays or its place in the commu-nity when we think about each ecosystem service out of context. When we simply look at a parcel of land for its potential credit value for sage-grouse habitat, we may lose sight of the value of that land overall. What role is it playing in the community? Is there cultural importance to the current land use? What role could the land play in protecting other species or ecosystem services? Maybe pigeonholing a parcel into the category of sage-grouse habi-tat exacts high opportunity costs and hampers its potential development for other types of important resources. A changing climate and landscape may make current habitat ill-suited down the line. For example, we may ham-string future community members by valuing a particular type of inflexible land use over other potential future land uses. With REDD+, for example, we may constrain communities into being forest-based or constrain them by removing forests as the source of their livelihood through now-prohibited activities. Yet at the same time, if we don't pick some environmental amenity as our priority driving factor now, a given area may be developed and may be permanently unavailable for conservation.

We should be careful in assessing the value of the environmental benefits from a proposed project or program. For example, in the biodiversity offset examples, scientists seek to calculate some type of credit or dollar value for the preservation actions. These are hard numbers to determine. Moreover, we have concerns regarding additionality. Ensuring against additionality may be particularly difficult in terms of conservation easements, REDD+, or Payments for Ecological Services. Are the restrictions in conservation agree-ments or payments for preservation actions that would not have occurred but for the existence of the conservation easement or payment scheme? For example, if we pay a rancher to restrict her land to ranching, we may not have gained anything if she had no intention or potential of converting her land to less environmentally friendly uses. Paying someone not to chop down a forest doesn't gain us much on the mitigation front if there was never any risk of that forest being chopped down. This reality also means that where regulations prohibit environmentally harmful activities (e.g., conversion of wetlands), private or additional agreements to prohibit the same activity may yield little or no benefit. Even where we might consider a benefit obtained because such restrictions add security against land conversion, it may not be the best use of land conservation funds.

None of the ideas we shared here offer permanent solutions to the species extinction crisis. They are stopgap, emergency legal mechanisms that buy (in some cases, literally) time for us to transition to a non-hydrocarbon based economy and for the planet to heal and rebound from heat and chaos. Poorly designed projects with poor management and projects that pay no attention to the needs of local human communities that depend on non-human communities may facilitate ecologically damaging human development and hence may simply accelerate biodiversity loss in the face of climate change, undermining humans' own options for adaptation and survival. If done well, however, creative biodiversity projects offer enhanced resilience for local human and non-human communities in the present, bandages to staunch wounds while we find the moxie to address the underlying causes of species extinction.

The next round of IPCC reports should tackle these methods head on. While thinking about equity and other considerations have normative aspects, scientists are well positioned to be able to consider the various protection tools at issue and examine their long-term viability.

Chapter 5
The Local Official and Climate Change

Stephen R. Miller

REBECCA:

He wrote Jane a letter and on the envelope the address was like this: It said: Jane Crofut; The Crofut Farm; Grover's Corners; Sutton County; New Hampshire; United States of America. . . . Continent of North America; Western Hemisphere; the Earth; the Solar System; the Universe; the Mind of God—that's what it said on the envelope. . . . And the postman brought it just the same.

—THORNTON WILDER, OUR HOUSE Act 1 (1938)

In all but the largest cities, including most fast-growth cities, local officials are volunteers that hold other jobs and typically receive little, if any, compensation for their governmental work.[1] This fact is true even for those local officials, members of the planning commission and the city council, who most directly control the city's development, making what are arguably the most important long-term decisions that will shape cities' futures.[2] For those commissioners and council members, merely reading the weekly staff reports that accompany individual projects that require adjudications and engaging in the more comprehensive legislative actions related to specific plans, neighborhood plans, or business districts can be an overwhelming task.[3] Further, public meetings often begin right after work and can last into the wee hours of the morning.[4]

It is in the hands of these local officials, however, that the task of forming the United States' overall land use pattern rests.[5] Indeed, because the country's land use pattern relies so heavily upon this patchwork of volunteers,

---

1. C. GREGORY DALE ET AL., THE PLANNING COMMISSIONERS GUIDE 1-3 (2013); *see also* CITY OF BOISE, IDAHO, CITY CODE §2-01-03 (2015) ("Unless otherwise provided in this ordinance, all members of any Boise City Boards and Commissions shall serve without compensation.").
2. DALE ET AL., *supra* note 1, at 1-3.
3. *Id.*
4. *Id.*
5. *Id.* at 5-15.

most of whom are not experts in development, there has long been a skepticism about whether the country can ever have a coherent land use policy.[6] This potential problem is notable in the context of climate change. Although it is well-known that land use patterns can affect climate change—particularly regarding the relation between land use development and transportation infrastructure—even the most aggressive efforts to address climate change have largely ignored land use. For instance, California's Global Warming Solutions Act of 2006,[7] the most significant greenhouse gas (GHG) emission reduction strategy in force at present, places almost no importance on land use in GHG emissions reductions, even despite the fact that the state had adopted the country's most aggressive mandate to link land use and transportation planning.[8]

This disconcerting disconnect—that those with the power to alter land use patterns are those least likely to actually effect such change—found its way into the Intergovernmental Panel on Climate Change's (IPCC's) most recent series of reports, which are collectively referenced as the Fifth Assessment Report (AR5).[9] All IPCC reports, of course, remain deeply scientific enterprises aimed at recording and determining the pace of climate change.[10] In addition to this scientific investigation, however, the IPCC assessments have also provided detailed, worldwide analyses of major socio-ecological factors related to climate change and, in particular, addressed how those factors might assist with mitigation or adaptation to climate change.[11] Among the socio-ecological factors considered in this latest AR5 was a substantial analysis of why the endeavors to change land use patterns, which hold such promise for addressing climate change, have failed.[12] These sections, while

---

6. *See* PAUL G. LEWIS, SHAPING SUBURBIA: HOW POLITICAL INSTITUTIONS ORGANIZE URBAN DEVELOPMENT 32 (1996).

7. CAL. A.B. 32 (2006), California's Global Warming Solutions Act of 2006 (HEALTH & SAFETY CODE §§38500 et seq.).

8. CAL. S.B. 375 (2008), Sustainable Communities and Climate Protection Act of 2008.

9. The IPCC Fifth Assessment consists of three reports and a synthesis report. *See* INTERGOVERNMENTAL PANEL ON CLIMATE CHANGE, CLIMATE CHANGE 2013: THE PHYSICAL SCIENCE BASIS (2013) [hereinafter 2013 IPCC PHYSICAL SCIENCE REPORT]; INTERGOVERNMENTAL PANEL ON CLIMATE CHANGE, CLIMATE CHANGE 2014: IMPACTS, ADAPTATION, AND VULNERABILITY (2014) [hereinafter 2014 IPCC ADAPTATION REPORT]; INTERGOVERNMENTAL PANEL ON CLIMATE CHANGE, CLIMATE CHANGE 2014: MITIGATION OF CLIMATE CHANGE (2014) [hereinafter 2014 IPCC MITIGATION REPORT]; INTERGOVERNMENTAL PANEL ON CLIMATE CHANGE, CLIMATE CHANGE 2014: SYNTHESIS REPORT (2014) [hereinafter 2014 IPCC SYNTHESIS REPORT]. Collectively, these four reports constitute the IPCC Fifth Assessment (AR5). All reports from the Fifth Assessment are available at http://www.ipcc.ch/report/ar5/.

10. For a summary review of the scientific data related to climate change, see 2014 IPCC SYNTHESIS REPORT, *supra* note 9, at 2-16.

11. *See generally* 2014 IPCC ADAPTATION REPORT, *supra* note 9; 2014 IPCC MITIGATION REPORT, *supra* note 9.

12. *See infra* Sections II, III, and IV.

global in scope, also offer substantial perspective and insight for the local official in the United States.

This chapter seeks to make these insights into land use development from the AR5 more readily accessible to the U.S. local official and, in particular, will also place a special emphasis on issues facing local officials in fast-growth cities that have yet to establish a concerted response to climate change. The chapter will first investigate how the IPCC can provide a common language for cities to talk about climate change as a global problem and, in particular, discuss several sections of the AR5 of interest to local officials. The chapter will then investigate how the AR5 can provide a framework for working through the institutional problems that can cause local governments to fail in addressing climate change. While politics will always play a role in the effectiveness of governmental responses to climate change,[13] the AR5 provides a much-needed framework for discussing how the functioning of government itself can also serve as an impediment. Perhaps the most succinct statement to this effect in the AR5 is that "[o]vercoming the lack of political will, restricted technical capacities, and ineffective institutions for regulating or planning land use will be central to attaining low-carbon development at a city-scale."[14] This chapter will use this AR5 framing statement—addressed here in the order of technical capacity, institutional effectiveness, and political will—in investigating both global problems facing local officials and those that are specific to local officials operating under the U.S. land use legal rules.

Finally, while I write here in an academic capacity, my thinking is also informed by my service as a planning commissioner on Boise, Idaho's Planning and Zoning Commission. Boise is a fast-growth city located in the American Mountain West, which is one of the United States' fastest growing regions. This chapter draws on that experience as a commissioner in considering how addressing climate change in emerging cities differs from the excellent work on climate change already being done in some of the nation's larger cities.

I. Reading the Fifth Assessment as a Local Official

The AR5's three content reports, each written by a working group of scholars and experts, comprise thousands of pages and are summarized in a

---

13. *See, e.g.*, Philip Bump, *Jim Inhofe's Snowball Has Disproven Climate Change Once and for All*, Wash. Post (Feb. 26, 2015), https://www.washingtonpost.com/news/the-fix/wp/2015/02/26/jim-inhofes-snowball-has-disproven-climate-change-once-and-for-all/.

14. 2014 IPCC Mitigation Report, *supra* note 9, §12.6.

fourth synthesis report that has its own heft.[15] Few people are likely to read the AR5 in its entirety. For the local official tasked with addressing climate change in an urban environment, much of the AR5's most relevant information can be found in reviewing just a few sections of chapters outlined here. For those seeking a general familiarity with the IPCC's scientific conclusions, the synthesis report's summary report for policymakers provides an excellent overview.[16]

The IPCC presents its detailed study of urban environments in several sections of two chapters. The first relevant sections are in the chapter addressing cities and climate change adaptation. That chapter appears in Working Group II's report on climate adaptation, *Climate Change 2014: Impacts, Adaptation, and Vulnerability*, as *Chapter 8: Urban Areas*.[17] Within this chapter, Section 8.4 specifically addresses urban environment governance challenges related to adaptation to climate change.[18]

The second relevant set of sections appears in the chapter addressing cities and climate change mitigation. That chapter appears in Working Group III's report on climate mitigation, *Climate Change 2014: Mitigation of Climate Change*, as *Chapter 12: Human Settlements, Infrastructure, and Spatial Planning*.[19] Within this chapter, Sections 12.5 through 12.8 specifically addresses urban environment governance challenges in mitigation.[20]

While numerous other sections of the Fifth Assessment address urban environment governance to varying degrees,[21] investigating just these several pages of the larger report provides the opportunity to focus on the legal and policy issues that most affect urban areas and through which local officials are most accustomed to taking action.

II.   Restricted Technical Capacities

Many fast growing cities do not have the technical capability to address climate change, an unfortunate reality because it is these fast-growth communities where the most impact can be made in creating land use patterns

---

15.   *See supra* note 9.
16.   *See* 2014 IPCC Synthesis Report, *supra* note 9, at 2-31.
17.   2014 IPCC Adaptation Report, *supra* note 9: *Chapter 8: Urban Areas*.
18.   *Id.* at §8.4.
19.   2014 IPCC Mitigation Report, *supra* note 9: *Chapter 12: Human Settlements, Infrastructure, and Spatial Planning*.
20.   *Id.* at §§12.5-12.8.
21.   Both *Chapter 8: Urban Areas*, 2014 IPCC Adaptation Report, *supra* note 9, and *Chapter 12: Human Settlements, Infrastructure, and Spatial Planning*, 2014 IPCC Mitigation Report, *supra* note 9, are worth reviewing in their entirety for the local official seeking additional information.

that provide mitigation and adaptation strategies.[22] This section evaluates several legal structures discussed in the Fifth Assessment that fast-growth cities with limited technical capacities can implement without greatly increasing spending.[23]

For cities with limited technical capacities, one of the most important first steps is simply to build a common language for discussion of climate issues, which can then be used to help establish a common vision for future planning.[24] Building a supportive legal culture in which local officials feel able to frame this common language and common vision is especially important. For instance, many fast-growth cities find themselves resource constrained and thus use their limited legal resources to address the most immediately salient legal issues of the day, which might involve legal aspects of annexation, subdivisions, and applying existing land use regulations. That kind of focus, however, does not provide the necessary legal training necessary for local government attorneys to gain expertise in the process and substance of fitting climate change-based local legislation and adjudication into the legal framework of federal, state, and local laws. The result can be that, when faced with litigation, or even the threat of a backlash, by climate change deniers, property rights absolutists, and the like, local government legal staffs feel inadequately prepared to defend climate change policies and regulations. In turn, this failure to prepare for the legal arguments that surround climate change measures can encourage those advisors to recommend less aggressive climate protections than might be warranted by local circumstances and permitted under law. Of course, a respect for local concerns is warranted, but too often a few objectors can hijack a local governmental process and use threats of legal action to challenge activities that are well within legal requirements.[25] Providing local legal advisors trained in legal aspects of climate change will prove immensely valuable to any community where such changes may face opposition.

---

22. *See Executive Summary*, 2014 IPCC ADAPTATION REPORT, *supra* note 9 ("Urban governments are at the heart of successful urban climate adaptation because so much adaptation depends on local assessments and integrating adaptation into local investments, policies, and regulatory frameworks (high confidence). [8.4]"); *id.* ("Urban centers around the world face severe constraints to raising and allocating resources to implement adaptation. . . . [8.3, 8.4]")).

23. *See generally Chapter 8: Urban Areas*, 2014 IPCC ADAPTATION REPORT, *supra* note 9, and *Chapter 12: Human Settlements, Infrastructure, and Spatial Planning*, 2014 IPCC MITIGATION REPORT, *supra* note 9.

24. 2014 IPCC ADAPTATION REPORT, *supra* note 9, §8.4.2.1.

25. These challenges often take the form of regulatory takings claims. *See, e.g.*, Nollan v. California Coastal Comm'n, 483 U.S. 825 (1987) (exactions require a nexus with the project); Dolan v. City of Tigard, 512 U.S. 374 (1994) (exactions must be "roughly proportional" to the project); Koontz v. St. Johns River Water Mgmt. Dist., 133 S. Ct. 2586 (2013).

The local government's common vision regarding climate change also needs to be clearly articulated to all decisionmakers in affected jurisdictions.[26] It is surprisingly common that well-intentioned local development plans take years to develop, only to be ignored in practice. The disconnect between planning and application is often the result of a lack of concerted effort to convey the new plans to all decisionmakers: city councils, planning commissions, and numerous other local bodies. All of these local officials have a great deal of impact in affecting the same city, but they often act independently. They all must be informed of the common vision—whether it be espoused simply in a mission statement for the city, a comprehensive plan, or detailed zoning regulations—as well as how each can effectively work in concert with the others to achieve the desired ends.

Fast-growth cities also need to develop their technical capacity in the face of rapid change. As most development professionals know, recessions are often the best time to do long-term planning because they afford staff and the industry time to grapple with complex issues. On the other hand, recessions are often a time when political forces call for reduced regulation to stimulate the economy. As a result, in many fast-growth areas, staff will likely need to find ways to train themselves about climate issues even while working under heavy caseloads of boom cycles. An approach used by many cities engaging in local environmental regulations has been to phase in such regulations through several steps. For instance, when San Francisco implemented its green building regulations in the midst of a housing boom, the first regulatory step was a reporting phase that did not require any mandatory level of green building compliance.[27] This reporting-only phase gave the staff time to learn green building codes, to experiment with ways to effectively communicate the relative efficiency of buildings in staff reports, and to give the regulated community time to understand how to meet the procedural reporting requirements and also to experiment with approaches to meeting substantive green building requirements in a cost-effective manner.[28] When San Francisco then moved to a reporting and mandatory compliance requirement within a year, it first started by requiring a relatively low level of regulatory compliance that gradually increased.[29] This three-tiered approach—reporting, minimal compliance, and then increased compli-

---

26. 2014 IPCC ADAPTATION REPORT, *supra* note 9, §§8.4.1.2., 8.4.2.1.
27. *Green Building Ordinance*, CITY & CTY. OF SAN FRANCISCO, CAL., http://sfdbi.org/green-building-ordinance (last visited Oct. 9, 2015); *see also* CITY & CTY. OF SAN FRANCISCO, CAL., *Administrative Bulletin 093: Implementation of Green Building Regulations* (Jan. 1, 2014), *available at* http://sfdbi.org/sites/sfdbi/files/AB-093.pdf (last visited Oct. 9, 2015).
28. *Id.*
29. *Id.*

ance—could prove equally useful for fast-growth areas trying to increase the technical capacities of their staffs in addressing climate change.

Fast-growth areas should also consider engaging urban vulnerability and risk assessments for both existing urban areas and areas where growth is expected.[30] Efforts to address climate change mitigation and adaptation need information about the local landscape.[31] Because most states do not require individualized environmental review of private projects, local officials need to devise an efficient way to map vulnerabilities and risk, plan for them, and then hold the line against risk-prone development in the noted areas.[32] Resources for such detailed analysis are often tight in fast-growth communities, but several legal approaches could facilitate better decisionmaking. For instance, areas of vulnerability and risk could take, as starting points, analysis from other federal or state agencies that provide general guidance on flood or fire risk.[33] In those areas, and perhaps even in some reasonable buffer areas adjacent thereto, the local government could require a heightened showing from applicants, or a presumption against development that could be rebutted, to justify an entitlement.

III.   Ineffective Institutions for Regulating or Planning Land Use

The Fifth Assessment identified "[t]he urban institution conundrum": "rapidly urbanizing cities—cities with the greatest potential to reduce future GHG emissions—are the cities where the current lack of institutional capacity will most obstruct mitigation efforts."[34] The same is true with regard to adaptation efforts as well.[35] This section looks at several aspects of why local development institutions are ineffective and what local officials can do with an eye towards addressing climate change.

Among the reasons urban development institutions fail is not only resources, but also organizational design. Three examples serve to illustrate

---

30.   2014 IPCC ADAPTATION REPORT, *supra* note 9, §8.4.1.4.
31.   *Id.*
32.   *See* DANIEL R. MANDELKER, NEPA LAW AND LITIGATION §§12:1 (2d ed. 2015) ("Fifteen states and the District of Columbia followed the congressional lead and adopted environmental policy acts modeled on NEPA.").
33.   *See, e.g., Flood Map Service Center,* FED. EMERGENCY MGMT. SERV., https://msc.fema.gov/portal (floodplain maps and planning documents); WESTERN GOVERNORS' ASS'N, COMMUNITY GUIDE TO PREPARING AND IMPLEMENTING A COMMUNITY WILDFIRE PROTECTION PLAN (2008), http://www.forestsandrangelands.gov/communities/cwpp.shtml (planning for wildfires in the wilderness-urban interface.
34.   2014 IPCC MITIGATION REPORT, *supra* note 9, §12.6.1.
35.   2014 IPCC ADAPTATION REPORT, *supra* note 9, §8.4.3.4.

these failures and their effect on climate change planning: ineffective commission structures; ineffective public participation structures; and ineffective alliance of staff professional goals with climate change goals.

A.   *Overcoming Ineffective Commission and Permitting Structures*

The proliferation of land use controls in the last 100 years has led to the belief, in some cities, that there is a need for multiple boards or commissions to review different parts of a project.[36] For instance, the rise of historic preservation has led many advocacy groups to create a specific historic preservation committee or commission.[37] In some cities, these commissions give recommendations to planning commissions; in other cities, these commissions have equal status as planning commissions in determining whether a project obtains a certificate of appropriateness or similar entitlement.[38] Other commissions or committees common in many cities include design review boards that apply design guidelines, and transportation-focused groups that address traffic-related issues.[39] Add to these approval complications the bifurcation of land use and building permits, and it becomes clear that decisions about any one project can become highly segmented. This fragmentation can cause problems that lead to either over-regulation—in which case the various regulatory bodies fail to see the burdens imposed by other regulators and duplicate regulation—or under-regulation, in which case the developer can segment the approval process in a manner that frustrates holistic decisionmaking and collective review of the project.

Such problems could affect climate change in a number of ways, several of which are discussed here. First, climate change factors should be integrated into permitting processes at the front-end of the development cycle. For instance, the building efficiency of a project should be a factor in whether it

---

36. For instance, Boise is a prime example of a still small but fast-growth city with multiple agencies. *See, e.g.*, CITY OF BOISE, IDAHO, CITY CODE §§2-02-01 et seq. (Airport Commission); *id.* §§2-06-01 et seq. (Planning-Zoning Commission); *id.* §§2-07-01 et seq. (Development Impact Fee Advisory Committee); *id.* §§2-16-01 et seq. (Public Works Commission); *id.* at §§2-17-01 et seq. (Arts and History Commission); *id.* §§2-20-01 et seq. (Irrigation Commission); *id.* §§2-21-01 et seq. (Housing and Community Development Advisory Committee); *id.* §§2-23-01 et seq. (Foothills Conservation Advisory Committee); *id.* at §§2-25-01 et seq. (Boise City Accessible Parking Committee); ADA COUNTY HIGHWAY DIST., *Policy Manual*, http://www.achdidaho.org/AboutACHD/PolicyManual.aspx (district controls all roads in Boise City).
37. CITY OF BOISE, IDAHO, CITY CODE §4-13-03 (2015) (designating Boise City Historic Preservation Commission as entity tasked with reviewing historic buildings).
38. *Id.*
39. *See supra* note 37.

obtains a discretionary land use permit.[40] However, in most American jurisdictions, the building permit, and compliance with efficiency codes, occurs
in a typically ministerial review and against energy codes that are often not
sufficient to meet climate change mitigation necessities.[41] Decisionmaking
could be improved by integrating even energy code compliance into land use
entitlement processes, something easily done by placing such goals into the
comprehensive plans with which most conditional use permits for larger land
use projects must comply.[42] If the project does not meet the comprehensive
plan energy mandates, it might not receive the discretionary land use entitlement, even if it might otherwise meet the ministerial requirements of an
outdated building code.

Second, local permitting should require demonstration of compliance with
other state and federal laws prior to obtaining the local permit. Local land
use decisionmaking is often not effectively coordinated with other state and
federal agency processes that evaluate the project for compliance with other
laws, which may currently include, or may come to include, climate change
mitigation and adaptation.[43] The facts of *Sackett v. Environmental Protection
Agency* provide a useful example.[44] In *Sackett*, local officials issued building permits for a project applicant's local code-compliant home near a lake;
the applicant proceeded to build on the bases of those properly issued local
permits.[45] However, the U.S. Environmental Protection Agency issued an
administrative compliance order to stop work when the project was already
under construction because, the agency argued, the project was placing fill
material into a jurisdictional wetland and thus needed a Clean Water Act
§404 permit from the U.S. Army Corps of Engineers.[46] While the outcome
of the *Sackett* case ultimately turned on a procedural question of administrative law,[47] the facts of the case illustrate important institutional issues regard-

---

40. *See, e.g.*, City & Cty. of San Francisco, Cal., General Plan, *Environmental Protection Element,
     Objective 13, Enhance the Energy Efficiency of Housing in San Francisco*, http://www.sf-planning.org/
     ftp/general_plan/I6_Environmental_Protection.htm#ENV_EGY_12 (last visited Oct. 9, 2015).
41. *See, e.g.*, 7 Miller & Starr Cal. Real Est. §25:25 (4th ed. 2015):
        As a general rule, the building official is required to issue a permit if the application is in
        order, the proposed use is one permitted by the zoning ordinance, the proposed structures
        comply both with zoning conditions and with the applicable building codes, and any other
        conditions imposed on the development or subdivision approval.
42. *See supra* note 40.
43. 2014 IPCC Mitigation Report, *supra* note 9, §12.5.3.
44. 132 S. Ct. 1367 (2012).
45. Complaint for Declaratory and Injunctive Relief, Sackett v. United States Environmental Protection
     Agency, 2010 WL 7634112 at *7 (2010) ("[The Sacketts] applied for and obtained the requisite
     building permits.").
46. Sackett v. United States Environmental Protection Agency., 132 S. Ct. at 1370.
47. *Id.* at 1371 (holding that the administrative compliance order was a final agency action for purposes
     of the Administrative Procedure Act and thus petitioners could seek judicial review of the order under

ing the lack of integration of local government and other permits. Many local governments issue land use and building permits with standard conditions, which typically include the requirement that the project applicant must comply with all other state and federal laws. Problems arise, however, where local government issues land use and building permits without verifying compliance with those other laws. As in the case of *Sackett*, the local government likely could have foreseen the necessity of a Clean Water Act fill permit for a home being built near a lake—even though the Sacketts as developers contested that requirement—but the local government did not require that the fill permit be on file or otherwise ensure compliance with other laws before issuing its building permits.[48] This is poor institutional practice.

It is true that it can be difficult for local governments, especially those in states that do not require environmental review of private projects, to ensure compliance with the raft of potentially applicable state and federal environmental regulations. However, local governments need not shoot in the dark: the local government could simply have a policy of sharing all applications with local offices of state and federal permitting officials seeking their guidance, as is common with the lead agency and cooperating agency distinction under the National Environmental Policy Act (NEPA).[49] By using the local government permit as the coordinating permit for compliance with other state and federal laws, local officials can ensure that a situation like that in *Sackett* is avoided, which also aids the project applicant in ensuring that the applicant does not necessarily spend money or time on a project that will run afoul of other regulations. This coordinated approach, while valuable for many land use and environmental purposes, would also prove useful in ensuring climate change mitigation and adaptation compliance. Further, it should be noted that this process should not lengthen the entitlement timeframe because the project applicant cannot properly begin construction until all permits are obtained in any case.

B.   Overcoming Ineffective Public Participation

The last several decades have seen a great emphasis on public participation in local government decisionmaking.[50] This has included, among other changes, increased participation for neighborhood groups, as well as increasing access

---

the Act).

48.   *Id.* at 1370.

49.   40 C.F.R. §1501.5 (2015) (duties of lead agencies); 40 C.F.R. §1501.6 (2015) (duties of cooperating agencies).

50.   *See, e.g.,* LAWRENCE SUSSKIND ET AL., MEDIATING LAND USE DISPUTES: PROS AND CONS (POLICY FOCUS REPORT) 2-5 (Ann LeRoyer ed., Lincoln Institute of Land Policy 2000).

to GIS tools that permit the community to offer their own project alternatives.[51] Nevertheless, despite these additional procedural and technological tools to enhance community engagement, public participation routinely fails to prove effective in basic ways. Most importantly, public participation is typically focused on quasi-judicial proceedings against particular projects where the community shows up solely to oppose the project. In these situations, despite hours-long meetings in which tens or even hundreds of community members offer comments, there is typically no real discussion of project alternatives. Instead, public participation typically involves a litany of reasons that oppose the particular project.

This is a poor use of the public process. Surely, in some cases, the project under review deserves wholesale rejection. However, if the project complies with the community's basic land use documents—the comprehensive plan, zoning, and so on—then it is likely not without some merit. A better public participation process would address not only whether the project should be approved in its current iteration, but more importantly, how the project might be altered or otherwise provide mitigations that would make the project acceptable to the community.[52] This broader analysis requires a far more searching review of community goals than simply rejection or acceptance of the project; indeed, it invites conversation between city officials, the community, and the developers as to what the future of the community should be. That conversation is seldom had in quasi-judicial proceedings, but it should be, especially in situations where climate change mitigation and adaptation are at stake.

Further, in many communities, public participation is simply not a component of those processes where the real planning for the future takes place: in the legislative determinations of how to structure the comprehen-

---

51. Craig Anthony Arnold, *The Structure of the Land Use Regulatory System in the United States*, 22 J. LAND USE & ENVTL. L. 441, 476 (2007) (noting that "increasingly neighborhood residents are actively participating in developing plans and land use regulations for their neighborhoods through techniques like design charrettes, scenario development, impact assessment, [and] participatory land use mapping").

52. Some have argued that the current air of uncertainty created by *Koontz* would make such consideration of alternatives more difficult. *See* Lee Anne Fennell & Eduardo M. Peñalver, *Exactions Creep*, 2013 S. CT. REV. 287, 287-88 (2014) ("By beating back one form of exactions creep—the possibility that local governments will circumvent a too-narrowly drawn circle of heightened scrutiny—the Court [in *Koontz*] left land use regulation vulnerable to the creeping expansion of heightened scrutiny under the auspices of its exactions jurisprudence."). On the other hand, it is ironic that environmental review statutes typically require the presentation of project alternatives and thus, in those states with mini-NEPAs, the environmental review process necessitates that the land use process also envision alternatives. *See* CAL. PUB. RES. CODE §21002 (2015) (California Environmental Quality Act requires that "public agencies should not approve projects as proposed if there are feasible alternatives or feasible mitigation measures available which would substantially lessen the significant environmental effects" of the project.).

sive plan and zoning. For the interested public seeking to make a difference with regard to climate change, participation in these legislative processes is instrumental to ensuring that the community's development rules are climate-friendly.[53] Local officials can make climate change part of the legislative process by actively engaging the conversation in a manner that is appropriate to the community.[54] This engagement can include public meetings, but, increasingly, online and social media participation can be valuable. Many local communities have adapted climate action plans over the last decade, but many have taken the approach of primarily providing a common language for engaging climate rather than providing actionable regulatory compliance measures.[55] The common language assists with the previously noted goal of providing a common vision, but ultimately communities will need to find a way to move climate compliance from policy to law.

C.   Overcoming Staff Reluctance to Engage

While staff can be a great resource both for implementing existing policies as well as creating new policies, there are often significant barriers to staff effectively addressing long-term problems such as climate change. These impediments can be doubly strong in fast growth communities.

First, planning departments are often funded from fees paid by developers.[56] This mandate for planning departments to "pay their own way" can create a culture in which leadership establishes a mandate to please its perceived customer—the developer—because the department's continued existence is dependent upon such applications. Clearly, such a mindset can make it difficult to have hard conversations with developers; it can also obscure calls in existing plans to require or encourage types of development that may not be popular with the community's extant development sector but that might assist with climate mitigation or adaptation. Staff who work under such conditions can find themselves evaluated on the basis of how they please the customer-developer rather than with respect to the verve with which they

---

53.   2014 IPCC ADAPTATION REPORT, *supra* note 9, §8.4.2.2.
54.   *See* Maarten K. van Aalsta et al., *Community Level Adaptation to Climate Change: The Potential Role of Participatory Community Risk Assessment*, 18 GLOBAL ENVTL. CHANGE 165 (2008).
55.   *See, e.g., California Jurisdictions Addressing Climate Change*, CAL. OFFICE OF PLANNING & RESEARCH (July 7, 2014), http://www.ca-ilg.org/sites/main/files/file-attachments/california_jurisdictions_addressing_climate_change_pdf_0.pdf (list of local governments in California that have adopted plans "to address climate change and/or to reduce GHG emissions").
56.   *See, e.g.,* Facts, City & Cty. of San Francisco Planning Dept., http://www.sf-planning.org/index.aspx?page=3419 (noting that, in 2012, total revenue was $24,604,399 and fees accounted for $19,630,295 of costs with just $1,905,311 in General Fund support).

maintain the integrity of the code or exhibit creativity in assisting project applicants with climate-friendly alternatives.

Second, planning is an occupation in which there is continued ambivalence about professionalization.[57] While many planning departments in major cities require some form of advanced graduate work in planning for their staff, fast growth areas often do not. As a result, many planners faced with the inordinate challenges of fast growth have no formal training in the history of land use regulation, much less regarding cutting-edge strategies for addressing long-term issues like climate change. What training that does occur in fast-growth areas tends to focus on assisting processing of applications—making the day-to-day business of the department function smoothly—rather than on contemplating alternatives that could improve a community's mitigation of and adaptation to climate change. In these circumstances, with project applications piling up and pressure from developers to get to a hearing, finding time to learn about climate change, much less draft language and engage departmental leadership on the issue, can feel like trying to shoot the moon.

D.   The Fifth Assessment's Contributions

Into the midst of these failed institutional structures, several potential approaches discussed in the AR5 could show promise. First, an emphasis on learning to bundle tools could prove valuable.[58] In this approach, rather than asking staff and commissions to view climate change as an overwhelming monolithic problem to tackle, the emphasis becomes on helping the staff and commissions to start with a tool here or there that, perhaps, might have a co-benefit with an existing need of the community.[59] For instance, reducing the urban heat island effect with shade trees on streets can prove popular from an urban design perspective even absent climate change adaptation goals.[60] With this incremental approach, the institutional components of the city familiarize themselves with tools slowly over time but at a pace where it does not feel overwhelming.[61]

---

57. *Becoming a Planner*, Am. Planning Ass'n, https://www.planning.org/aboutplanning/becominga-planner.htm ("In 2004, 43 percent of all APA members (note: approximately one-sixth of the APA members are planning commissioners, officials, or students, who do not have a degree in planning) had earned a master's degree in planning.").
58. 2014 IPCC Mitigation Report, *supra* note 9, §12.5.3.
59. *Id.*
60. *See also* Lawrence Susskind et al., Managing Climate Risks in Coastal Communities: Strategies for Engagement, Readiness and Adaptation (2015) (providing numerous examples of same).
61. *Id.*

Another approach recommended by the AR5 is the use of pilot projects and sectoral approaches.[62] Pilot projects provide a similar sense of incremental change and also minimize the potential risk because, should the pilot fail, the status quo would be restored.[63] Sectoral approaches, such as first addressing impervious pavement in commercial building, makes sense because they can seek out projects that might have a desire for green building mandates.[64]

Finally, while most efforts at regionalism have failed over the past several decades, there is still good reason for fast-growth institutions to think regionally, even if governance is not regional. For instance, it is well-known that opportunities to reduce vehicle miles traveled have been lost where land uses around regional rail stations are not zoned to require close residential and mixed-use developments that would permit pedestrian access to the station.[65] Achieving this kind of zoning, however, requires coordination between local land use planners and the typically inter-governmental rail agency. While such coordination would seem natural, the number of failed opportunities around rail stations indicates that even basic collaboration on land use planning at the regional scale remains complicated.

IV.   The Lack of Political Will

This section addresses how local officials in fast-growth cities can engage climate change in a meaningful way while still addressing those pressing concerns that are foremost in the minds of some elected and appointed officials. The greatest concern of local officials in addressing climate change should be to provide the public space required to facilitate the ongoing conversation necessary to create a common vision around action, noted previously.[66] Achieving this common vision at the local level would have several components.

First, in many locations local government is not a partisan office, and that status has a valuable contribution to make to climate change politics.[67]

---

62. 2014 IPCC Adaptation Report, *supra* note 9, §8.4.1.2.
63. *Id.*
64. *Id.*
65. Robert Cervero et al., BART @ 20 Series: Land Use and Development Impacts 2 (1995), http://www.uctc.net/papers/308.pdf (noting that the Bay Area region's regional rail, BART, "largely failed to attract high-density residential development around stations").
66. 2014 IPCC Adaptation Report, *supra* note 9, §8.4.2.1.
67. *Partisan vs. Nonpartisan Elections*, Nat'l League of Cities, http://www.nlc.org/build-skills-and-networks/resources/cities-101/city-officials/partisan-vs-nonpartisan-elections ("According to a 2001 survey, 77 percent of the responding cities have nonpartisan elections, and 23 percent have partisan elections.").

Where local officials are not bound to party allegiances, they should feel freer to speak openly about climate change without concern for the talking points of their respective political parties.

Even where local official elections are partisan, a second component to providing meaningful space for discussion of climate change would be an open embrace by all local officials, no matter what the party allegiance, of the existing scientific consensus regarding climate change—that it is occurring, and that human emissions of GHGs are a significant cause. For instance, a conservative politician concerned about the effects of climate change regulation should limit concern to precisely that—the effects of regulation—rather than maintaining an unhelpful obfuscation about the facts on climate change. Embracing the scientific consensus would permit even conservative local politicians to realistically represent their interests and, potentially, seek out novel solutions that do not rely so heavily on command-and-control regulation but which might instead use the market to make the changes that the climate needs.

Third, politicians should not sacrifice climate policy, or the environment generally, on the altar of economic development. Many fast-growth areas have propelled their rise by offering low-cost living and a low cost of business operations. Where that strategy proves successful in luring development, local officials can feel hemmed in by what may feel like a tenuous balance and believe that any amount of raising taxes or costs would threaten the whole development scheme. Local officials need to provide a rhetoric true to the local community that emphasizes both environmental stewardship and economic development. Those cities that have done so, while they have missed out on some major low-end manufacturing facilities, have found themselves attracting high-wage earners and the companies that seek to employ them, ultimately proving that climate stewardship can be a valuable component of sustainable growth.[68]

Fourth, it is not uncommon that local officials will offer to take on the costs of environmental compliance for large companies through economic development agreements, a fact that further undercuts the importance of the environment to business because it permits corporations to place all of the costs of their externalities onto the local community's tax base. In essence, this strategy forces the local community to pay for a clean environment while the polluting corporation pays nothing. These types of deals should not be permitted because they take away from the corporations the price signal of

---

68. See, e.g., Development Agreement, CITY OF TWIN FALLS, IDAHO (constructing a waste water facility treatment for yogurt company free of cost to the company) (on file with author).

the social costs of their businesses, which would otherwise encourage the companies to operate in climate friendly ways.

Fifth, local officials should focus on co-benefits of climate change tools; for instance, a climate adaptation strategy that focuses on hazard mitigation might lead to less development in floodplains.[69] Those same non-developed floodplains could potentially be used for a greenbelt or other public amenity that ultimately raises property values of nearby non-floodplain properties. Through such a strategy, the local government obtains both a climate adaptation benefit and the new amenity, the bike path through a local park, which is a benefit shared by the developer through higher housing prices on nearby lands.

Sixth, local officials in fast-growth communities routinely find themselves short of resources for even some of the most basic functions.[70] Under such circumstances, it is easy to ignore long-range planning, which is the kind of planning most likely to mediate the urban community's response to and effects on climate change.[71] Local officials can illustrate the importance of climate change, as well as long-range planning, by protecting funding sources for positions within the local government that address these issues from cuts that may seem more expedient. The specifics will depend on each local government's budget structure; however, consider a situation, as discussed previously, where a planning department is funded by developer fees. Such a department might find it difficult to justify giving even one employee the time to consider climate change impacts arising from the city's growth, especially where developers are unlikely to reward the department for doing so. A local government can illustrate the importance of climate change by securing such a position from another funding source—whether through the general fund or another department with an alternative funding mechanism—that gives that position some autonomy and the ability to speak with some independence.

In addition to taking the above steps to create the space for a common vision around climate change, local officials should take several additional steps that would prove useful both in addressing climate change as well as in improving land use policy in a fast-growth region. First, building a forum for local governments, business leaders, and community groups to work together on growth is an important objective. Despite planning's rise over the last century, many of the country's most notable places—even comprehensive

---

69.   2014 IPCC Mitigation Report, *supra* note 9, §12.8.
70.   2014 IPCC Adaptation Report, *supra* note 9, §8.4.2.1.
71.   2014 IPCC Adaptation Report, *supra* note 9, tbl. 8-4.

plans—have come about as a result of the efforts of either individual private businesses or coalitions involving private businesses. For instance, Daniel Burnham's 1909 *Plan of Chicago* was not written at the behest of the city, but rather for the Commercial Club of Chicago, a collection of the city's largest business interests.[72] San Francisco, often considered a prime example of the regulatory planning approach, obtained the outlines of its modern form after World War II under the guise of the Bay Area Council, another collection of the city's most prominent business leaders.[73] Today, the proposed revival of Las Vegas' historic downtown is occurring not under the direction of city planners, but through the largesse and vision of the founder of a global shoe company with its headquarters located nearby.[74] Salt Lake City has engaged a public-private approach, Envision Utah, which has provided a regional forum and changed the relationship to planning in a town not known for its acquiescence to regulation.[75] These examples illustrate that great planning does not need to be adversarial to business interests and, in the United States, is more likely to succeed when it engages those interests to create a coherent regional vision.

These past experiences with business interests assisting planning efforts are not without their faults. Chief among them is that historically marginalized groups, whether they be racial minorities or low-income individuals, have been treated poorly and often had to deal with environmental justice concerns. By bringing representatives of those communities into the conversation about climate change planning early on, the planning group could ensure that such regional visions also provide an equitable distribution of opportunity and environmental protection for all residents.[76]

---

72. DANIEL H. BURNHAM & EDWARD H. BENNETT, PLAN OF CHICAGO: PREPARED UNDER THE DIRECTION OF THE COMMERCIAL CLUB DURING THE YEARS MCMVI, MCMVII, AND MCMVIII (Charles Moore ed., 1908).

73. MARVIN T. BROWN, CORPORATE INTEGRITY: RETHINKING ORGANIZATIONAL ETHICS AND LEADERSHIP 153 (2005):
    The Bay Area Council in the San Francisco Bay Area provides a good example of the business leader type of corporate/city relationship. It not only participated in urban renewal during the 1960s, but continues to be active today. Founded in 1945 by business leaders, the Bay Area Council began developing plans and policies for the whole San Francisco Bay region, from San Jose to Santa Rosa. Its strategy has been one of funding research and providing proposals for local government to implement.

74. Susan Berfield, *Tony Hsieh Is Building a Startup Paradise in Vegas*, BLOOMBERGBUSINESS (Dec. 30, 2014), http://www.bloomberg.com/bw/articles/2014-12-30/zappos-ceo-tony-hsiehs-las-vegas-startup-paradise.

75. *Mission and History*, ENVISION UTAH, http://envisionutah.org/about/mission-history ("As a neutral facilitator, Envision Utah brought together residents, elected officials, developers, conservationists, business leaders, and other interested parties to make informed decisions about how we should grow. Empowering people to create the communities they want is still our goal.").

76. For general information on environmental justice, see *Federal Interagency Working Group on Environmental Justice*, U.S. ENVTL. PROT. AGENCY, http://www3.epa.gov/environmentaljustice/interagency/ (last visited Oct. 9, 2015).

V. Conclusion

Land use patterns develop incrementally and under supervision of thousands of local bodies with small jurisdictions. It is easy, then, to imagine the result of such decisions as equally local and small and without import to global problems like climate change. If the AR5's sections on socio-ecological factors, and land use in particular, do anything, they should end dismissive attitudes toward the local factors in climate change. In Thornton Wilder's mid-20th century classic, *Our House*, a little girl receives a letter addressed to her, and then to ever-expanding measures of social life until, at last, the address spirals toward space, placing her in "the Universe, the Mind of God."[77] In that moment, the little girl sees her place in the world and, moreover, the interconnectedness of big and small. That moment in *Our House* is both profound and common, and it may be that bringing the AR5, and climate change, to local governments beyond our major cities will require a similar approach. The AR5—along with the climate change mitigation and adaptation measures it proposes—invites local officials to link big effects to small decisions and to provide a profound but common language for climate change. In this sprit, all local officials should shoot for the moon with their feet on the ground.

---

77.   Thornton Wilder, Our House Act 1 (1938).

Chapter 6
Taming the Super-Wicked Problem of Waterfront Hazard Mitigation Planning: The Role of Municipal Communication Strategies

Sarah J. Adams-Schoen

[T]he policy process, and government in general, is rife with information, and this provides a critical but often overlooked dynamic in politics.[1]

In the Adaptation Report of the Fifth Assessment Report (AR5), the Intergovernmental Panel on Climate Change (IPCC) identifies floods in urban riverine and coastal areas as among the key climate-related risks for North America.[2] Not surprisingly for residents of coastal and riverine communities devastated by recent extreme weather events, the Adaptation Report acknowledges that risks related to sea-level rise, increased frequency and duration of extreme precipitation events, and increasingly intense coastal storms are not only future risks, but are current risks that are already manifesting in property and infrastructure damage, ecosystem and social system disruption, public health impacts, and water quality impairment.[3] The Adaptation Report identifies the current risk level for North American coastal cities as "medium" and projects that, with a 2° Centigrade (C) increase in global average temperatures over pre-industrial levels, coastal urban areas will have to implement "high adaptation" just to maintain the current risk level of

---

Author's Note: The author would like to thank Brian Walsh (Touro Law 2016) for his assistance with this chapter.

1. BRYAN D. JONES & FRANK R. BAUMGARTNER, THE POLITICS OF ATTENTION: HOW GOVERNMENT PRIORITIZES PROBLEMS 2 (2005).
2. INTERGOVERNMENTAL PANEL ON CLIMATE CHANGE, CLIMATE CHANGE 2014: IMPACTS, ADAPTATION, AND VULNERABILITY 23 (2014) [hereinafter 2014 IPCC ADAPTATION REPORT].
3. *Id.* at 6.

medium.[4] With a 4°C increase, even high adaptation is projected to have little efficacy—indeed, the IPCC reports that under a 4°C pathway North American coastal cities will face high risk levels even if they implement high adaptation.[5] Given that staying within a 2°C pathway appears unlikely,[6] policymakers should heed the IPCC's projections by implementing waterfront development policies consistent with increasingly severe flood risks in both current and expanded flood zones.[7]

Notwithstanding the magnitude of present and future risks to coastal and riverine communities, however, waterfront development policies have shifted only incrementally. The result has been the continued siting of residential communities and critical infrastructure in vulnerable waterfront areas and the expansion and entrenchment of policies, behaviors, and preferences that, at best, fail to mitigate risk and, at worst, heighten risk. Even communities that have otherwise undertaken robust climate change mitigation and adaptation planning continue to base waterfront development policies on irrationally discounted risk projections and embrace communication strategies that obfuscate the risk and ultimately undermine the communities' ability to adequately respond to the risks. The literature on "wicked" and "superwicked" policy problems suggests that, in the current context of heightened risk aversion following a major disaster like Hurricanes Sandy[8] or Katrina, municipal governments in the affected areas have an opportunity to transform waterfront development policies consistent with scientific evidence on climate related risks. Shifting waterfront development policies toward resilience likely begins with official communications that accurately portray risk, including waterfront and hazard mitigation plans, flood risk maps, and comprehensive planning processes, which can facilitate changes in zoning and building codes and private market behavior consistent with near- and long-term risks.

---

4. *Id.* at 23.
5. The 2014 IPCC Adaptation Report characterizes the projected risk under a 4°C increase, even with high adaptation, to be approximately halfway between "medium" and "very high." *Id.*
6. *See* Veerabhadran Ramanathan & Yan Feng, *On Avoiding Dangerous Anthropogenic Interference With the Climate System: Formidable Challenges Ahead*, 105 PROC. NAT'L ACAD. SCI. 14245, 14245 (2008) (estimating global warming of 2.4°C even if greenhouse gas concentrations held to 2005 levels).
7. Throughout this chapter, the word "policy" denotes governmental strategies in response to a problem, including communications, plans, and rules, both informal and formal.
8. This chapter refers to Sandy as a "hurricane" because, "although Sandy made landfall [near Brigantine, New Jersey] as an extratropical low, its strong winds, heavy rains and storm surge had been felt onshore for many hours while Sandy was still a hurricane." ERIC S. BLAKE ET AL., TROPICAL CYCLONE REPORT: HURRICANE SANDY (AL182012) 22-29 OCTOBER 2012 4 n.6 (National Hurricane Center Feb. 12, 2013).

I. Using the Construct of "Wicked" Policy Problems to Shift Waterfront Development Policy to a New Equilibrium

Framing waterfront development in the context of climate change as a "wicked" or "super-wicked" problem may help guide municipalities toward policy strategies that account for risk on a timeframe commensurate with the life of new developments and infrastructure. Since 1973, public policy scholars and others have been using the term "wicked" to describe and analyze strategies for addressing social planning problems that cannot be successfully resolved with traditional linear, analytical approaches.[9] Characteristics of wicked problems include, among other things, that the problems are difficult to define, not entirely solvable, socially complex, and characterized by interdependencies that can result in conflicting goals for the various stakeholders. Wicked policy problems also tend to exist in complex systems such that attempts to address the problems lead to unforeseen or undesirable consequences and responses to wicked problems typically involve changing behavior.[10] When Horst Rittel and Melvin Webber introduced the concept of wicked problems, they argued that current modes of policy analysis promoted rather than solved these complex problems. However, as Kelly Levin et al. later observe, "[w]hile Rittel and Webber usefully highlight features of problems that decision makers ought to consider when determining which decision tool to apply, wicked problems arguably describe most policy problems."[11] Thus Levin et al. introduced the term "super-wicked" to describe anthropogenic climate change and other intractable problems that are characterized by the key features of wicked problems as well as four additional features: (1) time is running out, (2) those who cause the problem also seek to provide a solution, (3) the central authority needed to address the problem is weak or nonexistent, and (4) irrational discounting occurs that pushes responses into the future.[12] These features in concert "create a tragedy because our governance institutions, and the policies they generate (or fail to generate), largely respond to short-term time horizons even when the cata-

---

9. Horst W.J. Rittel & Melvin M. Webber, *Dilemmas in a General Theory of Planning*, 4 Pol'y Sci. 155, 160-69 (1973).

10. *See id.* at 161-64 (identifying 10 characteristics of wicked problems).

11. Kelly Levin et al., *Overcoming the Tragedy of Super Wicked Problems: Constraining Our Future Selves to Ameliorate Global Climate Change*, 45 Policy Sci. 123, 127 (2012).

12. Levin et al. first identified climate change as a super-wicked problem in a conference paper in 2007. *See* Kelly Levin et al., *Playing It Forward: Path Dependency, Progressive Incrementalism, and the "Super Wicked" Problem of Global Climate Change*, presented at International Studies Association Convention, Chicago, Ill., Feb. 28-Mar. 3, 2007.

strophic implications of doing so are far greater than any real or perceived benefits of inaction."[13]

While anthropogenic climate change is the prototypical example of a "super-wicked" problem, waterfront hazard mitigation planning and related lawmaking also embody the attributes of a super-wicked policy problem.[14] As with national and international climate issues, climate-related waterfront risks embody the characteristics of wicked problems. Climate-related waterfront risks have multiple causal factors, including coastal erosion and storms, dam failure, disease outbreak, floods, landslides, land subsidence, building collapse, infrastructure failure, and utility disruptions.[15] High levels of disagreement exist about the nature of the risks and their potential solutions.[16] And, the motivation and behavior of individuals is a key part of any solution. Indeed, a range of cognitive processes affect assessment of redevelopment in the wake of disaster and often "militate in favor of development even where such development is 'irrational' in the market sense that risks outweigh benefits."[17] Climate-related waterfront risks are also characterized by the four additional "super-wicked" attributes.

A. Time Is Running Out

Infrastructure lock-in and increasing flood and storm surge risk levels over time mean that time is not costless. The U.S. population is expected to grow to 420 million by 2050, resulting in the projected construction between 2007 and 2050 of 89 million new or replaced homes and 190 billion square feet of new offices, institutions, stores, and other nonresidential buildings.[18] Based on these projections, two-thirds of homes and buildings in existence in 2050 will be built between 2007 and then.[19] Given that more than one-half the U.S. population lives in coastal watershed counties and population den-

---

13. Levin et al., *supra* note 11, at 124.

14. This is not to say that waterfront hazard mitigation in the context of a changing climate embodies all the characteristics that make anthropogenic climate change a super-wicked problem. *See* Richard J. Lazarus, *Super Wicked Problems and Climate Change: Restraining the Present to Liberate the Future*, 94 Cornell L. Rev. 1153, 1161-87 (2009) (asserting that national climate change legislation presents a super-wicked problem as a result of the nature of climate change itself, human nature, and the nature of U.S. lawmaking institutions).

15. *See, e.g.*, City of New York, 2014 New York City Hazard Mitigation Plan 47-48 (2014).

16. *See, e.g.*, Niki L. Pace, *Wetlands or Seawalls? Adapting Shoreline Regulation to Address Sea Level Rise and Wetland Preservation in the Gulf of Mexico*, 26 J. Land Use & Envtl. L. 327, 329 (2011); *see also* National Oceanic and Atmospheric Administration (NOAA), State of the Coast: Shoreline Armoring: The Pros and Cons, http://stateofthecoast.noaa.gov/shoreline/shoreline_armoring.html.

17. *See generally* Justin Pidot, *Deconstructing Disaster*, 2013 B.Y.U. L. Rev. 213, 242-43 (2013).

18. Reid Ewing et al., Growing Cooler: Evidence on Urban Development and Climate Change 8 (2008).

19. *Id.*

sity continues to grow in these counties,[20] it seems likely that, absent policies that limit waterfront development, a large portion of new homes and buildings, as well as related infrastructure, will be constructed in waterfront areas.

On a personal scale, time is not costless for those who are rebuilding in, relocating to, and choosing to remain in hazardous areas where future property damage and public health problems including loss of life are foreseeable results of new and continued waterfront development. Thus, not surprisingly, the IPCC highlights the importance of "city and municipal governments acting *now* to incorporate climate change adaptation into their development plans and policies and infrastructure investments."[21]

B.   The Same Actors Both Cause and Seek to Solve the Problem

Those who contribute to the problem of increased waterfront risks also seek to end the problem. For example, many waterfront property owners use shoreline armoring[22] in an attempt to protect their property from erosion and flood risks, while this same armoring often leads to the "unintended . . . consequences [of] vertical erosion, loss of downdrift sediment, and erosion of flanking shores."[23] Likewise, following Sandy, many waterfront municipalities amended their zoning and building codes to facilitate and encourage development and redevelopment in floodplains, notwithstanding the heightened risks that would occur as a result of increasing impermeable surface areas, which tends to increase flood risk, and attracting greater numbers of people into vulnerable areas.[24]

Indeed, even a report on achieving hazard-resilient coastal communities published by the National Oceanic and Atmospheric Administration (NOAA) and the U.S. Environmental Protection Agency (EPA) encourages

---

20.   NAT'L OCEANIC & ATMOSPHERIC AGENCY, NATIONAL COASTAL POPULATION REPORT: POPULATION TRENDS FROM 1970 TO 2020 11 (2013).

21.   2014 IPCC ADAPTATION REPORT, *supra* note 2, at 541 (emphasis added).

22.   "Armoring" refers to the use of hard structures to protect shoreline properties from flooding and erosion, including, for example, bulkheads, seawalls, groins, and revetments. Pace, *supra* note 16, at 338.

23.   *Id.* (citing Scott L. Douglass & Bradley H. Pickel, *The Tide Doesn't Go Out Anymore: The Effect of Bulkheads on Urban Bay Shorelines*, 67 SHORE & BEACH 19, 19 (1999)).

24.   *See, e.g.*, NEW YORK CITY BUILDING CODE (NYCBC), app. G, §304.1.1 (2014) (requiring one- to two-family residences be flood-proofed to two feet above Base Flood Elevation); *id.* at §302.1.1 (requiring 30 feet of ramp for a 30-inch rise). Depending on the amount of stairs or ramping required to access the elevated structure, the structure may need to be shifted back from the street, thereby occupying space that had previously been the backyard, and addition of lengthy switchback ramps and stairs needed to access an elevated first floor may increase the impermeable area of the structure. *See* CITY OF NEW YORK, COASTAL CLIMATE RESILIENCY: RETROFITTING BUILDINGS FOR FLUID RISK 42-43 (2014); *see also* OREGON DEP'T OF LAND CONSERVATION, WATER QUALITY MODEL CODE AND GUIDE BOOK 4.44 (2000) (discussing disruptions caused by building impervious surfaces in floodplains).

rebuilding in coastal areas, albeit with design and siting decisions based on smart growth principles.[25] The report's 10 "smart growth and hazard mitigation strategies specifically for coastal and waterfront communities" do not include any suggestion that waterfront development be restricted or limited and only one strategy that would have this effect,[26] despite recognition that "[i]nfill development may increase risk if existing development is in a hazard-prone location" and "[k]eeping development out of flood-prone areas protects lives and property and allows alternative uses of the land, such as public waterfront parks and recreation areas."[27] Conflicting messages like these from stakeholders committed to increasing resilience reflect economic and political realities, to be sure, but they also illustrate the super-wicked nature of the problem presented by waterfront development in the context of a changing climate.

C.   Weak or Nonexistent Central Authority to Address the Problem

Authority over waterfront hazard mitigation is fragmented and diffuse. Although federal and state law delegates much of the authority relevant to climate change adaptation to municipal governments, municipal governments' ability to adequately respond to climate-related hazards is often constrained by unmet needs for funding and technical support and a lack of complimentary state and federal laws and policies.[28] In 2011, approximately 90% of all U.S. cities surveyed by the Massachusetts Institute of Technology in a joint project with ICLEI-Local Governments for Sustainability reported that they face challenges securing funding for adaptation, and only 6% reported that the federal government understood the realities they face with respect to adaptation.[29] Likewise, the U.S. Government Accountability Office (GAO) concluded in a 2013 report that, although the federal government plays a

---

25. ACHIEVING HAZARD-RESILIENT COASTAL & WATERFRONT SMART GROWTH: COASTAL AND WATER-FRONT SMART GROWTH AND HAZARD MITIGATION ROUNDTABLE REPORT 6 (2013). Strategy three is to "[p]rovide a range of housing opportunities and choices to meet the needs of both seasonal and permanent residents" and strategy seven is to "[s]trengthen and direct development toward existing communities, and encourage waterfront revitalization." Id.

26. Strategy 6 is to "[p]reserve open space, farmland, natural beauty, and the critical environmental areas that characterize and support coastal and waterfront communities." Id. at 6.

27. Id. at 8.

28. See generally John R. Nolon, Climate Change and Sustainable Development: The Quest for Green Communities, Part II, PLAN. & ENVTL. L., Nov. 2009, at 3, 5. But see Community Risk and Resiliency Act, 2014 N.Y. Laws 355 (directing state agencies to prepare model municipal laws taking into consideration sea-level rise and other climate-related events and "develop additional guidance on the use of resiliency measures that utilize natural resources and natural processes to reduce risk").

29. JOANN CARMIN ET AL., PROGRESS AND CHALLENGES IN URBAN CLIMATE ADAPTATION PLANNING: RESULTS OF A GLOBAL SURVEY 22-24 (2012). ICLEI-Local Governments for Sustainability is an association of more than 1,000 cities, towns, and metropolises committed to sustainability. See ICLEI-

critical role in producing the information needed to facilitate informed local infrastructure adaptation decisions, this information is not easily accessible to local decisionmakers.[30] The governors, mayors, and other local leaders on the President's Task Force on Climate Preparedness and Resilience also concluded in their report to the President in November 2014 that "projects and investments are being advanced without adequate and coordinated consideration of the project design or alternatives relative to climate impacts . . . , a direction that generates unacceptable public health, safety, and financial risks for communities."[31] Similarly, a 2014 Georgetown Climate Center report on how to improve federal programs to support local climate change preparedness found that many local governments "have been looking to the federal government for help and guidance, only to run into challenges tapping into federal programs and resources."[32]

Additionally, with respect to waterfront hazard mitigation in particular, a complex web of more than a dozen local, state, and federal laws implemented by an even greater number of agencies, departments, commissions, and task forces create a policy regime characterized by fragmentation and diffuse authority.[33] Waterfront policies and projects also often implicate state common law and statutory public trust doctrine[34] as well as federal takings jurisprudence.[35] Furthermore, even at the sub-state levels waterfront policies tend to be scattered throughout numerous

---

LOCAL GOVERNMENTS FOR SUSTAINABILITY, WHO WE ARE, ICLEI.ORG, http://www.iclei.org/about/who-is-iclei.html (last visited Jan. 18, 2016).

30. U.S. GOV'T ACCOUNTABILITY OFFICE (GAO), GAO REPORT: FUTURE FEDERAL ADAPTATION EFFORTS COULD BETTER SUPPORT LOCAL INFRASTRUCTURE DECISION MAKERS 80 (Apr. 12, 2012).

31. See THE WHITE HOUSE, PRESIDENT'S STATE, LOCAL, AND TRIBAL LEADERS TASK FORCE ON CLIMATE PREPAREDNESS AND RESILIENCE: RECOMMENDATIONS TO THE PRESIDENT 20 (Nov. 2014).

32. GEORGETOWN CLIMATE CTR., PREPARING OUR COMMUNITIES FOR CLIMATE IMPACTS: RECOMMENDATIONS FOR FEDERAL ACTION 5 (2014).

33. See, e.g., The Coastal Zone Management Act, 16 U.S.C. §1454 (2012); Submerged Lands Act of 1953, 43 U.S.C. §1312 (2006); Coastal Barrier Resources Act, 16 U.S.C. §1452(2)(K) (2006); New York State Waterfront Revitalization of Coastal Areas and Inland Waterways Act, N.Y. COMP. CODES R. & REGS. tit. 19, §600.1(c) (2012); Tidal Wetlands Act (TWA), N.Y. COMP. CODES R. & REGS. tit. 6, §661.1 (2012); New York Coastal Erosion Hazard Area Act (CEHA), N.Y. ENVTL. CONSERV. LAW §34-0102(5) (McKinney 2012); NEW YORK CITY DEPARTMENT OF CITY PLANNING, THE NEW WATERFRONT REVITALIZATION PROGRAM 3 (2002); Zoning Resolution Text, N.Y.C. DEP'T OF CITY PLAN'G (Apr. 28, 2015); see also N.Y. Exec. Law §§910-923 (authorizing local waterfront revitalization plans); N.Y. COMP. CODES R. & REGS. tit. 19, §601 (2012) (implementing optional LWRP provisions); see generally Sarah J. Adams-Schoen, Sink or Swim: In Search of a Model for Coastal City Climate Resilience, 40 COL. J. ENVTL. L. 433, 473-79 (2015) (discussing web of federal, state, and local laws applicable to New York City waterfront).

34. See The Underwater Lands Bill, Act of Aug. 7, ch. 791, §3, 1992 N.Y. Laws 4028, 4029 (codified as amended at N.Y. PUB. LANDS LAW §75 (McKinney 2014)).

35. See, e.g., New Creek Bluebelt, Phase 4 v. City of New York, No. D42904 (N.Y App. Div. Nov. 19, 2014) (finding reasonable probability that city wetlands designation is a regulatory taking under federal Constitution).

plans including local comprehensive plans, waterfront revitalization plans, and hazard mitigation plans.[36] Although in most jurisdictions zoning laws must be consistent with a municipality's comprehensive plan,[37] which may be interpreted to include all relevant planning activities,[38] and local, state, and federal actions must be consistent with any local waterfront revitalization plan,[39] often the numerous plans setting forth waterfront policies in a municipality fail to cross-reference one another, are developed by various planning authorities that may not collaborate with one another, and ultimately may contain conflicts.[40] With respect to this fragmentation at the planning level, a roundtable of experts from the fields of smart growth, hazard mitigation, climate change adaptation, and coastal management recognized the need to link hazard mitigation and land use planning processes, further research the potential for one plan to serve multiple planning requirements, and provide tools and technical assistance to better integrate plans at the local level.[41] In the meanwhile, however, the existing fragmentation means that central authority over waterfront hazard mitigation remains weak or nonexistent.

---

36. *See, e.g.*, City of New York, PlaNYC: A Stronger, More Resilient New York 57-65 (June 2013) [hereinafter Stronger, More Resilient] (setting forth 37 initiatives to increase resilience of city's waterfront); N.Y.C. Dep't of City Planning, Vision 2020: New York City Comprehensive Waterfront Plan (March 2011) [hereinafter Vision 2020]; N.Y.C. Dep't of City Planning, The New Waterfront Revitalization Program 3 (2002); N.Y.C. Dep't of City Planning, The New York City Waterfront Revitalization Program: New York City Approved Revisions Pursuant to Section 197-a of the City Charter (2013); City of New York, 2014 New York City Hazard Mitigation Plan (2014).

37. *See* Patricia E. Salkin, 1 N.Y. Zoning Law & Prac. §4:03 (reporting that enabling statutes in most states require zoning to be in accordance with the comprehensive plan); Edward J. Sullivan & Jennifer Bragar, *Recent Developments in Comprehensive Planning*, 46 Urb. Law. 685, 689-90 (2014) (reporting trend in case law toward view that comprehensive plan is at least a factor in judicial analysis of zoning law).

38. *See, e.g.*, N.Y. Town Law §272-a(2)(a) (defining comprehensive plan as "the materials, written and/or graphic, including but not limited to maps, charts, studies, resolutions, reports and other descriptive material that identify the goals, objectives, principles, guidelines, policies, standards, devices and instruments for the immediate and long-range protection, enhancement, growth and development of the" municipality).

39. *See* 16 U.S.C. §§1456(c)(1)-(2) & (d) (2015); 15 C.F.R. pt. 930 (2015); *see, e.g.*, 42 N.Y. Exec. Law §916 (McKinney 2014) (requiring "state agency program actions be undertaken in a manner which is consistent to the maximum extent practicable with the approved [local] waterfront revitalization program [LWRP]," including reviews conducted under the state environmental quality review act"); N.Y. Comp. Codes R. & Regs. tit. 10, §97.12(d)(13) (2015) (providing for state environmental impact review based on effects of proposed action on applicable policies of LWRP as opposed to state WRP when municipality has an approved LWRP).

40. *See* Stronger, More Resilient, *supra* note 36, at 40 (concluding that "[e]fforts by [the multiple] agencies [with regulatory authority in the coastal zones] are not completely aligned" and "[t]his lack of unified and coordinated regulatory oversight can lead to delayed and unpredictable waterfront activity, complicating the achievement of important public goals, including coastal resiliency").

41. NOAA, Achieving Hazard-Resilient Coastal & Waterfront Smart Growth: Coastal and Waterfront Smart Growth and Hazard Mitigation Roundtable Report 11 (2013).

D. Irrational Discounting of Climate-Related Waterfront Risks Pushes Responses Into the Future

Examples of local government plans, reports, executive orders, and other communications that irrationally discount climate related waterfront risks abound—even in jurisdictions that are otherwise undertaking robust climate adaptation initiatives. For example, following Hurricane Sandy, state and local governments along the East Coast of the United States characterized the storm as "unthinkable," "unique," and the "perfect storm."[42] Implicit (and sometimes explicit) in these communications was the message that the magnitude of and devastation from Sandy were unforeseeable and that Sandy was a "worst case scenario" that resulted from the confluence of highly improbable factors. Although containing some elements of truth, each of these characterizations is potentially misleading.

Rather than being "unthinkable," the magnitude and devastation of the storm was foreseeable. Prior to the storm, numerous sources including state and local government agencies had projected extreme flooding and significant property damage for vulnerable coastal areas along the east coast of the United States. New York and New Jersey had both adopted master plans and issued reports predicting the growing dangers from continued waterfront development.[43] More than eight years before Sandy, Princeton University reported that the rapid population growth in New Jersey's "coastal counties was setting the scene for monumental environmental damage and property loss."[44]

Notwithstanding the foreseeability of rising sea levels and storm surges, however, heavy development of vulnerable flood prone areas continued. On Staten Island, "developers built more than 2,700 mostly residential structures in coastal areas at extreme risk of storm surge flooding between 1980 and 2008, with the approval of city planning and zoning authorities. . . ."[45] The devastation of these areas during Sandy and other extreme weather events

---

42. Cavan Sieczkowski, *Hurricane Sandy Damage Photos: Superstorm's "Unthinkable" Aftermath Revealed (PICTURES)*, HUFFINGTON POST (Oct. 30, 2012), http://www.huffingtonpost.com/2012/10/30/hurricane-sandy-damage-photos-superstorm-unthinkable-aftermath_n_2044099.html ("Chris Christie said the wreckage is 'beyond anything I thought I'd ever see.' Adding, 'The level of devastation at the Jersey Shore is unthinkable,' according to CNN.").

43. *See* Maxine Burkett, *Duty and Breach in an Era of Uncertainty: Local Government Liability for Failure to Adapt to Climate Change*, 20 GEO. MASON L. REV. 775, 782 n.46 (2013) (citing New York and New Jersey master plans and reports predicting the growing dangers from continued development).

44. John Rudolf et al., *Hurricane Sandy Damage Amplified by Breakneck Development of Coast*, HUFFINGTON POST (Nov. 12, 2012, 12:15 PM), http://www.huffingtonpost.com/2012/11/12/hurricane-sandy-damage_n_2114525.html.

45. *See* John Rudolf et al., *Hurricane Sandy Damage Amplified by Breakneck Development of Coast*, HUFFINGTON POST (Nov. 12, 2012, 12:15 PM), http://www.huffingtonpost.com/2012/11/12/hurricane-sandy-damage_n_2114525.html.

included loss of lives, displacement of thousands of residents and businesses, and massive property and infrastructure losses.[46] Ultimately, New Jersey suffered economic losses from Hurricane Sandy of $9 to $15 billion[47] and New York suffered economic losses of $19 billion.[48]

Since Sandy, by repeatedly employing language like "unique" and "worst case scenario" to describe Sandy,[49] local governments continue to give the impression that the storm was an anomaly that is unlikely to recur. Although Sandy was indeed unprecedented in some respects (for example, it had the lowest recorded sea-level pressure of a storm making landfall north of North Carolina in the United States[50]), a storm of Sandy's magnitude is not unprecedented in the region, and a different set of circumstances could have made Sandy even more devastating than it was. Since 1900, the New York City region has experienced storms with higher wind speeds,[51] more rain,[52] and peak surges 10 feet or higher above mean low tide.[53] Moreover, although a number of idiosyncratic factors combined to increase Sandy's devastation, Sandy itself was not a worst-case scenario. Had Sandy struck at high tide in Western Long Island Sound, as opposed to near high tide in New York Harbor and along the Atlantic Ocean, modeling by the storm surge research team at the Stevens Institute of Technology projects that Sandy's peak surge would have been four feet higher than it was.[54] The city of New York provides most of this information in publicly accessible reports; however, these reports tend to highlight—through themes, headers, and executive summaries—characterizations of the storm as an anomaly unlikely to occur again.[55]

---

46. See Burkett, supra note 43, at 782 ("At least two fatalities in Staten Island occurred in developments completed as recently as the 1990s in coastal areas at extreme risk of storm surge flooding." (citations omitted)).

47. Id.

48. Id.

49. See, e.g., Michael R. Bloomberg, Foreword, in STRONGER, MORE RESILIENT, supra note 36 (referring to Sandy as "the worst natural disaster ever to hit New York City").

50. BLAKE ET AL., supra note 8, at 6.

51. STRONGER, MORE RESILIENT, supra note 36, at 21 ("[Sandy's] 80-mile-per-hour (mph) peak wind gusts fell well short of other storms that have hit New York City, including Hurricane Carol in 1954 (up to 125-mph gusts) and Hurricane Belle in 1976 (up to 95-mph gusts).").

52. Id. ("Previous storms also brought much more rain with them. Sandy dropped a scant inch in some parts of New York, far less than the 5 inches of rain dropped on the city during Hurricane Donna in 1960 or the 7.5 inches during the April 2007 nor'easter.").

53. See id. at 21 (discussing 1821 hurricane (13-foot storm surge) and Hurricane Donna in 1960 (10-foot storm surge)); BEN STRAUSS ET AL., NEW YORK AND THE SURGING SEA: A VULNERABILITY ASSESSMENT WITH PROJECTIONS FOR SEA LEVEL RISE AND COASTAL FLOOD RISK, CLIMATE CENTRAL RESEARCH REPORT 11, 16 (2014) (noting that storms today are intensified in terms of surge height and other variables as a result of higher sea levels and arguing that Sandy's surge height has been misreported as 14 feet at the Battery and that Sandy's peak storm surge was actually nine feet).

54. See STRONGER, MORE RESILIENT, supra note 36, at 21 (describing projected impacts under a western Long Island Sound high-tide scenario).

55. See, e.g., STRONGER, MORE RESILIENT, supra note 36.

Exacerbating the discounting effect of this messaging, a theme that New York City and New Yorkers are tougher than climate change is woven throughout the city's voluminous climate resilience reports. For example, the June 2013 post-Sandy report, *Stronger, More Resilient New York*, tells a persuasive story of toughness and machismo:

> The underlying goal of this report is resiliency. That is, to adapt our city to the impacts of climate change and to seek to ensure that, when nature overwhelms our defenses from time to time, we are able to recover more quickly.

> In short, we have to be tough.

> And toughness, as we all know, is one of the defining traits of New Yorkers.

> In just the first few years of this century, we have been through the September 11, 2001 terrorist attacks, financial crises and blackouts, and now, Sandy. With each challenge, we have become more united as a city.

> We must come together again with an even stronger commitment to slow the progress of climate change while simultaneously preparing for the changes already evident around us—and those yet to come.

> . . . . .

> The time has come to make our city even tougher.[56]

Newer reports issued under the de Blasio administration carry the toughness theme forward with, among other things, use of the tag line "One City, Built to Last," reminiscent of Ford Truck's 1990s ad campaigns ("Built to Last" and "Built Ford Tough").[57] The underlying message appears to be that New York City and its residents are tougher than climate change. Illustrative of this, the inside cover of *A Stronger, More Resilient New York* provides the following definition of "resilient":

> res•il•ient [ri-zil-yuhnt] adj.

> 1. Able to bounce back after change or adversity. 2. Capable of preparing for, responding to, and recovering from difficult conditions.

> Syn.: TOUGH

> See also: New York City[58]

---

56. *Id.* at 6 (emphasis in original). The "toughness" theme is also reinforced through images. *See, e.g., id.* at 6.

57. *See* City of New York, One City, Built to Last 20 (Revision 1.1 2014); Tanya Gazdik, *Ford Boosts Ad Spending Behind Jwt's "Built to Last" Campaign*, AdWeek (Feb. 9, 1998, 12:00 AM), http://www.adweek.com/news/advertising/ford-boosts-ad-spending-behind-jwts-built-last-campaign-23668.

58. Stronger, More Resilient, *supra* note 36, at 2.

Consistent with a theme that suggests New Yorkers are tougher than climate change, the city's plans eschew retreat strategies and instead boast about continued development of waterfront areas. For example, the city reported in its Clean Waterfront Plan that "New Yorkers are taking advantage of the waterfront for recreation, housing, and new business opportunities in record numbers,"[59] and in its coastal management plan that "[n]ew housing on waterfront property has helped the city accommodate the influx of nearly one million new residents. Since 1992, [when the city adopted its first waterfront plan,] more than 20,000 new residential units have been built on waterfront blocks, with nearly 6,000 additional new units in the development pipeline."[60] By touting waterfront development, New York City and other municipalities discount waterfront hazards, promote building in—and attract populations to—vulnerable areas, and irrationally delay appropriate responses to known risks.

II. Coastal Cities' Commitment to Rebuild Can Reinforce Maladaptive Path-Dependent Processes and Fail to Take Advantage of a Window of Opportunity to Entrench Support for More Resilient Waterfront Policies

The local government toolbox contains a variety of tools that can be used to create more resilient waterfronts, including various planning processes, zoning code amendments, building code amendments, moratoria, conservation easements, transferable development credits, tax incentives, exactions and condemnation, buyouts, public education and private information disclosure requirements, and risk mapping tools.[61] The nature of the super-wicked class of problems, however, makes taking advantage of the tools in the local government toolkit difficult. The reward of risk mitigation tends to be ephemeral—either the absence of harm or, even worse from a political perspective, the reduction but not elimination of harm. Moreover, when the harm is something that would not occur (or is not perceived to be likely to occur) within the lifespan of a government or even within the lifespan of the voting public, the impetus to

---

59. N.Y.C. Local Law 55 of 2011: Clean Waterfront Plan 4 (2014).
60. Vision 2020, *supra* note 36, at 13.
61. *See* Anne Siders, Management Coastal Retreat: A Legal Handbook on Shifting Development Away From Vulnerable Areas 5-7 (Columbia Law School Center for Climate Change Law, 2013); *see generally* J. Grannis, Adaptation Tool Kit: Sea Level Rise and Coastal Land Use (Georgetown Climate Center, 2011); John R. Nolon, *Disaster Mitigation Through Land Use Strategies*, 23 Pace Envtl. L. Rev. 959, 976-77 (2006); J. Peter Byrne & J. Grannis, *Coastal Retreat Measures*, *in* The Law of Adaptation to Climate Change 267-306 (M. Gerrard & K. Kuh eds., 2012).

educate the public to the risk in order to garner support for spending political capital on mitigation is further reduced. Instead, given the lifespan of political power,[62] rather than educating constituents about medium- and long-term risks, elected officials may prefer to increase public support for actions that have immediate, visible effects—like increasing the tax base through development of high-value coastal properties[63]—by utilizing messaging and other strategies that actually increase the short-sightedness of the public. In this way, communications that irrationally discount waterfront development risks are both the cause and effect of the wicked nature of the problem.

Indeed, municipal plans that utilize themes of toughness and resistance may promote a cultural narrative of climate change that further entrenches status quo waterfront policies. Robin Kundis Craig has characterized coastal communities' preference for resistance over retreat strategies as a manifestation of a "technology will save us" cultural narrative that underlies many U.S. environmental laws and policies. Consistent with a technology will save us narrative, waterfront adaptation strategies focus on human control, minimize disruption and displacement of human activities, and ignore the potential for sea-level rise to overwhelm coastal technologies.[64]

Notwithstanding entrenched resistance to restrictions on waterfront development, disasters like Hurricane Sandy can create a window of opportunity to shift waterfront development policy to a new, more resilient policy equilibrium. For many residents of the northeastern United States who are still displaced and rebuilding more than three years after Hurricane Sandy, maintaining the current risk level of medium is not acceptable and a future with even greater risk levels is unthinkable.[65] In the wake of Sandy, 14 counties were declared federal disaster areas, 117 lives were lost, approximately 300,000 housing units were damaged or destroyed, 2,000 miles of roads were affected or closed, subways and tunnels were flooded, major power transmission and communication systems were damaged, and, more than three years after the storm, many residents remain displaced.[66] These experi-

62. *See* COLIN PRICE, TIME, DISCOUNTING, AND VALUE 125 (Blackwell, London 1993) ("although society may be regarded as immortal, a government achieving several terms in office still has a life-span shorter than that of an average human").

63. *See* JOHN R. LOGAN & HARVEY L. MOLOTOCH, URBAN FORTUNES: THE POLITICAL ECONOMY OF PLACE 57-63 (Berkeley, CA: Univ. of California Press, 1987) (describing municipal narratives of cost- and value-free growth and local political pressure for economic growth).

64. Robin Kundis Craig, *Learning to Live With the Trickster: Narrating Climate Change and the Value of Resilience Thinking*, PACE ENVTL. L. REV. (forthcoming 2016).

65. *See, e.g.*, Justin Gillis & Felicity Barringer, *As Coasts Rebuild and U.S. Pays, Repeatedly, the Critics Ask Why*, N.Y. TIMES, Nov. 18, 2012, http://www.nytimes.com/2012/11/19/science/earth/as-coasts-rebuild-and-us-pays-again-critics-stop-to-ask-why.html?pagewanted=all.

66. N.Y. STATE DEP'T OF STATE OFFICE OF PLANNING AND DEVELOPMENT, RFP 15-OPD-7 FOR GENERIC ENVIRONMENTAL IMPACT STATEMENT FOR LONG ISLAND TRANSFER OF DEVELOPMENT RIGHTS PROGRAM

ences have resulted in heightened climate risk aversion, which is reflected in many local government hazard mitigation plans.[67]

The heightened risk aversion that follows a major disaster creates an opportunity to shift waterfront development policy to a new equilibrium. Bryan Jones and Frank Baumgartner's ambitious empirical study of shifts in American policy from the end of the Second World War to the end of the 20th century suggests that a shift in focus, like the one following Sandy, provides a "window" during which policymakers may punctuate an otherwise stable policy.[68] Using pre- and post-9/11 terrorism policies as an illustration, Jones and Baumgartner assert that

> Shifting [policy] attention requires a major impetus, and some general intelligence about possible threats would not be enough. The natural tendency is to under-emphasize new threats, new ways of thinking of things, new ways to organize public bureaucracies, until and unless some significant threshold of urgency is crossed. At that point, major changes can occur. . . . Crises seem necessary to drive change.[69]

In the case of climate change generally and waterfront development policies specifically, identifying and taking advantage of this window is particularly important in light of the "time is running out" nature of the policy problem.

However, notwithstanding the magnitude of the devastation caused by Sandy, waterfront development policies have shifted only incrementally and for the most part have failed to shift toward resilient path-dependent processes, with the result being the continued siting of residential communities and critical infrastructure in flood zones. Illustrating this cycle of development, devastation, and redevelopment that is characteristic of many coastal communities,[70] New York City and State shifted course away from a state property acquisition program that would have permanently preserved properties as open space[71] and instead entered into a Memorandum of Understanding under which the city could purchase vulnerable waterfront properties

---

67. See, e.g., TOWN OF SOUTHOLD, NATURAL HAZARDS CHAPTER, in SOUTHOLD 2020: THE NEW COMPREHENSIVE PLAN FOR THE TOWN OF SOUTHOLD (final draft Sept. 16, 2013) (recognizing various risks from sea-level rise).

68. JONES & BAUMGARTNER, supra note 1, at 49-50 (discussing windows in which policy equilibria may be punctuated); id. at 21 (discussing data set and methodology).

69. JONES & BAUMGARTNER, supra note 1, at 51.

70. See SIDERS, supra note 61, at 1 (observing that Dauphin Island, Alabama, has been substantially destroyed and rebuilt 10 times in the past 40 years).

71. See Christine A. Fazio & Ethan I. Strell, Government Property Acquisition in Floodplains After Hurricane Sandy, Feb. 28, 2013, N.Y. Law J.; 42 U.S.C. §5107c(b)(2)(B)(ii); FEMA, HAZARD MITIGATION ASSISTANCE UNIFIED GUIDANCE: HAZARD MITIGATION GRANT PROGRAM, PRE-DISASTER MITIGATION

for redevelopment and resale.[72] Along the same vein, the city's comprehensive coastal management plan identifies as an achievement the rezoning of approximately 3,000 acres of shorefront land to enable redevelopment, about one-half of which was rezoned from non-residential to mixed-use and from lower to higher-density.[73]

These redevelopment policies and zoning code amendments are touted as resilience oriented, notwithstanding the fact that more than eight million New Yorkers live in areas vulnerable to flooding, storm surges, and other natural disaster-related risks,[74] and nearly one-half million of these residents live on 120 square miles of land that is less than six feet above the high-tide line.[75] Moreover, as a result of climate-related factors and land subsidence, sea level in New York City has risen 1.1 feet since 1900, approximately 1.2 inches per decade, a rate nearly two times the global average.[76] As Strauss et al. of Climate Central observe, "Looking forward under a fast sea-level rise scenario, [Climate Central] compute[s] a 3-in-4 chance of historically unprecedented coastal flooding in New York City by 2100—or a 1-in-10 chance under a slow rise scenario."[77] According to NPCC2, an ongoing body established by New York City law to regularly update and report on region-specific climate data and projections, sea-level rise is projected to accelerate as the century progresses, rising in New York City 11 to 21 inches by the 2050s, 18 to 39 inches by the 2080s, and as much as six feet by 2100 (over average 2000-2005 levels).[78]

PROGRAM, FLOOD MITIGATION ASSISTANCE PROGRAM, REPETITIVE FLOOD CLAIMS PROGRAM, SEVERE REPETITIVE LOSS PROGRAM 75, 94-97 (2010).

72. Memorandum of Understanding Between the State of New York and the City of New York Concerning the Purchase of Properties Affected by Superstorm Sandy (Dec. 16, 2013).

73. VISION 2020, *supra* note 36, at 13.

74. *Id.* at 207.

75. STRAUSS ET AL., *supra* note 53, at 8. This vulnerable land is also home to more than 1,500 miles of road, 1,200 EPA-listed sites, and 100 public schools. *Id.*

76. NEW YORK CITY PANEL ON CLIMATE CHANGE, CLIMATE RISK INFORMATION 2013: OBSERVATIONS, CLIMATE CHANGE PROJECTIONS, AND MAPS 8 (Cynthia Rosenzweig & William Solecki eds., 2013) (finding that approximately 45% of the observed sea-level rise of 1.2 inches per decade since 1900 is due to land subsidence, with the remaining sea-level rise driven by climate-related factors).

77. STRAUSS ET AL., *supra* note 53, at 11.

78. Cynthia Rosenzweig et al., *Building the Knowledge Base for Climate Resiliency: New York City Panel on Climate Change 2015 Report*, 1336 ANNALS N.Y. ACAD. SCI. 1, 11 (2015). *See also infra* Part III (discussing the city's robust, transparent, and science-based data collection, analysis, and benchmarking initiatives).

III.   Utilizing Transparent Risk Projections and Land Use Planning Processes to Expand and Entrench Support for Resilient Waterfront Policies

We know intuitively that climate change poses intractable obstacles and waterfront development restrictions are politically unpopular. So, why bother identifying these policy problems as wicked or super-wicked? The point certainly is not to sit around and lament the problems,[79] but rather to "tame" them.[80] The wicked and super-wicked constructs prove useful only insofar as they help inform responses to the problems. By identifying a problem as wicked or super-wicked, lawmakers and analysts can recognize from the outset that the problem is "highly resistant to resolution,"[81] avoid strategies that are known not to work with such problems, and utilize "policy analysis techniques that are consistent with, rather than ignore, the key features of this class of problems."[82]

Climate change generally and waterfront hazard mitigation specifically have temporal free rider challenges such that strategies to counteract these problems must overcome the tendency to give greater weight to immediate interests, discount future threats, and delay behavioral changes, even when doing so is contrary to medium- and long-term interests.[83] To overcome this, Levin et al. assert that policymakers need to address three diagnostic questions when addressing super-wicked problems: (DQ1) "What can be done to create stickiness making reversibility immediately difficult?"; (DQ2) "What can be done to entrench support over time?"; and (DQ3) "What can be done to expand the population that supports the policy?"[84] They posit that DQ2 and DQ3 are "prerequisites" because they must occur to develop path dependency to address super-wicked problems, while DQ1 is "useful" because it "[b]uys time," but is not a prerequisite "as long as increasing support over time kicks in quite quickly."[85]

---

79.   Chris Riedy, *Climate Change Is a Super Wicked Problem*, Planetcentric (May 29, 2013), http://chrisriedy.me/2013/05/29/climate-change-is-a-super-wicked-problem/.

80.   Rittel & Webber, *supra* note 9 (contrasting wicked and tame problems); John C. Camillus, *Strategy as a Wicked Problem*, Harv. Bus. Rev. online (May 2008), https://hbr.org/2008/05/strategy-as-a-wicked-problem (arguing that wicked problems cannot be solved, but can be tamed).

81.   Australian Public Serv. Comm'n, Tackling Wicked Problems: A Public Policy Perspective iii (2007).

82.   Levin et al., *supra* note 11, at 129.

83.   *See* Lazarus, *supra* note 14, at 1183 (discussing "'free riders,' who exploit the ecosystem commons to maximize their gains or minimize their losses by relying on others to make the necessary sacrifices").

84.   Levin et al., *supra* note 11, at 129.

85.   *Id.* at 130; *see also* Jones & Baumgartner, *supra* note 1, at 49 ("The general phenomenon of policies reproducing themselves through time is known as path dependency. Once a path is chosen, it tends to be followed. Moving off the path can be difficult." (citation omitted)). For example, rather than

Thus, focusing more on entrenchment and expansion, Levin et al. argue that small policy changes can trigger path-dependent processes that can gain durability and expand over time.[86] This approach has at least two benefits over one-shot approaches that focus on creating immediate stickiness. First, to create immediate stickiness, a policy would have to include features that make it difficult to undo and would as a result be subject to attack as anti-democratic.[87] Second, such a policy would likely entail a large shift from the status quo, an approach that tends to be met with resistance.[88] Ultimately, rather than focusing on one-shot policy changes (whether they create stickiness or not), Levin et al. suggest that focusing on norms, values, and coalition-building can "unleash[ ] path-dependent trajectories."[89] An approach to shifting policy equilibria by changing norms and values also finds support in a growing body of research that suggests that emotional responses to risk are an important component of rational risk regulation.[90] However, given the time-is-running-out nature of super-wicked problems, approaches that expand and entrench support incrementally must nevertheless be capable of changing behavior quickly.

Land use planning processes offer an opportunity to build coalitions and shift norms and values toward resilience. Participants in interactive planning processes not only influence the norms and values underlying the plan, but likely also experience shifts in their own values as a result of their participation. Many land use planning processes—for example, community engagement initiatives, visioning, and charrettes[91]—facilitate collaborative decisionmaking through intensive, personal engagement in project planning. These processes often engage participants in self-advocacy, public com-

---

developing skills related to relocation, students, developers, builders, and others respond to policies that promote rebuilding by developing skills related to armoring shores, buildings, and infrastructure against flood risks.

86. Levin et al., *supra* note 11, at 125.
87. *But see* Lazarus, *supra* note 14, at 1195-1204 (discussing and rejecting anti-democratic critique of policies that create stickiness).
88. Levin et al., *supra* note 11, at 125 ("one-shot 'big bang' policies for super wicked problems, which require behavioral change by all relevant populations immediately, either fail to garner adequate support or, in those rare cases where such policies are adopted, are likely to produce societal 'shocks' that hamper implementation and compliance, derailing a policy no matter how well designed").
89. *Id.*
90. Dan M. Kahan, *Two Conceptions of Emotion in Risk Regulation*, 156 U. Pa. L. Rev. 741, 744 (2008).
91. A charrette is a collaborative brainstorming session "intended to build consensus among participants, develop specific design goals and solutions for a project, and motivate participants and stakeholders to be committed to reaching those goals." Gail Lindsey et al., A Handbook for Planning and Conducting Charrettes for High Performance Projects 1 (Nat'l Renewable Energy Lab., 2d ed. 2012), *available at* http://www.nrel.gov/sustainable_nrel/pdfs/44051.pdf. *See also* Danielle Bergstrom et al., *The Sustainable Communities Initiative: The Community Engagement Guide for Sustainable Communities*, J. Affordable Housing & Community Dev. L., 2014, at 191, 194-95 (discussing strategies for engaging marginalized communities in traditional planning processes).

mitment to a vision, and validation of the vision through shared personal experiences. Research on changing deeply held beliefs suggests that these attributes—self-advocacy, public commitment, and validation through personal experience—can effect lasting, cognitively accessible changes in participants' deeply held beliefs.[92]

However, without transparent communication regarding waterfront risks, participants in land use planning processes are hobbled in their ability to engage with the issues. Analogizing to research on complex adaptive systems, John Nolon observes that effective communication of information is a key component in successful adaptation to stressful events.

> In nature and in human organizations, the systems that thrive are those that have established effective mechanisms for exchanging, evaluating, and reacting to information among their component parts. As stress occurs, information is gathered at the lowest level of the system and relayed to higher levels that digest and synthesize that information. Then, through continued communication, system behaviors are reordered to react and adapt to change. . . . Through continued and effective communication . . . the system adapts in unpredictable but generally successful ways as it deals with external events.[93]

By accurately communicating about risks, local governments can also increase the diversity of participants in the planning process, thereby involving actors who may be more amenable to punctuating policy equilibria. As Jones and Baumgartner observe,

> [An] oft-noted reason for the difficulty in shifting policy direction stems from continuity of participation in key governmental positions. . . . [E]nacting change often requires the involvement of a diverse range of policymakers. Many of these, including those in important gate-keeping positions, typically were involved in creating the earlier policy or at least in administering it.[94]

Failing to communicate accurately about waterfront risks limits those who understand the risks to insiders and experts, thereby exacerbating a lack

---

92. *See, e.g.*, Joshua Aronson et al., *Reducing the Effects of Stereotype Threat on African American College Students by Shaping Theories of Intelligence*, 38 J. Experimental Soc. Psychol. 113, 116-23 (2002) (empirical study identifying conditions for influencing persistent, cognitively accessible changes in attitudes including advocacy in a person's own words, public commitment, and validation by personal experience); *see generally* Sarah J. Adams-Schoen, *Of Old Dogs and New Tricks: Can Law Schools Really Fix Students' Fixed Mindsets*, 19 Legal Writing: J. Legal Writing Inst. 3, 23-31 (2014) (discussing and citing research on facilitating long-lasting, cognitively accessible changes in deeply held beliefs); John R. Nolon, *Champions of Change: Reinventing Democracy Through Land Law Reform*, 23 Pace Envtl. L. Rev. 905, 915 (2006) (analyzing changes within and among communities observed in author's experience working with local governments).
93. Nolon, *supra* note 92, at 916.
94. Jones & Baumgartner, *supra* note 1, at 49-50.

of diversity in the planning process that, as Jones and Baumgartner assert, makes change difficult.

IV.   Conclusion

In summary, discounting of risk in local government communications about climate change and waterfront development likely reinforces existing mal-adaptive path-dependent processes. By adopting toughness narratives, reject-ing retreat strategies outright, or otherwise discounting risks following a major storm like Hurricanes Katrina or Sandy, municipalities fail to take advantage of a window of opportunity in which public support likely exists for a shift to more resilient, albeit restrictive, waterfront development poli-cies. By recognizing waterfront hazard mitigation as a super-wicked problem, which is characterized by time-is-running-out features and which requires entrenchment and expansion of support for resilience in order to break the cycle of development, destruction, and redevelopment, local governments, with the support of federal and state governments, can and should begin to evaluate and seize upon opportunities to shift policies toward resilience. Such opportunities likely begin with official communications that accurately portray risk, including waterfront and hazard mitigation plans and flood risk maps, which can then lead to planning processes and changes in zoning and building codes and private market behavior consistent with near- and long-term risks.

Chapter 7
Effective Climate Change Decisionmaking: Scientific Consensus Plus a Hint of Religion?
Cinnamon Piñon Carlarne

> Effective decision-making to limit climate change and its effects can be informed by a wide range of analytical approaches for evaluating expected risks and benefits, recognizing the importance of governance, ethical dimensions, equity, value judgments, economic assessments and diverse perceptions and responses to risk and uncertainty.[1]

While ethics and morality have always played a role in the development of climate policy, the role of religion has been far more tenuous until very recently, particularly in relation to climate science. Long-standing tensions between science, environmentalism, and religion underpin this disjunction. As political will to respond to climate change has continued to waver even when confronted with solid empirical evidence about the existence and risks of human-induced climate change, however, the debate about climate change policy has widened to include more, and more varied voices, including religious voices. The compatibility of science and religion, however, continues to be a point of tension. This chapter explores the relationship between climate science and religion, focusing on how recent developments in these two areas are bringing this relationship into greater relief, and making this relationship of much greater importance to the future development of climate policy.

---

1. Intergovernmental Panel on Climate Change, Climate Change 2014: Synthesis Report 17 (2014), *available at* http://ar5-syr.ipcc.ch/topic_summary.php [hereinafter 2014 IPCC Synthesis Report].

I.   The Coexistence of Science and Religion

In the Synthesis Report of the Fifth Assessment Report (AR5), the Intergovernmental Panel on Climate Change (IPCC) embraces a multidisciplinary approach to addressing climate change that recognizes the role of norms in decisionmaking processes. Specifically, in discussing the foundations of decisionmaking about climate change, the IPCC determines that:

> effective decision-making to limit climate change and its effects can be informed by a wide range of analytical approaches for evaluating expected risks and benefits, recognizing the importance of governance, ethical dimensions, equity, value judgments, economic assessments and diverse perceptions and responses to risk and uncertainty.[2]

The IPCC then adds specificity to this statement, noting that "[s]ustainable development and equity provide a basis for assessing climate policies," that both "[m]itigation and adaptation raise issues of equity, justice and fairness," and that "[d]elaying mitigation shifts burdens from the present to the future."[3] Here, albeit indirectly, the IPCC—an objective, empirical body—acknowledges, if not legitimizes, the idea that sustainable development and equity provide valid normative principles upon which to base efforts to address climate change.

In the world of environmental law and policy, the idea that norms matter is unremarkable. Environmental law and policy choices can never be neutral. Sustainable development is a central, albeit imprecise, driving norm in systems of domestic and international environmental law. Similarly, environmental law—including climate change law—is infused with principles grounded in equity considerations.

One need only look at the international climate change regime to find evidence of the ways in which sustainable development and notions of equity provide guiding principles in ongoing efforts to implement and develop the regime. In relevant part, the United Nations Framework Convention on Climate Change (UNFCCC) characterizes the Earth's climate system as of common concern to humankind; articulates the importance of protecting the climate system for present and future generations; recognizes that the common responsibility to protect the climate system should be differentiated among parties on the basis of capacity; promotes a precautionary approach to addressing climate change; and recognizes the right to sustainable develop-

---

2.   *Id.*
3.   *Id.*

ment.[4] The UNFCCC is a fundamentally normative instrument grounded in the idea that the global community *should* act to prevent dangerous anthropogenic climate change for the good of present and future generations. It emphasizes that the roles of different state parties in fulfilling this task *should* be differentiated on the basis of equity concerns.

The UNFCCC, however, leaves the question of how these objectives should be implemented for the parties to the regime to work out. In practice, efforts to realize the treaty's principles in reality face persistent challenges.

In the AR5, however, the IPCC formally recognizes what the international climate legal regime demonstrates: the development of climate policy is inherently normative. It is influenced not only by how people perceive risks and uncertainties, but also by the role that different normative frameworks—whether, e.g., economic, social, or ethical in nature—play in this assessment process. The AR5 stops short of endorsing any particular normative framework. Instead, it simply notes that there is no framework that is capable of "identify[ing] a single best balance between mitigation, adaptation and residual climate impacts."[5]

The move in the AR5 toward recognizing the inherently complex nature of the climate change debate breathes a hint of, or at least a nod toward, normativity in an otherwise objective and neutral report. This nod toward the complexity of developing climate policy is a side-note in a report that otherwise remains a vehicle for offering the international community empirical evidence about climate change.

For many people involved in the climate change conversation, the assumption has long been that empirical evidence is and should be enough to prompt action. The evidence of anthropogenic climate change is so strong that, surely, when confronted with this information the public will determine that the risks are so great that they should care about, and demand action on climate change. Inevitably, then, on the basis of this empirical evidence and constituency concerns, policymakers will recognize the urgency of the situation and take action.

The basic premise is that the empirical data speaks for itself and the challenge is to make sure that the public and the policymakers have access to the data. The general assumption underlying this premise is that the reason why the international community has not coalesced around climate change to date is primarily because of a lack of understanding—i.e., people do not

---

4. May 9, 1992, 1771 U.N.T.S. 107, art. 3(1), *available at* http://www.unfccc.de/resource/conv/index.html [hereinafter UNFCCC].
5. *Id.*

understand the gravity of the problem and the key to understanding the gravity of the problem is to educate people with evidence.

As this and other chapters in this book demonstrate, the AR5 provides a wealth of robust empirical evidence about anthropogenic climate change, and the findings of the AR5 have been widely shared. Nevertheless, widespread concern and demand for action are still lacking.

Against this backdrop, this chapter explores the essential but inherently limited role that the IPCC, through its empirical assessment reports, can play in mobilizing collective awareness of the risks associated with climate change and widespread support for action on climate change. In particular, this chapter explores the increasing role of religion in converting climate science into climate action. Using Pope Francis' Encyclical Letter, *Laudato Si', On Care for Our Common Home*,[6] as a counterpoint, the chapter examines the uneasy, but also necessary and potentially symbiotic, relationship between empirical evidence and moral imperatives for mobilizing action on climate change.

II.   Foundations of Climate Change Decisionmaking: The World According to the IPCC

The IPCC's AR5 presents the most comprehensive overview of climate science to date. Expanding on the four preceding reports based on subsequent research and analysis, the AR5 paints a grim, unequivocal picture of, among other things, the impacts that humans have had on the climate system, the risks that these impacts pose for present and future generations, and some of the options humans have for limiting and alleviating future negative impacts. All of these discussions are grounded in data and reflect scientific consensus. In common with its predecessors, the AR5 carefully notes the degree of confidence as to each of the findings in the report. The AR5 is precise, careful, and conservative. The findings that it shares are adamant. The AR5 declares that "[h]uman influence on the climate system is clear" and that "warming of the climate system is unequivocal . . . many of the observed changes are unprecedented over decades to millennia."[7]

The report leaves little room for doubt as to the inevitability of warming or the gravity of the reality of a warming world. For those who worked on, awaited, or eventually read the report with an eye to deepening their understanding of climate science, the AR5 offers many detailed insights into the

---

6.   The Holy See, Encyclical Letter, *Laudato Si' of the Holy Father Francis, On Care for Our Common Home* ¶ 53 (2015) [hereinafter Papal Encyclical].

7.   2014 IPCC Synthesis Report, *supra* note 1, at 2.

physical science of climate change,[8] the economics of climate change,[9] and even the social science dimensions of climate change.[10] The report also provides guidance for assessing and managing the risks of climate change as well as options for mitigating and adapting to climate change.

Even beyond the audience that anticipated the release of the report, the AR5 made headlines. Although it is a highly technical and detailed report, the AR5 includes summaries of each part of the report for policymakers as well as a synthesis report, thus ensuring that the information contained therein is as accessible to as wide an audience as possible.

In the days following its release, the AR5 received ample attention in the global press. Related headlines declared: "U.N. Climate Change Report Delivers Stark Warnings"[11]; "U.N. Panel Issues Its Starkest Warning Yet on Global Warming"[12]; "Time Running Out to Meet Global Target"[13]; "Human Impact Is 'Unequivocal'"[14]; "Climate Change Fight Affordable, Cut Emissions to Zero by 2100"[15]; "Effects of Climate Change 'Irreversible'"[16]; and "Our Climate Change Future Is Terrifying and Emissions Need to Stop Completely as Soon as Possible."[17] For his part, U.N. Secretary General Ban

8. *See generally* INTERGOVERNMENTAL PANEL ON CLIMATE CHANGE, CLIMATE CHANGE 2013: THE PHYSI-CAL SCIENCE BASIS (2013).

9. *See generally* INTERGOVERNMENTAL PANEL ON CLIMATE CHANGE, CLIMATE CHANGE 2014: MITIGATION OF CLIMATE CHANGE, Ch. 3 (2014).

10. *See generally* INTERGOVERNMENTAL PANEL ON CLIMATE CHANGE, CLIMATE CHANGE 2014: IMPACTS, ADAPTATION, AND VULNERABILITY (2014).

11. Karl Ritter, *U.N. Climate Change Report Delivers Stark Warnings*, HUFFINGTON POST (Nov. 2, 2014, 7:35 AM), http://www.huffingtonpost.com/2014/11/02/un-climate-change-report_n_6089392.html.

12. Justin Gillis, *U.N. Panel Issues Its Starkest Warning Yet on Global Warming*, N.Y. TIMES (Nov. 2, 2014), http://www.nytimes.com/2014/11/03/world/europe/global-warming-un-intergovernmental-panel-on-climate-change.html?_r=0.

13. Alister Doyle, *Time Running Out to Meet Global Warming Target—U.N. Report*, THOMSON RE-UTERS (Apr. 6, 2014, 6:57 AM), http://www.reuters.com/article/2014/04/06/climate-un-id USL5N0MW3MA20140406.

14. Fiona Harvey, *IPCC Climate Report: Human Impact Is "Unequivocal,"* THE GUARDIAN (Sept. 27, 2013, 6:48 AM), http://www.theguardian.com/environment/2013/sep/27/ipcc-climate-report-un-secretary-general.

15. Alister Doyle, *Climate Change Fight Affordable, Cut Emissions to Zero by 2100: U.N.*, THOMSON REUTERS (Nov. 2, 2014, 9:28 AM), http://www.reuters.com/article/2014/11/02/us-climatechange-report-idUSKBN0IM08A20141102. *See also* Adam Vaughan, *Climate Change Report: Live Reaction to IPCC Conclusions*, THE GUARDIAN (Sept. 27, 2013, 12:01 PM), http://www.theguardian.com/environment/2013/sep/27/ipcc-climate-change-report-ar5-live-coverage (providing a running commentary on the release of the report).

16. Joby Warrick & Chris Mooney, *Effects of Climate Change "Irreversible,"* U.N. Panel Warns in Report, WASH. POST (Nov. 2, 2014), https://www.washingtonpost.com/national/health-science/effects-of-climate-change-irreversible-un-panel-warns-in-report/2014/11/01/2d49aeec-6142-11e4-8b9e-2ccdac31a031_story.html.

17. Chelsea Harvey, *U.N. REPORT: Our Climate Change Future Is Terrifying and Emissions Need to Stop Completely as Soon as Possible*, BUS. INSIDER (Nov. 4, 2014, 3:38 PM), http://www.businessinsider.com/un-climate-report-stop-all-greenhouse-emissions-2014-11#ixzz3f89hPx26.

Ki-moon helped launch the release of the report by declaring: "The heat is on. Now we must act."[18]

Through the media coverage, the fundamental point of the AR5—i.e., that there is scientific consensus that humans are influencing the climate system in such a way as to produce warming that could cause pervasive negative impacts—reached a general audience. While it may not be possible to know whom the coverage reached or the general effect of this widespread coverage, to some unquantified extent, it is likely that the release of the IPCC AR5 increased levels of awareness and concern about climate change.

But to what end? As previously discussed, the AR5 does not offer normative guidance on how to use the information that it provides. The absence of normativity is intentional. The principles governing the work of the IPCC dictate that the group be neutral and objective. Specifically, the IPCC is tasked with:

> assess[ing] on a comprehensive, objective, open and transparent basis the scientific, technical and socio-economic information relevant to understanding the scientific basis of risk of human-induced climate change, its potential impacts and options for adaptation and mitigation. IPCC reports should be neutral with respect to policy, although they may need to deal objectively with scientific, technical and socio-economic factors relevant to the application of particular policies.[19]

Pursuant to these principles, the AR5 identifies where consensus exists and provides information that can be used by policymakers (and others) in whatever way they see fit. Nothing more, nothing less.

The IPCC reports are also distinct because they bring together thousands of scientists from across the globe. The IPCC is open to all U.N. member countries. One hundred and ninety-five countries are members of the organization, making participation near-universal. The inclusive, multidisciplinary nature of the organization is unique. By bringing together scientists from multiple disciplines from across the globe to assess (rather than provide or create) information, the IPCC seeks to "provide rigorous and balanced scientific information to decision makers"—information that is "policy-relevant and yet policy-neutral, never policy-prescriptive."[20]

---

18.   Ban Ki-moon, *STATEMENT: Secretary-General's Video Message on Launch of IPCC Working Group I Report*, UNITED NATIONS (Sept. 27, 2013), http://www.un.org/sg/STATEMENTS/index.asp?nid=7152.
19.   *See Principles Governing IPCC Work*, at 1, http://www.ipcc.ch/pdf/ipcc-principles/ipcc-principles.pdf (as amended 2013).
20.   Intergovernmental Panel on Climate Change, *Organization*, https://www.ipcc.ch/organization/organization.shtml.

The IPCC was created to provide inclusive, objective, policy-neutral assessments, and it has sought to stay true to this mandate over time. In so doing, it serves an essential role. The global community, especially the Conference of the Parties (COP) to the UNFCCC as well as state policymakers, need a source of information that is not associated with any particular state, scientist, social movement, or political party. Climate policy is fraught with complex politics. Decisionmakers need a source of information that is as unbiased and unprescriptive as possible so that they can use the information to inform debates about how to structure climate policies that are inevitably normative and involve costs and benefits that will be unevenly distributed across space and time.

As the empirical evidence becomes more robust and, along the way, more alarming, there is a tendency to want the IPCC to accompany the evidence with equally robust normative statements about the urgent need for policymakers to act decisively to address the causes and consequences of climate change. If the IPCC were to adopt this approach, however, it would lose credibility. Given that the IPCC and climate science, generally, have already come under fire as a result of past errors and accusations of bias, the organization cannot afford to shift gears.[21]

Assume for the sake of argument that the IPCC serves an essential role and that it should not waver from this role. Assume further that the evidence that the AR5 presents is robust and as widely distributed as possible for a report of this kind. What more can the IPCC do to ensure that the information that it assesses and compiles stimulates the development of more, and more effective, climate policies?

---

21. The credibility of the IPCC came under fire as a result of errors—one key error in particular—in the Fourth Assessment Report. *See, e.g.*, Michelle S. Simon & William Pentland, *Reliable Science: Overcoming Public Doubts in the Climate Change Debate*, 37 WM. & MARY ENVTL. L. & POL'Y REV. 219, 221-22 (2012); Lauren Morello, *IPCC Admits Error on Himalayan Glacier Warning*, E&E News PM, Jan. 20, 2010, http://www.eenews.net/eenewspm/2010/01/20/archive/3?terms=IPCC+admits+error. In addition, the integrity of high-profile climate scientists came under fire around the same time when the e-mail accounts of several scientists were hacked. While the empirical findings of the scientists were not questioned, the drama and intrigue surrounding the event arguably harmed the credibility of individual, if not the collective group of climate scientists, in the eyes of at least some members of the public. *See, e.g.*, InterAcademy Council Committee to Review the Intergovernmental Panel on Climate Change, Climate Change Assessments: Review of the Processes and Procedures of the IPCC xiii-xiv (2010); Andrew C. Revkin, *Hacked E-Mail Data Prompts Calls for Changes in Climate Research*, N.Y. TIMES, Nov. 28, 2009, at A8; House of Commons, Sci. and Tech. Comm., The Disclosure of Climate Data From the Climatic Research Unit of East Anglia, Eighth Report of Session 2009-2010 (Mar. 31, 2010), at 5-7, *available at* http://www.publications.parliament.uk/pa/cm200910/cmselect/cmsctech/387/387i.pdf; Report of the International Panel Set Up by the University of East Anglia to Examine the Research of the Climate Research Unit 1-2, 1, 5 (Apr. 10, 2010), *available at* http://www.uea.ac.uk/mac/comm/media/press/CRUstatements/oxburgh [hereinafter Oxburgh Report]; The Independent Climate Change E-Mails Review 1, 22-24 (July 7, 2010), http://www.cce-review.org/.

This is an important question, but it is also an incomplete one. As the response to the release of Pope Francis' Encyclical Letter in 2015 reveals, empirical evidence—no matter how robust or how neutral—may never be enough to mobilize the concern, sense of personal responsibility, and, ultimately, the hope that is necessary to support collective action on climate change.

The release of Pope Francis' Encyclical begs the question: If empirical evidence, on its own, cannot motivate widespread efforts to address climate change, can it comfortably co-exist alongside ethical and moral imperatives? Can science and morality operate side-by-side to drive positive change? Given the inherently value-laden nature of responding to climate change, the next section explores the evolving role of religion in influencing awareness and perceptions of climate change alongside the increasingly strong empirical record.

III. Religion and Science: Uncomfortable Bedfellows?

Religion and science do not always make easy partners. Neither do religion and politics make comfortable bedfellows. This tension is particularly true in the context of environmental law and policy. In the Western world, environmentalists have historically spurned religious interference in the domain of environmental decisionmaking. Environmentalists have been wary of the inherently anthropocentric, sometimes unscientific, and often mechanistic views of the human-nature relationship associated (rightly or wrongly) with many world religions. Equally, many religious traditions have abstained from active involvement in environmental politics for many reasons, including internal disagreement over the question of the proper human-nature relationship, the relatively low priority of environmental issues on the religious agenda, and disinterest in engaging in secular partisan politics.

Climate change has begun to shift these boundaries. Indeed, the recent release of Pope Francis' Encyclical Letter, with its powerful call for action on climate change, has prompted a rethinking of the ability of science and religious-based moral imperatives to comfortably co-exist as drivers of environmental law and policy.

A.   Religion and Environmentalism: A Brief History

The United States was an early leader in developing a system of environmental law. In the United States, in common with other Western countries, the early origins of the system emerged from the ashes of secular despair over the ongoing devastation of the American wilderness and the pollution of America's growing cities. Inspired by the writings of Henry David Thoreau, Ralph Waldo Emerson, Aldo Leopold, John Muir, and Rachel Carson, the modern environmental movement drew its strength in part from the perceived failures of religious-based ideologies to foster sustainable human-nature relationships.[22] Thus, even while the early Romantic writers converged in finding spirituality and even religion in nature,[23] the religious roots of, for example, Emerson and Thoreau's writings did not translate to an intermingling of religious values with modern environmental decisionmaking.

In fact, the religious underpinnings of many of these influential writings identify the ways that Judeo-Christian religions encouraged an anthropocentric approach to nature that supported notions of human dominion over nature and views of nature as a human resource lacking in intrinsic value.[24] In the early days of the development of environmental policy, perceived failures of religious-based ideologies such as manifest destiny and man's dominion over nature[25]—whether textually valid or not[26]—drove a secular approach to environmental protection that was skeptical of religious interference. As a result, in the 20th century, environmentalism became a dominant form of secular religion,[27] with the rise of environmentalism even being characterized as part of "the fourth great religious awakening."[28]

---

22. For example, Emerson and Thoreau's earlier writings, in conjunction with those of the German writer Johann von Goethe and English writers William Wordsworth and Samuel Taylor Coleridge, helped inspire the Romantic movement of the 19th century, which "sought to make a case for nature as a prior sustaining context that humans need for the nurture of their soul." Shepard Krech et al., Encyclopedia of World Environmental History 459 (Routledge 2003). The notion of nature as central to the well-being of the human soul continues to be a defining feature in the United States, United Kingdom, and German environmental movements and is particularly engrained in Germanic notions of the value of nature. Muir later carried on the Romantic-Transcendentalist movement in the United States, embedding concepts of nature protection within a larger moral framework.

23. Daryl Fisher-Ogden & Shelley Ross Saxer, *World Religions and Clean Water Laws*, 17 Duke Envtl. L. & Pol'y F. 63, 81 (2006).

24. Troy L. Payne, *Comment: Cartesian Eco-Femdarkanism: She Comes From the Earth, Therefore We Are*, 37 Envtl. L. 201 (2007) (citing Donald Worster, Nature's Economy: A History of Ecological Ideals 28-29 (1994) (quoting Thoreau's unpublished journals)).

25. Christopher D. Stone, *Should Trees Have Standing?—Toward Legal Rights for Natural Objects*, 45 S. Cal. L. Rev. 450 (1972).

26. Fisher-Ogden & Saxer, *supra* note 23, at 98.

27. *See, e.g.*, Joseph L. Sax, Mountains Without Handrails: Reflections on the National Parks 104 (1980) (writing that he and his fellow preservationists were "secular prophets, preaching a message of secular salvation").

28. Robert H. Nelson, *Environmental Religion: A Theological Critique*, 55 Case W. Res. L. Rev. 51, 55 (2004) (suggesting that "a fourth great awakening in American life began in the 1960s, including the rise of the contemporary environmental movement, and its effects are still being felt"). Robert Nelson further notes that "American environmental groups derive much of their moral energy, their funding, their sense of purpose and their crusading drive from an 'environmental fundamentalism' that has grown up out of the fourth great religious awakening." *Id.* at 55.

As systems of environmental law developed into robust legal frameworks, a general skepticism of religious-based approaches to conservation persisted. As a result, the social movements and systems of environmental law in the United States are rooted in principles of ecology and economics, and to a lesser extent in a narrow system of secular ethics, while remaining largely detached from overt religious influence.

To many, however, the gap between the environmental movement and religion is both problematic and disingenuous. As Yandle and Buck note:

> The environmental movement (at least in its "deep" version) . . . has great similarities with the religious fundamentalisms sweeping the world. . . . For though it may appear that the environmental movement is "scientific" and hence "modern" whereas the religious fundamentalists are "non-scientific" and "pre-modern," they both share a fear and contempt of the modernity whose central features are rightly seen to be an instrumental rationality that undermines humankind's traditional relationship with God or Nature.[29]

While focusing on the "fundamentalist" branches of thinking within religious and environmental communities, Yandle and Buck's analysis holds true in relation to mainstream environmental politics, which remains inherently normative and value-laden even when those traits are not openly recognized.[30]

These critiques extend to environmentalists' approach to climate change. As Eric Dannenmaier points out:

> [e]ven the *National Review*, a conservative standard, publishes articles that challenge the orthodoxy of an "environmentalist religion," and decry the environmentalists' perspective on climate change thus: "In equally medieval

---

29. Bruce Yandle & Stuart Buck, *Bootleggers, Baptists, and the Global Warming Battle*, 26 Harv. Envtl. L. Rev. 177, 189 (2002) (quoting Deepak Lal, Unintended Consequences: The Impact of Factor Endowments, Culture, and Politics on Long-Run Economic Performance 108-09 (1998) (quoting Mary Douglas & Aaron Wildavsky, Risk and Culture 30 (1983)). Nelson has similarly characterized environmentalism, noting that:
> For many of its followers today, environmentalism has been a substitute for fading mainline Christian and progressive faiths-its religious quality obvious to any close observer of its workings. Its language is often overtly religious: "saving" the earth from rape and pillage; building "cathedrals" in the wilderness; creating a new "Noah's Ark" with laws such as the Endangered Species Act; pursuing a new "calling" to preserve the remaining wild areas.
> Robert H. Nelson, *Environmental Colonialism: "Saving" Africa From Africans*, Indep. Rev., June 22, 2003, at 65, 67.

30. *See* Michael Shellenberger & Ted Nordhaus, The Death of Environmentalism: Global Warming Politics in a Post-Environmental World 33 (2004), http://www.thebreakthrough.org/images/Death_of_Environmentalism.pdf [hereinafter The Death of Environmentalism], commenting that
> Environmentalists and other liberals tend to see values as a distraction from "the real issues"—environmental problems like global warming. . . . If environmentalists hope to become more than a special interest we must start framing our proposals around core American values and start seeing our own values as central to what motivates and guides our politics.

fashion, adherents of the environmentalist religion have launched an inquisition against scientific views that they consider heretical."[31]

In summing up some of the conservative critiques, Dannenmaier suggests that environmentalists "are perceived as apostates of science and reason; theirs is a belief-based religious calling dominated by 'crazy beliefs' and clouded judgment."[32] Not all critiques emerge from conservative quarters, however. Calls for a rethinking of environmentalism have become more vocal and more widespread in recent years from across a range of political perspectives. These calls are based, in part, on arguments that the modern environmental movement excludes consideration of a sufficiently wide set of values, including social values, in such a way as to render it anachronistic and dysfunctional.[33]

Yet, modern environmentalism continues to remain largely secular and, until very recently, religious institutions have played a marginal role in the development of environmental law and policy in the United States[34] and elsewhere. In recent years, however, the role of religious institutions in environmental policymaking has begun to change.

Empirical evidence demonstrating the pervasive and grave risks that climate change poses to the global community as a whole has prompted a more inclusive conversation about how values, including religious values,[35] influence policy choices in the climate change decisionmaking sphere.[36] For an increasing swathe of the population, the secular religion of environmentalism no longer offers a satisfying response to the ethical dilemmas that underpin efforts to address climate change. Within this gap, many people look to religion to provide "a strong baseline for value judgments from which to launch a pragmatic approach to sustaining our environment."[37] Even beyond the religious community, in their controversial essay, *The Death of Environmentalism: Global Warming Politics in a Post-Environmental World*, Michael Shellenberger and Ted Nordhaus call upon environmentalists to "tap into the creative worlds of myth-making, even religion, not to better sell narrow and

---

31.   Eric Dannenmaier, *Executive Exclusion and the Cloistering of the Cheney Energy Task Force*, 16 N.Y.U.
      ENVTL. L.J. 329, 370-71 (2008) (quoting Iain Murray, *Sir David King's Queenie Fit*, NAT'L REV., July
      23, 2004.)).
32.   *Id.*
33.   *See, e.g.*, THE DEATH OF ENVIRONMENTALISM, *supra* note 30.
34.   Lucia A. Silecchia, *Environmental Ethics From the Perspectives of NEPA and Catholic Social Teaching:
      Ecological Guidance for the 21st Century*, 28 WM. & MARY ENVTL. L. & POL'Y REV. 659, 667 (2004).
35.   However, again, there is a parallel movement to rethink environmentalism in such a way as to be
      more responsive to a larger set of social and cultural values. *See* THE DEATH OF ENVIRONMENTALISM,
      supra note 30.
36.   *See, e.g.*, KATHARINE HAYHOE & ANDREW FARLEY, A CLIMATE FOR CHANGE: GLOBAL WARMING FACTS
      FOR FAITH-BASED DECISIONS (FaithWords 2009).
37.   Fisher-Ogden & Saxer, *supra* note 23, at 81.

technical policy proposals but rather to figure out who we are and who we need to be."[38] Hence, while religion has been largely absent from the secular world of environmental decisionmaking over the past half century, climate change has renewed interest in the role of religion in this regard.

B.   The Papal Encyclical: The Escalation of Morality

The absence of religious values in modern environmentalism is attributable in part to its historical origins and the dominance of the secular environmental movement, but it also results from continuing tensions among religious leaders[39] concerning the proper relationship between humans and nature.[40] The lack of continuity within and between the world's religions on the appropriate human-nature relationship complicates efforts to rethink the role that religious values can play in environmental decisionmaking.

However, just as global climate change has inspired renewed dialogue amongst policymakers working across disciplines such as human rights, law of the sea, biodiversity, development, security and trade,[41] so has it prompted a rethinking of the role of religion in climate change decisionmaking. Climate change has brought about a new era in the religion-environment debate. Religious actors ranging from Muslim scholars, Catholic bishops, Evangelical Christians, the Church of England, the Society of Friends, interfaith alliances consisting of Hindus, Muslims, Christian, Buddhists, and beyond have begun engaging in cooperative efforts to imbue domestic and international climate debates with religious-based moral perspectives. Their efforts focus on both mobilizing religious constituencies and influencing the contours of political debate.[42]

Prior to the release of the AR5, religious dialogue played a small but still relevant part in influencing cultural perceptions of climate change and shap-

---

38. The Death of Environmentalism, *supra* note 30.
39. Fisher-Ogden & Saxer, *supra* note 23, at 68.
40. *E.g.*, rifts in the Christian community over notions of stewardship versus dominion.
41. Cinnamon Carlarne, *Good Climate Governance: Only a Fragmented System of International Law Away?*, 30 L. & Pol'y 4 (2008) (*Special Issue on Global Warming*); Michael Depledge & Cinnamon Carlarne, *Sick of the Weather: Climate Change, Human Health and International Law*, Opinion Piece, 9 Envtl. L. Rev. 231 (2007).
42. *E.g.*, John Copeland Nagle, *The Evangelical Debate Over Climate Change*, 5 U. St. Thomas L.J. 85 (2008); R. Bruce Hall, *Evangelicals and Environmentalists United*, New Scientist No. 2545, (Apr. 1, 2006) http://www.newscientist.com/article/mg19025454.700; Evangelical Climate Initiative, *Climate Change: An Evangelical Call to Action* 3 (2006), *available at* http://pub.christiansandclimate.org/pub/statement-booklet.pdf; John Tierney, *And on the Eighth Day, God Went Green*, N.Y. Times A31, Feb. 11, 2006; United States Conference of Catholic Bishops, *Global Climate Change: A Plea for Dialogue, Prudence, and the Common Good (Global Climate Change Statement)* (2001).

ing the ethical foundations of climate change debates.[43] Yet, religion and religious voices remained largely marginal to the larger global conversation. This changed in May 2015, when the Roman Catholic Holy Father released his Encyclical Letter. Prompted by the perceived harm that humans have "inflicted on [our common home] by our irresponsible use and abuse of the goods with which God has endowed her,"[44] the Pope uses the Encyclical Letter to declare that our modes of existence "have caused sister earth, along with all the abandoned of our world, to cry out, pleading that we take another course. Never have we so hurt and mistreated our common home as we have in the last two hundred years."[45]

With the release of the Papal Encyclical, Pope Francis used his pulpit to speak to the people in his worldwide parish—as well as to many others who do not adhere to Catholicism—in a way that no one else in the world is situated to do. For this reason alone, the release of the Encyclical marks a unique moment in the climate change debate.

At a very basic level, in the Encyclical Letter, the Pope makes a morality-based exhortation to conservation that, for many, may be much more difficult to ignore than a similar call from any other individual or social, epistemic, or political organization. The release of the Papal Encyclical thus brings religion and morality to the forefront of the climate debate in a new and dramatic way. Critically, for purposes of this chapter, the Papal Encyclical not only stimulates the moral debate about addressing climate change,[46] it also offers an unorthodox endorsement for climate science. In the Encyclical, the Pope draws upon both religious and rational arguments (grounded in the findings of science) to advance moral and spiritual goals. In this way, the Encyclical provides politicians, lawyers, and civil society with non-doctrinally grounded ways to think about climate change. In so doing, the Encyclical and the debate that it is prompting have the potential to change the tenor and intensity of the climate change conversation changes in, as of yet, undetermined ways.

---

43. *See, e.g.,* Cinnamon Carlarne, *Environmentalism as Modern Religion and Climate Change as the Secular Apocalypse: Reassessing the Role of Religion in Climate Change Decision-Making,* MUSLIM AND CHRISTIAN UNDERSTANDING: THEORY AND APPLICATION OF "A COMMON WORD" (2010).
44. Papal Encyclical, *supra* note 6, at ¶ 2.
45. Papal Encyclical, *supra* note 6, ¶ 53.
46. The Pope also calls for more intensive intra- and inter-religious dialogues, declaring that:
    The majority of people living on our planet profess to be believers. This should spur religions to dialogue among themselves for the sake of protecting nature, defending the poor, and building networks of respect and fraternity. . . . The gravity of the ecological crisis demands that we all look to the common good, embarking on a path of dialogue which demands patience, self-discipline and generosity, always keeping in mind that "realities are greater than ideas."
    Papal Encyclical, *supra* note 6, ¶ 201.

An underlying question for many advocates of climate change action, including many scientists and lawyers, concerns the practical impact of infusing morality, especially religious morality, into the heart of the climate change debates. That is, does framing climate change as an inherently moral issue substantiate empirical understanding both by widening the pool of actors who care about climate change, as well as by deepening the commitment of those who now view addressing climate change as a moral imperative? Or, does framing action on climate change as a religiously-driven moral imperative undermine our ability to develop rational, empirical-based approaches to addressing a massively complex problem?

In thinking through these questions, it is worth exploring very briefly the particular ways in which Pope Francis used his platform to influence the debate about climate change. To begin, Pope Francis characterizes the climate in a way that is familiar to both environmental lawyers and economists by defining the climate as "a common good, belonging to all and meant for all."[47] He then continues by using an ecology-based frame commonplace within the climate change debate, specifying that the global climate "is a complex system linked to many of the essential conditions for human life."[48] The Pope then adds intensity to the foundations of his call to action by declaring that:

> [c]limate change is a global problem with grave implications: environmental, social, economic, political and for the distribution of goods. It represents one of the principal challenges facing humanity in our day. Its worst impact will probably be felt by developing countries in coming decades. Many of the poor live in areas particularly affected by phenomena related to warming, and their means of subsistence are largely dependent on natural reserves and ecosystemic services such as agriculture, fishing and forestry.[49]

In framing the conversation about climate change and the environment, the Papal Encyclical makes numerous important moves. For purposes of this chapter, three in particular are important and will be discussed briefly, in turn.[50] First, the discussion of climate change is grounded in science. Second,

---

47. Papal Encyclical, *supra* note 6, ¶ 23.
48. *Id.*
49. *Id.* ¶ 25.
50. In the 180+ page Encyclical, Pope Francis makes many important contributions to the conversation about the environment, humanity, and morality, including a deep critique of the way in which our modern economy, focusing on contemporary forms of capitalism, and the way in which this system promotes unbridled exploitation of resources in a way that is not only detrimental to the natural environment but also deeply inequitable to the human population. *See, e.g.*, Papal Encyclical, *supra* note 6, ¶¶ 16, 162. The Pope's critique of modern society here and elsewhere is important but beyond the scope of this chapter. For a brief introduction to this topic, see Martin O'Neil, *The Pope's Radical*

the Pope weaves together the dual drivers of science and compassion-based morality in calling for a rethinking of the way in which humans use the resources of the earth. Third, underlying everything that the Pope says is a deep and abiding sense of hope—not hope that climate change is a farce, or even hope that we still have time to stop climate change full stop. Rather, the Pope's Encyclical displays profound hope in the power of the human spirit to prevail even in the face of a daunting challenge.

First, the Papal Encyclical draws upon the long empirical record created by the IPCC and the word-wide community of climate researchers to help ground the Pope's call for humanity to "recognize the need for changes of lifestyle, production and consumption, in order to combat this warming."[51] To do so, Pope Francis confirms that "a number of scientific studies indicate that most global warming in recent decades is due to the great concentration of greenhouse gases (carbon dioxide, methane, nitrogen oxides and others) released mainly as a result of human activity."[52] He continues by confirming that "[a] very solid scientific consensus indicates that we are presently witnessing a disturbing warming of the climatic system."[53] Then, instead of referring back to the work of climate researchers directly, he offers summaries of some of the key predictions that climate science has provided. For example, the Papal Encyclical summarizes key findings from climate research, noting that:

> melting in the polar ice caps and in high altitude plains can lead to the dangerous release of methane gas, while the decomposition of frozen organic material can further increase the emission of carbon dioxide. Things are made worse by the loss of tropical forests which would otherwise help to mitigate climate change. Carbon dioxide pollution increases the acidification of the oceans and compromises the marine food chain. If present trends continue, this century may well witness extraordinary climate change and an unprecedented destruction of ecosystems, with serious consequences for all of us. A rise in the sea level, for example, can create extremely serious situations, if we consider that a quarter of the world's population lives on the coast or nearby, and that the majority of our megacities are situated in coastal areas.[54]

In the following sections of the Encyclical, the Pope carefully explores distinct environmental issues, including water and the loss of biodiversity.

Economic Vision, Aljazeera America (June 24, 2015), http://america.aljazeera.com/opinions/2015/6/pope-francis-radical-economic-vision.html.

51. Papal Encyclical, *supra* note 6, ¶ 23.
52. *Id.*
53. *Id.*
54. *Id.* ¶ 24.

Throughout these sections, the gravity of the destruction of these environmental resources is grounded in an empirical understanding of the way that natural systems work and the ways in which humans influence these systems. In discussing the loss of biodiversity, for example, the Pope adopts an ecological approach to warn of the negative impacts of plundering the earth's resources based on "short-sighted"[55] economic objectives, cautioning that "the good functioning of ecosystems also requires fungi, algae, worms, insects, reptiles and an innumerable variety of microorganisms."[56]

As discussed below, although Pope Francis grounds his call for rethinking the relationship between humans and the environment in an empirical understanding of the human-nature dynamic, he is not advocating blind adherence to logic and rationality. Instead, Pope Francis adopts the words of his predecessor, Pope John Paul II, and endorses the view that "science and technology are wonderful products of a God-given human creativity."[57] He then uses the Encyclical to urge a rethinking of the relationship between science and faith based upon his belief that "science and religion, with their distinctive approaches to understanding reality, can enter into an intense dialogue fruitful for both."[58]

This framing leads to the second relevant move that Pope Francis makes in the Encyclical: a call for greater interweaving of science and religion in order to deepen the frame through which society understands the human-environment relationship. Referring to his namesake, Saint Francis, Pope Francis grounds his appeal for change in a fuller view of the relationship between humans and the environment. He advocates a perspective that understands that "an integral ecology calls for openness to categories which transcend the language of mathematics and biology, and take us to the heart of what it is to be human."[59] That is, from the Pope's perspective, it is impossible to understand the nature of the climate change challenge based on facts alone. These facts must be filtered through the Christian lens based on ideals of "harmony, justice, fraternity and peace."[60] This filter allows the challenges to be viewed simultaneously as scientific and human imperatives. Equally, this filter ensures that the empirical and ethical complexity of the challenges is visible.

---

55.   *Id.* ¶ 32.
56.   Papal Encyclical, *supra* note 6, ¶ 34.
57.   *Id.* ¶ 102 (quoting Pope John Paul II, *Address to Scientists and Representatives of the United Nations University, Hiroshima* (Feb. 25, 1981), 422:3 AAS 73 (1981)).
58.   *Id.* ¶ 62.
59.   *Id.* ¶ 11.
60.   *Id.* ¶ 82.

Adding these layers of analysis requires that society rediscover a "sense of responsibility for our fellow men and women upon which all civil society is founded."[61] Rediscovering this sense of responsibility will allow us more fully to appreciate the magnitude of the challenge, entailing, as it does, grave risks to human well-being in both the present and the future. In common with the international climate change regime, the Papal Encyclical calls for a rethinking of the human-environment paradigm based upon principles of intra- and intergenerational equity.[62] Rejecting the notion of human dominion over the earth, the Pope determines that there is a "relationship of mutual responsibility between human beings and nature."[63] As a result, "[e]ach community can take from the bounty of the earth whatever it needs for subsistence, but it also has the duty to protect the earth and to ensure its fruitfulness for coming generations."[64] Framed thusly, the enormous multigenerational ethical dimensions of climate change become essential parts of the conversation.

As previously discussed, however, Pope Francis' embrace of science as a necessary tool for understanding our world and our relationship to it is not unqualified. Running throughout the Encyclical is a cautionary tale about the risks of science and technology untempered by humility. The Pope reminds us that "science and technology are not neutral"[65] and cautions that "[m]odernity is has been marked by an excessive anthropocentrism"[66] that "has paradoxically ended up prizing technical thought over reality."[67] It is just these patterns—this untempered "undifferentiated and one-dimensional paradigm"—that has led us to our current predicament. In order to stop perpetuating these patterns, the Pope suggests, we must reinsert humanity into the equation. As the Pope advises, in order to renew our relationship with nature, we need a "renewal of humanity itself," because, ultimately, "[t]here can be no ecology without an adequate anthropology."[68] In the end, the possibility of, and hope for, a happy future relies on a "bold cultural revolution"[69] grounded in recognition that science and technology are not neutral.

---

61. Papal Encyclical, *supra* note 6, ¶ 25.
62. *Id.* ¶ 159.
63. *Id.* ¶ 67.
64. *Id.*
65. *Id.* ¶ 114.
66. Papal Encyclical, *supra* note 6, ¶ 116.
67. *Id.* ¶ 115.
68. *Id.* ¶ 118.
69. *Id.* ¶ 114.

In addition, and interestingly, the Papal Encyclical reflects a theme pervasive in academic literature today—a call for interdisciplinary thinking.[70] The Encyclical warns of the risks of over-specialization and the fragmentation of knowledge and issues a plea for interdisciplinary, inclusive communication.[71] In issuing this call, the Pope mirrors many climate researchers when he advocates increased inter- and cross-disciplinary communication. What is needed, he suggests, is "[a] broad, responsible scientific and social debate needs to take place, one capable of considering all the available information and of calling things by their name."[72]

In re-envisioning the world, the Pope calls for inter-religious dialogue, the integration of religion (or, at least, morality) into secular environmental dialogue, and the diversification and deepening of dialogue at all levels. His vision is one that, in common with many ongoing secular conversations, sees the need to embrace complexity. In the climate context, this manifests as a need to embrace the complexity that the empirical data reveals, as well as the moral complexity that is the necessary lens through which we view and make decisions using the empirical data. In the end, Pope Francis suggests, "any technical solution which science claims to offer will be powerless to solve the serious problems of our world if humanity loses its compass."[73] The harder question, of course, and the one for which Pope Francis can only offer his particular perspective,[74] is what that compass should look like and who

---

70. In key part, the Pope suggests:
     > Dialogue among the various sciences is likewise needed, since each can tend to become enclosed in its own language, while specialization leads to a certain isolation and the absolutization of its own field of knowledge. This prevents us from confronting environmental problems effectively. An open and respectful dialogue is also needed between the various ecological movements, among which ideological conflicts are not infrequently encountered.
     Id. ¶ 201.
71. Specifically, the Pope states: "specialization which belongs to technology makes it difficult to see the larger picture. The fragmentation of knowledge proves helpful for concrete applications, and yet it often leads to a loss of appreciation for the whole, for the relationships between things, and for the broader horizon, which then becomes irrelevant." Papal Encyclical, *supra* note 6, ¶ 110.
72. *Id.* ¶ 135. Interestingly, the Pope also embraces the importance of academic freedom, "[d]ue to the number and variety of factors to be taken into account when determining the environmental impact of a concrete undertaking, it is essential to give researchers their due role, to facilitate their interaction, and to ensure broad academic freedom." *Id.* ¶ 140.
73. *Id.* ¶ 200.
74. In part, Pope Francis suggests that we should let nature be our guide since, although some humans find it hard to accept, "the way natural ecosystems work is exemplary." *Id.* ¶ 22. This comment is made as part of a larger critique of our wasteful society. In full the Pope argues:
     > It is hard for us to accept that the way natural ecosystems work is exemplary: plants synthesize nutrients which feed herbivores; these in turn become food for carnivores, which produce significant quantities of organic waste which give rise to new generations of plants. But our industrial system, at the end of its cycle of production and consumption, has not developed the capacity to absorb and reuse waste and by-products. We have not yet managed to adopt a circular model of production capable of preserving resources for present and future generations, while limiting as much as possible the use of non-renewable resources,

should get to determine the morals, ethics, and values that drive decision-making processes.

Finally, the Encyclical is defined and elevated by Pope Francis' enduring optimism that "[h]uman beings, while capable of the worst, are also capable of rising above themselves, choosing again what is good, and making a new start, despite their mental and social conditioning."[75] One may not agree that either moral reasoning or hope must (or even can) rest in religion or religious teachings,[76] but through his powerful message of hope delivered to many millions of people, the Pope reinvigorates the climate change conversation by making it more accessible and less daunting to many people.

Hope in the power of humanity to cope with the challenge before us becomes ever more critical as the crisis grows ever more urgent. When a challenge is frightening and overwhelming, natural responses include freezing and doing nothing or feeling helpless and thus, again, doing nothing. As the empirical evidence has mounted, the headlines surrounding climate change have become increasingly dire and depressing. With climate-related headlines shouting "When the End of Human Civilization Is Your Day Job,"[77] "Killing Us Softly: The Industry of Lies Around Climate Change,"[78] "Global Warming May Fuel Terrorism,"[79] and "Humans Causing Catastrophic Ecosystem Shifts,"[80] it is easy to understand why the public might feel overwhelmed, alienated, and helpless in the face of climate change. Recognizing that recent efforts to prompt action on climate change have rested on the idea that fear is an essential driver, two prominent commentators noted that in order to make progress on climate change, "we need to stop trying to scare the pants off of

---

moderating their consumption, maximizing their efficient use, reusing and recycling them. A serious consideration of this issue would be one way of counteracting the throwaway culture which affects the entire planet, but it must be said that only limited progress has been made in this regard.

Id.

75. Papal Encyclical, *supra* note 6, ¶ 205.

76. For one clear and concise perspective on some of the ways that the Pope message both resonates with and creates tension with secular perspectives on the human-environment relationship, see Jedediah Purdy, *The Pope and I (Are Having a Complicated Weekend)*, HUFFINGTON POST GREEN, THE BLOG (June 21, 2015), http://www.huffingtonpost.com/jedediah-purdy/the-pope-and-i-are-having_b_7632200.html.

77. John H. Richardson, *When the End of Civilization Is Your Day Job*, ESQUIRE (July 7, 2015), http://www.esquire.com/news-politics/a36228/ballad-of-the-sad-climatologists-0815/.

78. Charles P. Pierce, *Killing Us Softly: The Industry of Lies Around Climate Change*, ESQUIRE (July 10, 2015), http://www.esquire.com/news-politics/politics/news/a36337/climate-change-liars/.

79. *Global Warming May Fuel Terrorism*, NEWS 24 (July 13, 2015), http://www.news24.com/Green/News/Global-warming-may-fuel-terrorism-report-20150713.

80. *Humans Causing Catastrophic Ecosystem Shifts, Study Finds*, THOMSON REUTERS (June 30, 2015), http://www.cbc.ca/news/technology/humans-causing-catastrophic-ecosystem-shifts-study-finds-1.3133752.

the American public."[81] Pope Francis' message of hope provides an opportunity to discover the ways in which hope, alongside empirical evidence and an inevitable sense of urgency, can impact efforts to address climate change.

The message of hope that the Pope spreads, however, is counterbalanced by the grim picture he paints of the way in which climate change will cause widespread suffering and what he perceives as the widespread indifference to such suffering.[82] Critiquing the selfishness of humans and the "lack of response to these tragedies involving our brothers and sister,"[83] the Pope calls for a renewed sense of responsibility for our fellow humans as well as more far-sighted approaches to caring for the ecosystems upon which we all depend. Here, he returns to a deeply ecological perspective as he reminds us that "[t]he human environment and the natural environment deteriorate together; we cannot adequately combat environmental degradation unless we attend to causes related to human and social degradation."[84]

In addition, the Pope's message of hope in the power of humanity to rise to the task at hand is tempered by his own depiction of the scale of the task. Pope Francis does not shy away from the seriousness of the situation. Rather he uses the story of struggle that the empirical evidence paints to demand action, declaring:

> Doomsday predictions can no longer be met with irony or disdain. We may well be leaving to coming generations debris, desolation and filth. The pace of consumption, waste and environmental change has so stretched the planet's capacity that our contemporary lifestyle, unsustainable as it is, can only precipitate catastrophes, such as those which even now periodically occur in different areas of the world. The effects of the present imbalance can only be reduced by our decisive action, here and now.[85]

The message is strong and decisive, and the Pope's embrace of empirical evidence, juxtaposed against his resounding call for action and his deep faith in the resilience of the human spirit, forges a call for action that is as powerful as one could imagine emerging from any platform, religious or secular.

Nevertheless, for some, the Pope's message may not resonate, coming as it does from a particular religious vantage point. Others might agree with the underlying message but differ about the degree to which religion is necessary or even compatible with efforts to structure climate change regimes.

---

81.   Michael Shellenberger & Ted Nordhaus, *The Long Death of Environmentalism*, http://thebreakthrough.org/archive/the_long_death_of_environmenta.
82.   Papal Encyclical, *supra* note 6, ¶ 25.
83.   *Id.*
84.   *Id.* ¶ 48.
85.   *Id.* ¶ 161.

For many others, however, Pope Francis' message may serve as an opening to thought, conversation, and action in a way that no message from a scientist, policymaker, or even low-level religious leader could. As Verchick argues, for many millions of people, the Pope may play the role of an indispensable climate change voucher.[86] Vouchers are "known individuals so liked and respected by others that they can successfully 'vouch' for large, complicated ideas and persuade them to take action."[87] As Verchick suggests, the Pope occupies a distinct space and has access to and credibility with a global audience in a way that no other leader does, whether religious or secular.

Accepting for the moment that, at least in terms of the size of the audiences, the IPCC's AR5 is the pinnacle of epistemic understanding of climate change, while Pope Francis' Encyclical is the pinnacle of moral opining on climate change, the juxtaposition of the two provides an unprecedented combination of evidentiary and normative support for addressing climate change. The AR5 and the Papal Encyclical may simply exist side-by-side in perpetuity with little interaction between them, or the Papal Encyclical might inspire a paradigm shift that allows more people to care more deeply about climate change, including climate science. Either way, one thing the Encyclical confirms is that value choices are intrinsic to assessing and responding to climate change. Equally, in many societies, religion plays a defining role in shaping value choices. As a result, henceforth, religion and religious perspectives are likely to play increasingly important roles in the climate change conversation. Moving forward, a key challenge for religious and secular activists and decisionmakers is to create a more open and transparent milieu for engaging with one another on an issue that transcends secular and spiritual divides.

IV.   Conclusion: We Are All St. Francis

In the wake of the release of the AR5, there was hope that the strength of the empirical evidence presented would provide the impetus needed to jump-start more assertive action on climate change. Thus far, this push has not happened. The IPCC reports have helped drive research and deepen understanding of and concern about climate change. Nevertheless, widespread support for action on climate change is still lacking. The lack of response results from many factors, but focusing on climate science, it is easy to ask:

---

86.   Here, borrowing the term that Verchick uses to discuss the Pope in his blog. Robert Verchick, *Why the Climate Movement Needs a Green Pope, and a Super Voucher*, Center for Progressive Reform (CPR) Blog (June 18, 2015), http://www.progressivereform.org/CPRBlog.cfm?idBlog= 5183431D-FBD7-3589-BCA091A0791F2439.

87.   *Id.*

What more could be done? How much clearer and more doomsday do the assessment reports have to be before enough people care enough to support effective action?

The fundamental problem with this framing, however, is that science and empirical evidence can never be enough. As Richard Shellenberger and Ted Nordhaus suggest, "more, better, or louder climate science will not drive the transformation of the global energy economy."[88] This is not to say that we do not need more and better science. We do. The better the information is, the better off we are in terms of crafting mitigation and adaptation strategies. Equally, more and better communication of science will also help. However, no matter how much, how solid, or how loud the science is, it will never be enough on its own to either mobilize the masses or maneuver the tricky, value-laden process of political decisionmaking. The Papal Encyclical does not solve the problem, but it helps spread the message of climate change and it ignites the already smoldering debate about the inherently value-laden decisionmaking processes that we are facing.

One might disagree with the Pope or question the compatibility of the message he spreads with larger church policies. But at the end of the day, religious values "are core to many people in the world", and whether one is a religious advocate, an agnostic, or an atheist, it is essential that the climate conversation is open to and engages multiple points of view in order to develop culturally informed, effective, and sustainable climate policies.[89] This is not to suggest that religion offers a panacea to troubled climate politics; clearly, it does not. Interjecting religion into climate politics creates ample opportunities for chaos and backtracking because there is neither religious consensus on the realities of climate change nor religious consensus on the proper political response to climate change among those religious traditions that accept human-induced climate change as a reality. Yet, excluding religion is neither a viable nor a desirable option, and the Pope, using his unique and powerful pulpit, has issued a profound call for action grounded in science and informed by morality.

In framing the Encyclical Letter, Pope Francis looked to his namesake, Saint Francis, as an "example par excellence of care for the vulnerable and of an integral ecology lived out joyfully and authentically."[90] In Pope Francis' description of Saint Francis, we see both a description of the person the Pope

---

88.   Richard Shellenberger & Ted Nordhaus, *The Long Death of Environmentalism* (Feb. 25, 2011), http://thebreakthrough.org/archive/the_long_death_of_environmenta.
89.   Fisher-Ogden & Saxer, *supra* note 23, at 65.
90.   Papal Encyclical, *supra* note 6, ¶ 10.

seemingly hopes to be as well as a vision of the type of person he thinks every citizen should be. According to Pope Francis, Saint Francis:

> is the patron saint of all who study and work in the area of ecology, and he is also much loved by non-Christians. He was particularly concerned for God's creation and for the poor and outcast. He loved, and was deeply loved for his joy, his generous self-giving, his openheartedness. He was a mystic and a pilgrim who lived in simplicity and in wonderful harmony with God, with others, with nature and with himself. He shows us just how inseparable the bond is between concern for nature, justice for the poor, commitment to society, and interior peace.[91]

This vision of Saint Francis—as a human deeply in tune not just with nature, but with a scientific understanding of it, deeply revered by people across religious divides, and living a simple life underpinned by an inclusive sense of compassion—is the vision Pope Francis has for our world and the individuals in it.

We have many miles to go before our climate change governance systems reflect and thus facilitate these qualities. Returning to where we began, in the AR5, the IPCC declares that:

> Effective decision-making to limit climate change and its effects can be informed by a wide range of analytical approaches for evaluating expected risks and benefits, recognizing the importance of governance, ethical dimensions, equity, value judgments, economic assessments and diverse perceptions and responses to risk and uncertainty.[92]

This statement, and the larger report, is not an open call to the religious leaders of today to define the course of action on climate change. It does, however, recognize that we now have enough evidence and knowledge to support robust action to address climate change. The next step is to mobilize support for action and analyze what kinds of policies are both effective and socially and culturally sustainable. This effort requires more than epistemic evidence; it requires a much deeper call to action and a much more inclusive and thoughtful decisionmaking process. Together, the AR5 and the Papal Encyclical provide the tools we need to understand the parameters of the challenge and to deepen and widen the conversation about what comes next.

The relationship between science and religion remains uneasy. This unease, however, pales in the face of the existential challenge that climate change presents. This challenge requires uncomfortable conversations and

---

91. *Id.*
92. 2014 IPCC Synthesis Report, *supra* note 1, at 76.

necessitates uneasy partnerships. The olive branches being extended between scientific and religious communities are a start. We need more conversations and more voices. Our climate system is a common good; decisions about how we share and care for that good are not the exclusive domain of any discipline, religion, or politics but, instead, require as broad and inclusive a conversation as possible.

Chapter 8
Agnostic Adaptation
Katrina Fischer Kuh

Adaptation planning and implementation at all levels of governance are contingent on societal values, objectives, and risk perceptions *(high confidence)*. Recognition of diverse interests, circumstances, social-cultural contexts, and expectations can benefit decision-making processes. Indigenous, local, and traditional knowledge systems and practices, including indigenous peoples' holistic view of community and environment, are a major resource for adapting to climate change, but these have not been used consistently in existing adaptation efforts. Integrating such forms of knowledge with existing practices increases the effectiveness of adaptation.

Decision support is most effective when it is sensitive to context and the diversity of decision types, decision processes, and constituencies *(robust evidence, high agreement)*. Organizations bridging science and decision making, including climate services, play an important role in the communication, transfer, and development of climate-related knowledge, including translation, engagement, and knowledge exchange *(medium evidence, high agreement)*.

—Intergovernmental Panel on Climate Change, Climate Change 2014: Impacts, Adaptation, and Vulnerability 26 (2014).

Public beliefs about climate change in the United States remain polarized, and public debate about climate change is marked by notable vitriol. Although the majority of Americans now think that climate change is occurring, nearly one in five Americans do not believe that climate change is happening.[1] Thirteen percent of Americans are characterized as "doubtful" with respect to climate change, meaning that they are "uncertain whether global warming is occurring or not, but believe that if it is happening, it is attributable to natural causes, not human activities," and another 13% of Americans are characterized as "dismissive" with respect to climate change, meaning that they are "certain that global warming is not happening and are likely to

---

1. Yale Project on Climate Change Communication, Climate Change in the American Mind 5 (March 2015) (reporting the results of national surveys).

"regard the issue as a hoax" and to be "strongly opposed to action to reduce the threat."[2] Moreover, public debate reflects sustained controversy about the form, content, and propriety of climate speech. Energy companies are alleged to have hired public relations firms to manufacture public uncertainty about climate science in a manner akin to efforts to spread disinformation about the health effects of smoking.[3] Presidential administrations of both stripes have been accused of silencing agency scientists with contrary climate views.[4] State government workers have purportedly been instructed not to even use the terms "climate change" or "global warming."[5] That efforts to prepare society to adapt to climate change are being developed amidst this rancorous, polarized scrum explains the intuitive appeal of climate change agnosticism as a means to protect adaptation policy.

Agnostic adaptation means adaptation without the "why"—the divorce of adaptation from knowledge or acceptance of anthropogenic climate change. Adaptation is agnostic when one prepares for or responds to an actual or projected climate change-induced impact (e.g., a farmer plants a drought-resistant crop) without acknowledging that the adaptation is probabilistically or in fact necessary because of anthropogenic climate change (i.e., that drought conditions are caused or exacerbated by humans' emissions of carbon dioxide and other greenhouse gases).

At the individual level, agnostic adaptation is natural and ubiquitous. When it is uncomfortably hot, people turn on air conditioners, flee to the beach, and visit local park sprinklers just as they gradually and logically update the stock of boots, umbrellas and coats in their closets to match the weather they have become accustomed to experiencing—most often with nary a thought of climate change. Considering how adaptation policy should approach agnostic adaptation is, however, more difficult. Should our domestic adaptation policy connect adaptation to anthropogenic climate change? Should it tolerate, or even facilitate, agnostic adaptation?

---

2.   Connie Roser-Renouf et al., *Global Warming's Six Americas in October 2014: Perceptions of the Health Consequences of Global Warming and Update on Key Beliefs* 7-8 (October 2014), *available at* http://climatechangecommunication.org/sites/default/files/reports/Six-Americas-October-2014%5B1%5D.pdf.

3.   Union of Concerned Scientists, Smoke, Mirrors & Hot Air: How ExxonMobil Uses Big Tobacco's Tactics to "Manufacture Uncertainty" on Climate Change (Feb. 2007); Complaint, Native Village of Kivalina et al. v. ExxonMobil Corp. et al., No. 08-1138 (N.D. Cal. Feb. 26, 2008) (alleging civil conspiracy related to climate disinformation campaign).

4.   *E.g.*, Andrew C. Revkin, *Bush Aide Edited Climate Reports*, N.Y. Times A15, June 8, 2005, http://query.nytimes.com/gst/fullpage.html?res=9E0DE1D71338F93BA35755C0A9639C8B63&pagewanted=all; Kimberly A. Strassel, *The EPA Silences a Climate Skeptic*, Wall St. J., July 3, 2009, http://www.wsj.com/articles/SB124657655235589119.

5.   Tristram Korten, *In Florida, Officials Ban Term "Climate Change,"* Miami Herald, Mar. 8, 2015, http://www.miamiherald.com/news/state/florida/article12983720.html.

Numerous government policies or programs are purposefully oriented toward preparing for or adjusting to climate change impacts. For example, executive orders direct federal agencies to promote adaptation in various ways, including by preparing Agency Adaptation Plans.[6] The U.S. Department of Agriculture (USDA) Farm Service Agency Climate Change Adaptation Strategy includes the following:

> Action 2: FSA will partner with the REE mission area, as well as NGOs, to publicize and/or make available decision support tools at field offices, facilitating their outreach. An example of such a tool to encourage use of seasonal climate information in farm management decisions is Agroclimate, a project of the Southeast Climate Consortium (Agroclimate 2011).[7]

The Agroclimate website provides detailed information to help farmers better manage climate risks, including those associated with climate change, and features climate risk analyses, drought indices, and a cooling/heating degree days calculator.[8] Although there are a few references to climate change on the website, it is a fair characterization that the website downplays the connection between anthropogenic causes, climate change, and the adaptation measures that it advances.[9] The website's description of the causes for changes in temperature illustrates its careful treatment of anthropogenic climate change and climate science:

---

6. Exec. Order No. 13514, 74 Fed. Reg. 52117 (Oct. 8, 2009). Agencies are also instructed to direct federal funding to support climate resilience and to design and implement "land- and water-related policies, programs, and regulations . . . to make the Nation's watersheds, natural resources, and ecosystems, and the communities and economies that depend on them, more resilient in the face of a changing climate." Exec. Order No. 13653, 78 Fed. Reg. 66819 (Nov. 6, 2013).

7. USDA FARM SERVICE AGENCY CLIMATE CHANGE ADAPTATION STRATEGY 39-40 (June 2012).

8. AgroClimate, Tools for Managing Climate Risk in Agriculture, http://agroclimate.org/fact-sheets-climate.php (lasted visited July 25, 2014). AgroClimate is a product of the Southeast Climate Consortium, a coalition of six universities funded in part by governmental agencies and programs with the mission "to use advances in climate sciences, including improved capabilities to forecast seasonal climate and long-term climate change, to provide scientifically sound information and decision support tools for agricultural ecosystems, forests and other terrestrial ecosystems, and coastal ecosystems of the Southeastern USA." Southeast Climate Consortium, Mission, http://www.seclimate.org/mission.php (last visited July 25, 2014).

9. A paper that can be downloaded from the site discusses rainfall intensity and includes one sentencing in a section titled "Climate Change Projections" that provides: "Warmer air can hold more water vapor, and if temperatures continue to rise, the projections of future climate suggest there will be continued increases in high-intensity rain events." DANIEL DOURTE & CLYDE FRAISSE, SOUTHEAST CLIMATE EXTENSION, RAINFALL INTENSITY CHANGES IN THE SOUTHEASTERN U.S. (2014), *available at* http://agroclimate.org/climate/Rain-intensity-changes-southeastern-US.pdf. A paper titled "Climate Trends in the Southeast: Temperature" includes a section, "Causes of Changes in Temperature," which is excerpted in text below. The site also offers a carbon footprint calculator tool indexed to different crops. AgroClimate, Carbon Footprint Calculator, http://agroclimate.org/tools/Carbon-Footprint/ (last visited June 4, 2015).

Some variations in average temperatures across regions are related to changes within the region itself, and others are caused by large-scale, global changes in the climate. Within an area, temperatures can vary naturally from year to year depending on the soil conditions and the rainfall and cloudiness that have occurred over the area. Wet years tend to be cooler than dry years since the precipitation and rain prevent the sun from heating the ground. Dry years also tend to be the hottest years since the sun's energy goes into heating the land and air. Over time, an area's average temperatures can change because of changes in land use. For example, cooling can occur as bare fields revert to forests, or warming can occur as pavement replaces grass when cities expand. Temperatures also change from one year to the next because of longer-term cycles in the global atmosphere, such as El Niño. . . . El Niño winters tend to be cooler and wetter than normal because of a strong stream of tropical air over Florida and southern Alabama and Georgia. Large volcanic eruptions, such as Tambora in 1815 and Krakatoa in 1883, can cause widespread cooling for several years after the eruption occurs. Solar activity also causes small changes in incoming energy over time. Temperature increases in the Southeast since the 1970s mirror increases in temperatures that have occurred across the US and the world as a whole. Most scientists believe that these increases in temperature are due to increases in greenhouse gases, which trap heat near the surface of the earth rather than releasing it back into space. These trends are likely to continue for the next century.[10]

The Agroclimate website, then, appears to provide an example of how adaptation policy may tolerate, if not deploy, agnostic adaptation in some contexts.

The example chosen here, involving the communication of adaptation strategies to farmers in the southeastern United States, provides a good illustration of the most obvious rationale for incorporating agnostic adaptation into adaptation policy. Many in the United States reject anthropogenic climate change,[11] and levels of belief in and concern about climate change vary greatly by region and appear to be relatively low in the southeastern United States.[12] Perhaps agnostic adaptation outreach will make skeptical or simply unconcerned individuals more receptive to taking adaptive measures. Per-

---

10. SOUTHEAST CLIMATE EXTENSION, CLIMATE TRENDS IN THE SOUTHEAST: TEMPERATURE, *available at* http://agroclimate.org/climate/Temperature-Trends.pdf (last visited June 4, 2015).

11. Gallup Politics, *One in Four in U.S. Are Solidly Skeptical of Global Warming* (Apr. 22, 2014) (presenting the results of detailed polling of American regarding attitudes toward and beliefs about climate change), *available at* http://www.gallup.com/poll/168620/one-four-solidly-skeptical-global-warming. aspx (last visited July 27, 2014).

12. Kevin Dennehy, *Yale Study Maps U.S. Climate Opinion in Unprecedented Geographic Detail*, YaleNEWS (Apr. 6, 2015); *see also* Yale Project on Climate Change Communication, Yale Climate Opinion Maps, *available at* http://environment.yale.edu/poe/v2014/ (last visited June 4, 2015).

haps farmers in the southeast are more likely to use and trust an agricultural adaptation website that downplays anthropogenic climate change, thereby rendering the agnostic adaptation policy more effective. And perhaps, because the benefits of effective adaptation accrue locally and to individuals, there is ample incentive for individuals and communities to adapt regardless of their beliefs about why there is a need to adapt.

Perhaps, but agnostic adaptation policy also suggests some potential concerns. Excising anthropogenic climate change information from adaptation outreach, or simply downplaying the connection between the need to adapt and anthropogenic climate change, could undermine mitigation efforts by obscuring a potentially powerful rationale for mitigation policy—the fact that climate change will threaten the individuals who are the subject of adaptation outreach. Ultimately, mitigation is a necessary part of successful adaptation because our capacity to adapt could be overwhelmed.[13]

The question thus becomes whether agnostic adaptation policy is better at promoting adaptation in the long run. This analysis would require weighing any short-term benefit from more effectively spurring adaptive behaviors in skeptical communities against any longer term influence on the pace and scale of mitigation.

Additionally, as a practical matter, agnostic adaptation outreach may make it more difficult to structure adaptation policy to promote mitigation co-benefits (decrease emissions) and avoid adverse mitigation side-effects (increased emissions).[14] Moreover, agnostic adaptation policy is also somewhat unpalatable from the perspective of international climate justice. Some of the most compelling normative claims for the United States to contribute to international adaptation and mitigation efforts rest upon recognition of anthropogenic climate change and the United States' historic and present contribution of greenhouse gas emissions. Agnostic adaptation may enhance our already superior domestic adaptation capacity in a manner that handicaps the development of public and political support for international adaptation assistance.

---

13. Gary W. Yohe et al., *Global Distributions of Vulnerability to Climate Change*, 6 INTEGRATED ASSESSMENT J. 35, 36, 43 (2006) (emphasizing that "[e]xtreme climate change overwhelms the abilities of all countries to adapt" and that "[w]ith high climate sensitivity, by 2100 much of the world may need not only high adaptive capacity but also significant emissions mitigation to have been implemented in order to avoid high levels of vulnerability").

14. It is hard to promote or discourage an adaptive measure in part because it reduces or produces emissions without first acknowledging that emissions contribute to climate change. For a discussion of the need for and benefits of holistic climate change governance considering both mitigation and adaptation, see Katherine Trisolini, *Holistic Climate Change Governance: Towards Mitigation and Adaptation Synthesis*, 85 U. COLO. L. REV. 615 (2014).

As adaptation policy takes shape in the United States, it would seem that a critical examination of agnostic adaptation is in order. Ultimately, evaluating agnostic adaptation policy requires the resolution of a series of empirical questions: Will adaptation outreach be more effective at achieving on-the-ground adaptation in some areas and contexts if it does not attribute the need for adaptation to climate change and/or attribute climate change to human causes? What effect does coupling (or uncoupling) adaptation outreach with (or from) information about anthropogenic climate change have on attitudes toward climate science, mitigation policy and international adaptation assistance?

In chief, these questions are better suited to resolution by the social, psychological, and communication sciences[15]; that they are resolved and appropriately reflected in adaptation policy, however, presents a legal and policy task. While there are no clear and ready answers to basic questions about the efficacy and advisability of agnostic adaptation, some existing research that bears on these questions is reviewed below. Although preliminary, on the whole existing evidence suggests that adaptation provides a promising context for structuring conversations about climate change that avoid ideologically triggered polarization. This suggestion, in turn, raises the question whether agnostic adaptation approaches that obscure connections between anthropogenic climate change and adaptation are necessary and perhaps even counterproductive to the extent that they miss an opportunity for climate learning.

I.   Can We Expect Agnostic Adaptation Strategies to Enhance Adaptation in Climate-Skeptic Communities?

Common experience suggests, and psychological and social science evidence confirms, that climate science and climate policy often engender strong cultural or ideological reactions that are often polarizing and render healthy debate difficult.[16] Agnostic adaptation seeks to avoid the "Greenhouse

---

15. The website Climate Access compiles research into climate change communication, including with respect to adaptation outreach. Climate Access, Resource Hub, http://www.climateaccess.org/resource-hub.

16. *E.g.*, Dan M. Kahan & Donald Braman, *Cultural Cognition and Public Policy*, 24 YALE L. & POL'Y REV. 149, 165 (2006):

> By virtue of the power that cultural cognition exerts over belief formation, public dispute can be expected to persist on questions like the deterrent effect of capital punishment, the danger posed by global warming, the utility or futility of gun control, and the like, even after the truth of the matter has been conclusively established.

Holy War"[17] by sidestepping subjects perceived to provoke these reactions. This includes downplaying or obscuring the fact that the climate modeling that motivates and guides most adaptation efforts incorporates projections grounded in anthropogenic climate change.

Notably, the agnosticism strategy is also employed in the context of mitigation. In the mitigation context, agnostic mitigation strategies divorce actions to reduce greenhouse gas emissions from climate mitigation, climate science, and/or anthropogenic climate change by encouraging reductions in energy use or emissions for reasons other than avoided climate change, such as energy independence or thrift.[18] Some agnostic mitigation efforts have had notable success. The Kansas Climate and Energy Project (CEP), for example, achieved up to a 5% reduction in energy use in some Kansas towns through an energy conservation campaign that purposefully did not reference climate change at all, instead focusing on thrift, economic development through green jobs, and the "creation care" obligation of Christians.[19] The group's website explains, "Although we believe global warming is the defining challenge of our generation, CEP consciously decided to sequester the climate conversation. We focused instead on finding common ground with people across the state."[20]

It is understandable why our experience with mitigation would seem to recommend agnostic adaptation. Indeed, some research suggests that merely associating a program with climate change (whether in the context of mitigation or adaptation) reduces support for the program among conservatives, "reinforc[ing] the conclusion that political ideology is one of the single most important factors in determining an individual's attitudes and beliefs concerning climate change . . . and is substantially larger than the impact of how the message was framed."[21] However, there are important distinctions

---

17. Robert R.M. Verchick, *Culture, Cognition, and Climate*, 2016 U. Ill. L. Rev. ___, 41 (forthcoming 2016).

18. Roger A. Pielke Jr., *The Case for a Sustainable Climate Policy: Why Costs and Benefits Must Be Temporally Balanced*, 155 U. Pa. L. Rev. 1843, 1850 (2007):
    Ultimately, motivating local action to mitigate global climate change calls for an indirect strategy, focused on the ways in which emissions-producing activities are embedded in broader community concerns. The primary benefit of an indirect approach is that it avoids many of the political debates about climate change science that have plagued international efforts to address this issue.

19. Leslie Kaufman, *In Kansas, Climate Skeptics Embrace Cleaner Energy*, N.Y. Times A1 (Oct. 18, 2010), http://www.nytimes.com/2010/10/19/science/earth/19fossil.html.

20. The Climate and Energy Project, *Our Story*, http://www.climateandenergy.org/page.7.our-story (last visited June 4, 2015).

21. Amanda R. Carrico et al., *Does Learning About Climate Change Adaptation Change Support for Mitigation?*, 41 J. Envtl. Psychol. 19, 24 (2015) (reporting the results of an empirical study in which conservatives were significantly more supportive of a financial assistance program to farmers when it was not associated with climate change).

between the mitigation and adaptation contexts, and agnosticism may be neither needed nor advisable in the context of adaptation. Emerging research indicates that: (1) it may be possible to "disentangle" adaptation from polarizing climate issues without ignoring climate science or anthropogenic climate change; and (2) adaptation may be a context particularly suitable for such disentangling to occur.[22]

The disentanglement principle has been proposed as a communication strategy for overcoming division and polarization regarding scientific evidence. This strategy proposes that "the entanglement of opposing factual beliefs with people's identities as members of one or another cultural group" has led to polarization with respect to science in various contexts; one proposed solution is to "*disentangle* knowledge and identity when communicating" about that science.[23] The disentanglement strategy builds on cultural cognition research that suggests that individuals tend to reject scientific conclusions and related empirical claims when those conclusions and claims appear to compel a policy response that the individual finds unpalatable as a result of the individual's cultural worldview. (Notably, cultural worldview is more predictive of views on a number of controversial issues, including climate change, than any other factor, including ideology.[24]) For example, those with individualist and hierarchical worldviews tend to be opposed to policy solutions often closely associated with the response to climate change (such as increased controls on emitters) while those with communitarian and egalitarian worldviews tend to support the same, thus leading to polarization between the groups with respect to the underlying climate science.[25] However, priming subjects with information about a mitigation policy that does not trigger cultural group identity because it is more palatable to individualists and hierarchs (for example, geoengineering or investment in nuclear energy instead of carbon-emission limits) leads to less polarization regarding the underlying climate science.[26]

The disentanglement principle is consistent with the intuition underlying agnostic adaptation—i.e., that it is helpful to avoid topics that invoke cul-

22. Dan M. Kahan, *What Is the "Science of Science Communication"?*, J. Sci. Comm., Issue 3 2015, at 9-10, *available at* http://jcom.sissa.it/sites/default/files/documents/JCOM_1403_2015_Y04.pdf.

23. *Id.* at 8.

24. Kahan & Braman, *supra* note 16, at 158 ("Indeed, cultural worldviews predicted individual beliefs about the seriousness of these risks more powerfully than any other factor, including gender, race, income, education, and political ideology.").

25. *Id.* at 169 ("Shown a solution that affirms their identities, individualists and hierarchists, as in the case of tradeable emission permits, can be expected to display less resistance—not just politically, but cognitively—to the proposition that global warming is a problem after all."); Kahan, *supra* note 22, at 8.

26. Kahan & Braman, *supra* note 16, at 170-71.

tural group identity and lead to polarization, particularly in the climate context. Broadly speaking, agnostic adaptation could be viewed as a means of disentangling adaptation from discussions of mitigation policy and climate science that often invoke cultural group identity. So, for example, the Agroclimate website's apparent downplaying of climate change may be understood as a pragmatic effort to avoid alienating those within the agricultural community whose individualist and hierarchical worldviews might cause them to distrust or reject climate-associated policies. However, the application of the disentanglement principle in the context of climate adaptation is likely more nuanced. Proponents of the disentanglement principle cite to the Southeast Florida Regional Climate Compact, which identified numerous mitigation and adaptation measures, as an example where a highly participatory, locally salient "*process* disentangled the question of 'what should we do with what we know,' a question that unifies Southeast Floridians, from 'whose side are you on,' the divisive question that shapes the national climate science debate."[27] That disentanglement appears to have occurred in the context of the Southeast Florida Regional Climate Compact suggests that care in framing the way that climate science, adaptation policy, and mitigation policies are presented and discussed can achieve disentanglement; it may not be necessary to ignore or downplay climate science in the manner of agnostic adaptation to avoid polarization.

Moreover, not only may disentanglement without agnosticism be possible, but adaptation may provide a particularly good context for getting past climate polarization and engaging in productive discussion and action that acknowledge anthropogenic climate change. In other words, adaptation may provide a platform for discussing climate science in a manner less likely to become entangled with ideology and world view because "adaptation is more congenial to a wider range of citizen values" since "most adaptation efforts are more local, tangible, and accessible."[28] For example, a largely climate-skeptic community might be comfortable talking about climate-driven projections of future flooding in the context of identifying local actions to avoid tangible, flood-related harms to local interests in a process that is accessible

---

27.   Kahan, *supra* note 22, at 10.
28.   Verchick, *Culture, Cognition and Climate, supra* note 17, at 36. *See also* Michael B. Gerrard, *Introduction and Overview, in* The Law of Adaptation to Climate Change 11 (Gerrard & Kuh eds.) (2012): There is a sense in which adaptation actions are easier to justify . . . . [T]he benefits of mitigation tend to be remote in time and space. . . . But many adaptation measure have short-term, specific, local benefits in terms of protecting against already occurring climate-related events and natural weather variability. While certain mitigation actions may impede economic development, many adaptation actions promote development by upgrading infrastructure, buildings, or agricultural equipment.

because it builds on preexisting flood control efforts and includes local planners and stakeholders.

For similar reasons, adaptation policy may not trigger "solution aversion"
to the same extent as mitigation policy. The solution aversion model posits
that common climate mitigation policies (such as pollution taxes and emission restrictions) contradict the ideology of some individuals (for example
proponents of free markets), thereby causing those individuals to be skeptical
of the underlying climate science.[29] Adaptation policies on the whole, particularly when embedded in preexisting local structures and programs, do not
appear to trigger the same ideological distaste and thus may not be as likely
to spur solution aversion.[30] For example, one individual involved in an EPA
pilot project, convened on behalf of the president's Adaptation Task Force to
bring together stakeholders to consider incorporating climate resilience into
traditional disaster recovery in Iowa, offered the following observations:

> During the Iowa pilot project meetings, participants noted that while politi-
> cians and residents were reluctant to talk about climate change in the con-
> text of pollution control, sometimes questioning the underlying science, these
> same people were often willing to learn about climate change and future
> scenarios within the context of hazard mitigation and disaster planning. . . .
> Perhaps not everyone was convinced that anthropogenic climate change was
> beyond argument, but no one dismissed the idea of anticipating larger and
> larger floods.[31]

The evidence, both empirical and anecdotal, described above suggests that
agnostic adaptation may not be necessary for effective adaptation outreach
even in climate-skeptical communities. For a variety of reasons, adaptation
policy is on the whole inherently more attractive and less ideologically or
culturally polarizing than mitigation policy. That agnostic adaptation may
not be *necessary* to effectively implement adaptation policy in climate-skeptic
communities leads to a related and potentially more important question,

---

29.   Troy H. Campbell & Aaron C. Katy, *Solution Aversion: On the Relation Between Ideology and Motivated
      Disbelief*, 107 J. Personality & Soc. Psychol. 809, 811 (2014):
           The solution aversion model . . . predicts that people will be skeptical of scientific evidence
           supporting the existence of a problem, to the degree that the existence of the problem di-
           rectly implies solutions that threaten a person's cherished beliefs and ideological motives. . . .
           When located in the context of climate change and debates over the science surrounding it,
           this framework predicts that the denial of scientific evidence will vary across people, specifi-
           cally along ideological lines, to the extent the proposed solution to the scientific problem is
           discordant with ideological positions.
30.   *See generally* Bo MacInnis et al., *The American Public's Preference for Preparation for the Possible Effects of
      Global Warming: Impact of Communication Strategies*, 128 Climatic Change 17, 24 (2015) (finding
      that 74% of Americans express a preference for preparing for climate change, although support for
      preparation is higher among Democrats than Republicans).
31.   Verchick, *supra* note 17, at 40-41.

namely whether engaging in agnostic adaptation on those communities might give rise to a missed opportunity. Can adaptation serve as a "gateway to climate learning"[32] and, if so, do we forego that gateway opportunity by engaging in agnostic adaptation?

II. How, if at All, do Adaptation Policies (Agnostic or Otherwise) Influence Understanding of or Attitudes About Climate Science and Climate Mitigation?

Very little research has been done that directly addresses how, if at all, adaptation policies (agnostic or otherwise) influence understanding of or attitudes about climate science and climate mitigation. In a study published in 2015, researchers considered, inter alia, how information about an adaptation strategy (in this case, one that acknowledged anthropogenic climate change) influenced subjects' attitudes toward climate change and climate mitigation.[33] Subjects were given one of three articles. Each article described a financial assistance program to help farmers purchase a new technology for increasing the efficiency of water use in farming practices. The technology was presented respectively as part of a farm technology assistance program, a global warming mitigation program, or a global warming adaptation program. Subjects were then questioned on a number of topics, including their support for the financial assistance program, perceived risk from global warming, and the relative political priority of global warming. A few results are of particular present interest. As already discussed above, conservatives were less likely to support the financial assistance program when it was associated with climate change (either mitigation or adaptation).[34] However, "moderates who received the adaptation article rated climate change as a significantly higher political priority than those who received the purse control . . . and mitigation control articles" and "were significantly more supportive of the plan in the adaptation condition than in the mitigation control condition."[35]

The study's authors concluded that the study provided partial support for the risk salience hypothesis, or the prediction that "learning about adaptation information may make climate change impacts more salient and thus increase concern about climate change and support for preventive measures."[36] Moreover, while the study results could be viewed as supporting agnostic adapta-

---

32. *Id.* at 35.
33. Carrico et al., *supra* note 21, at 19-29.
34. *Id.* at 24.
35. *Id.*
36. *Id.* at 20.

tion because conservatives disfavored the financial assistance program when it was associated with climate change, suggesting that conservatives might be less inclined to engage in adaptation expressly connected to climate change, the adaptation frame used in the study articles was rather simple. The discussion above illustrates how adaptation provides an opportunity for engaging citizens in adaptation processes that defuse some of this ideological response, "[a]nd if we find that appeals to adaptation soften the skepticism of climate deniers, we may make wider inroads for climate change mitigation as well."[37]

Further research to understand the implications of how we connect adaptation policy to climate change (or not) is clearly needed.[38] It may be, for example, that even adaptation outreach that is on its face agnostic, in that it declines to acknowledge or downplays climate change, may nonetheless build understanding and acceptance of climate science in skeptical participants because that science is so deeply and inextricably embedded in the climate modeling that underlies adaptation policy. However, taken together, existing research suggests that there may indeed be a risk that by divorcing anthropogenic climate change from adaptation policy, agnostic adaptation could forego an opportunity to build public concern about climate change.

III.   Conclusion

We come to climate adaptation chastened by the ideological impasse over climate science in the context of climate mitigation. One common sense response that seems to be finding at least some traction is to attempt to dodge polarization when presenting adaptation policy to climate-skeptical audiences by minimizing or avoiding the connection between adaptation and anthropogenic climate change. Tailoring climate messages to communities is arguably consistent with the observation and exhortation of the Intergovernmental Panel on Climate Change that "[a]daptation planning and implementation at all levels of governance are contingent on societal values, objectives, and risk," "[r]ecognition of diverse interests, circumstances, social-cultural contexts, and expectations can benefit decision-making processes," and "[d]ecision support is most effective when it is sensitive to context and the diversity of decision types, decision processes, and constituencies."[39]

---

37.   Verchick, *supra* note 17, at 36.
38.   I am not aware of any studies of the potential effect of agnostic adaptation on attitudes about climate science and mitigation (standing alone or compared to adaptation efforts that acknowledge climate change).
39.   INTERGOVERNMENTAL PANEL ON CLIMATE CHANGE, CLIMATE CHANGE 2014: IMPACTS, ADAPTATION, AND VULNERABILITY 26 (2014).

We should, however, approach agnostic adaptation with caution. We do not have persuasive evidence that agnostic adaptation will be more effective at achieving on the-ground-adaptation even in climate-skeptic communities and some research suggests that the polarization that agnostic adaptation seeks to avoid may be less of a problem in the adaptation context, particularly when adaptation processes are thoughtfully structured to disentangle ideology and science. Additionally, beyond achieving on-the-ground adaptation, adaptation outreach may have the potential to improve understanding and acceptance of climate science and increase recognition of the need for mitigation. Agnostic adaptation could prevent the realization of these important co-benefits.

Chapter 9
Responding to Climate-Related Harms: A Role for the Courts?
Shannon Roesler

Some unique and threatened systems, including ecosystems and cultures, are already at risk from climate change (*high confidence*).

Climate-change-related risks from extreme events, such as heat waves, extreme precipitation, and coastal flooding, are already moderate (*high confidence*).

Risks are unevenly distributed and are generally greater for disadvantaged people and communities in countries at all levels of development.[1]

These quotations come from three of the five "reasons for concern" identified by the Intergovernmental Panel on Climate Change (IPCC) as "starting point[s] for evaluating dangerous anthropogenic interference with the climate system."[2] In a report that understandably focuses much attention on the heightened probability and magnitude of harm associated with further warming in the future, the risks identified in the first two quotations stand out because they *already* exist. Some communities, including coastal villages in the Arctic and small island states, are *already* facing threats to their very existence. In addition, the risks associated with extreme weather events are widespread and *already* here. When these risks are considered alongside the reality that they are "unevenly distributed" and "generally greater for disadvantaged people," they present policy questions not only about long-term adaptation planning, but also about immediate disaster response and aid.

As poor and developing nations participated in international climate negotiations this past December, they were keenly aware of the costly burdens of adaptation and response to climate-related harms. Reports from the recent climate talks suggest that the "rift" between rich and poor countries over climate financing threatened to derail the negotiations toward a cli-

---

1. INTERGOVERNMENTAL PANEL ON CLIMATE CHANGE, CLIMATE CHANGE 2014: IMPACTS, ADAPTATION AND VULNERABILITY 12 (2014), *available at* https://www.ipcc.ch/report/ar5/wg2/ [hereinafter 2014 IPCC ADAPTATION REPORT].
2. *Id.*

mate treaty.[3] Developed countries had pledged $100 billion a year to compensate less-developed countries for climate-related loss and damage and to fund adaptation measures.[4] Fundraising efforts have raised billions, but have fallen far short of the $100 billion goal.[5] Although the final climate agreement recognizes the pressing need to address climate-related loss and damage, it does not contain specific binding commitments by developed nations toward this end.[6]

Without an international compensation scheme, vulnerable communities are largely left to seek remedies through domestic political processes and courts. This chapter investigates the role of U.S., and in particular federal, courts in mitigating and redressing climate harms. To date, plaintiffs seeking damages from private defendants, such as oil companies, utilities, and automobile manufacturers, have not had an opportunity to litigate the merits of their cases. Courts routinely dismiss these suits on threshold issues, finding that common law actions are displaced by statutory law or are nonjusticiable under the U.S. Constitution. Suits seeking to force governmental action that would mitigate climate harms have suffered similar fates. The recurring theme in these cases is that actual litigation of these issues would threaten the constitutional separation of powers among the executive, legislative, and judicial branches. In other words, in a democratic society, resolution of these questions should be left to political processes, rather than the courts.

This chapter seeks to interrogate the assumptions behind this separation-of-powers narrative. Using the example of Alaska Native communities in the Arctic, the first section provides a brief overview of the present and imminent climate harms that these communities face. This is followed by a discussion of the courts' general reluctance to hear cases in which plaintiffs seek to redress or mitigate these harms. The final section asks what we can learn about the role of courts in a democratic society by looking at the separation-of-powers narrative through the lens of two interdisciplinary approaches to law and society: legal geography and socio-legal studies. In overlapping and different ways, these two "lenses" undermine the premise that climate change litigation threatens the constitutional separation of powers that underpins the

---

3.   Dean Scott, *"Lack of Trust" on Climate Aid Still Divides Wealthier, Poorer Nations Ahead of Talks*, 46 ENV'T REP. (BNA) 2002 (July 3, 2015); *see also* Eric J. Lyman, *UN Climate Negotiation Leaders Trim Paris Document*, 46 ENV'T REP. (BNA) 2258 (July 31, 2015) (noting that "little progress" has been made on issues, such as loss and damage and adaptation financing, which are of critical importance to developing nations).

4.   Scott, *supra* note 3.

5.   *Id.*

6.   United Nations Framework Convention on Climate Change, Conference of the Parties, Paris Agreement, art. 8, *in* Decision 1/CP.21 (Adoption of the Paris Agreement) (2015), U.N. Doc. FCCC/CP/2015/L.9/Rev.1, *available at* https://unfccc.int/resource/docs/2015/cop21/eng/l09r01.pdf.

democratic rule of law. In the end, opening the courthouse doors to this type of litigation may actually further fundamentally democratic ends.

I.　Imminent Threats and Mounting Costs in the Arctic

In cases where communities are under serious threat from coastal erosion and sea-ice melt, the threat is imminent and the costs are steep. For example, in 2003, the U.S. Government Accountability Office (GAO) reported that coastal erosion and flooding had affected 184 of 213 Alaska Native communities.[7] In 2009, the GAO reported that 31 Native villages face "imminent threats" and that 12 of the 31 villages had decided to relocate or consider partial or complete relocation.[8] Given the rapid rate of warming in the Arctic, the number of villages facing an imminent threat is likely higher today than it was in 2009.

These threats result in real and quantifiable *current* costs. In 2006, the U.S. Army Corps of Engineers (the Corps) estimated the costs of relocating the Alaska Native Village of Newtok at $80 to $130 million.[9] Estimates of the costs to relocate other villages are either comparable or much higher. For example, it could cost as much as $400 million to move the inhabitants of the Village of Kivalina.[10] Even though Alaska Native communities are generally small (ranging from a couple to several hundred people), they are located in remote areas often accessible year-round only by airplane, a reality that makes relocation extremely expensive. The costs will only grow as flooding and coastal erosion pose increasing threats to homes, infrastructure, and the way of life in more of these communities.

Funding to relocate these villages must come from somewhere other than the local communities. Most Alaska Native villages are self-sustaining communities closely tied to the sea and river ecosystems where they hunt and fish for food. Federal funding is essential, but villages often fail to qualify for the disaster-mitigation programs that the Federal Emergency Management Agency (FEMA) administers. A village may lack a FEMA-approved disaster-mitigation plan, which is a prerequisite for mitigation funding, and even if such a plan is in place, it does not guarantee funding.[11] FEMA makes funding decisions based on the cost-effectiveness of a project, and the high

---

7.　See U.S. Gov't Accountability Office (GAO), Alaska Native Villages: Limited Progress Has Been Made on Relocating Villages Threatened by Flooding and Erosion 12 (GAO-09-551) (2009).

8.　*Id.* at 12.

9.　See *id.* at 29.

10.　See Native Village of Kivalina v. Exxonmobil Corp., 663 F. Supp. 2d 863, 869 (N.D. Cal. 2009).

11.　See U.S. GAO, *supra* note 7, at 22.

costs of new infrastructure (in comparison to the small numbers of people relocated) make relocation projects costly.[12] In addition, the nature of the risk (in this case, gradual coastal erosion) may frustrate attempts to obtain a federal disaster declaration, and serious obstacles prevent many villages from participating in the National Flood Insurance Program.[13]

In addition to the difficulty in qualifying for federal disaster funding, these villages also face serious challenges in the planning and decisionmaking phases of relocation. Decisions regarding relocation depend on the coordination of efforts by local, state, and federal authorities. The impacts of gradual coastal erosion and flooding are not governed by one federal or state agency.[14] Federal funding may be administered by multiple agencies, including the Corps, FEMA, and the Department of Housing and Urban Development. Without clear structures for information sharing and coordination, decisionmaking is inefficient at best. Indeed, the authors of the IPCC report on climate impacts note that "limited integration or coordination of governance" can hinder adaptation efforts.[15]

II.   Climate Change Litigation and the Constitutional Separation of Powers

Given the considerable difficulties in obtaining governmental assistance, it is not surprising that one Alaska Native village turned to the courts for relief. In 2008, the Village of Kivalina sued oil, energy, and utility companies in federal district court, alleging that the defendants' greenhouse gas emissions have caused global warming, which is, in turn, causing massive coastal erosion and increasing the risks of extreme weather and flooding.[16] On appeal, the U.S. Court of Appeals for the Ninth Circuit affirmed the district court's dismissal, concluding that under U.S. Supreme Court precedent, the Clean Air Act displaces claims for damages pursuant to the federal common law of public nuisance.[17] The majority concluded its opinion by acknowledging the seriousness of the problem, but characterizing it as one not amenable to judicial action: "Our conclusion obviously does not aid Kivalina, which itself is being displaced by the rising sea. But the solution to Kivalina's dire circumstance must rest in the hands of the legislative and executive branches

---

12.   *See id.* at 22-23.
13.   *See id.* at 23-24.
14.   *See id.* at 36.
15.   2014 IPCC ADAPTATION REPORT, *supra* note 1, at 26.
16.   *Native Village of Kivalina*, 663 F. Supp. 2d 863.
17.   Native Village of Kivalina v. Exxonmobil Corp., 696 F.3d 849, 858 (9th Cir. 2011).

of government, not the federal common law."[18] In other words, if the court were to allow the Village of Kivalina's suit to proceed to the merits, it would transgress the constitutional limits placed on the judiciary.

The concurring judge's conclusion that the Village of Kivalina lacked standing to bring suit under Article III of the Constitution is also grounded in separation-of-powers concerns. Indeed, as a jurisdictional doctrine intended to ensure the existence of an Article III "case or controversy," standing doctrine is often described as a means of securing "the proper—and properly limited—role of the courts in a democratic society."[19] Since the latter half of the twentieth century, the Supreme Court's standing doctrine has limited access to the federal courts unless a plaintiff can show a "personal injury fairly traceable to the defendant's allegedly unlawful conduct and likely to be redressed by the requested relief."[20] Courts routinely apply a three-part test, asking whether the plaintiff has alleged: (1) a concrete and particularized injury (an "injury-in-fact"), (2) a causal link between the injury and the defendant's conduct (the "fairly traceable" requirement), and (3) the likelihood that a favorable decision will redress the injury (the "redressability" requirement).[21]

The district court judge and concurring judge on appeal both concluded that the Village of Kivalina lacked Article III standing because it could not show a causal connection between its injury (its disappearing land) and the conduct of the oil, energy, and utility companies.[22] Neither judge questioned that the defendants had been and continued to be contributors to the warming of the planet through their emissions of greenhouse gases. Both opinions also do not question the causal link between global warming and the erosion of Arctic land caused by melting sea ice. The link, however, between the Village's injury and the conduct of these *specific* defendants appeared too remote in both time and space. Both judges emphasized that the Village of Kivalina's harm is a result of a long history of greenhouse gas emissions from numerous sources whose emissions cannot be differentiated from each other, making the link between the defendants' emissions and village's harm too attenuated to support standing.[23]

The causation requirement for standing has also posed problems for plaintiffs seeking to force governmental action to reduce greenhouse gas emissions.

---

18. *Id.*
19. Allen v. Wright, 468 U.S. 737, 750 (1984).
20. *Id.* at 751.
21. Lujan v. Defenders of Wildlife, 504 U.S. 555, 560-61 (1992).
22. *Native Village of Kivalina*, 696 F.3d at 868-69; *Native Village of Kivalina*, 663 F. Supp. 2d at 880-81.
23. *Native Village of Kivalina*, 696 F.3d at 868-69; *Native Village of Kivalina*, 663 F. Supp. 2d at 880-81.

Indeed, shortly after the Ninth Circuit dismissed *Native Village of Kivalina*, it dismissed a citizen suit by environmental organizations to compel Washington state agencies to set and enforce greenhouse gas emissions standards for five oil refineries.[24] In *Washington Environmental Council v. Bellon*, the environmental plaintiffs sought to enforce provisions in the state's Clean Air Act implementation plan that required the use of reasonably available control technology (RACT) by the oil refineries for all pollutants of concern, which, according to the plaintiffs, included greenhouse gases.[25] Although the district court had granted the plaintiffs the relief they sought, the Ninth Circuit panel vacated the lower court's decision, concluding that it lacked Article III jurisdiction.[26] Once again, the court found the causal connection between the plaintiffs' alleged injuries (which ranged from various aesthetic and recreational injuries to individual property damage and health-related injuries) and the defendants' conduct (here, the agencies' failure to set and enforce standards) too attenuated to establish standing.[27] In addition, because the defendants' contribution to global warming was relatively small and "scientifically indiscernible," even the most stringent of emissions standards could not slow the pace of warming and thereby redress the plaintiffs' climate-related harms.[28]

The Ninth Circuit's denial of a petition for rehearing en banc in *Bellon* prompted the dissent of three judges. Judge Ronald Gould's dissenting opinion is a defense of standing based largely on *Massachusetts v. EPA*, the landmark Supreme Court decision that opened the door to greenhouse gas regulation under the Clean Air Act.[29] According to Judge Gould, the Court's standing analysis in *Massachusetts* supports constitutional standing when plaintiffs seek governmental action—however tentative or small—that may redress incremental damage.[30] What is perhaps most striking about Judge Gould's dissent, however, is his charge that the majority's resolution of the case is detrimental to the public welfare because it "relegates judges—and the general public—to the sidelines as climate change progresses."[31] By removing

---

24. Wash. Envtl. Council v. Bellon, 732 F.3d 1131 (9th Cir. 2013).
25. *Id.* at 1140.
26. *Id.* at 1147.
27. *Id.* at 1145.
28. *Id.* at 1147.
29. In a five-four opinion, the Court held that Massachusetts had standing to challenge EPA's denial of a rulemaking petition requesting that EPA regulate greenhouse gas emissions from new motor vehicles. Massachusetts v. EPA, 549 U.S. 497, 526 (2007).
30. Wash. Envtl. Council v. Bellon, 741 F.3d 1075, 1180 (9th Cir. 2014) (Gould, J., dissenting from denial of petition for rehearing en banc).
31. *Id.* at 1081.

the threat of the citizen suit, he feared that state action to mitigate climate change "will be less forceful and less frequent."[32]

The dissenting judge's focus on public harm is striking because modern standing doctrine distinguishes between private (or individual) interests and public interests, giving courts jurisdiction over individual interests and leaving public interests to the political branches. In fact, the Supreme Court has given this distinction considerable weight, holding that even the U.S. Congress may not convert the "public interest in proper administration of laws" into an individual right cognizable in a federal court.[33] The concern is that citizen suits based only on the generalized interest in the rule of law encroach on the Executive's constitutional role in enforcing the law.[34] Standing doctrine therefore privileges *individual* rights or injuries, differentiated in some way from the generalized public interest.

This distinction is justified as a means of guarding against judicial overreach and preserving the separation of governmental powers essential to the democratic rule of law, namely, a conception of the rule of law that arises out of liberal democratic commitments to individual liberties and rights. Standing doctrine is justified as a means of safeguarding the separation of powers that protects these democratic values.

When standing doctrine stops climate change litigation at the courthouse doors, it should therefore further the democratic values that underlie the constitutional commitment to governmental separation of powers. A close analysis suggests that it does not. In fact, as the next section demonstrates, climate change litigation may be consistent with—and even further—the deeper commitments to democratic rule of law upon which these constitutional doctrines are premised.

III. Is Climate Change Litigation Contrary to Democratic Values?

A constitutional commitment to the separation of powers clearly contemplates the existence of an independent, but limited, judicial power. The precise contours of this power are, however, the subject of intense debate across various academic disciplines. Legal and political theorists essentially agree that the judicial power includes the interpretation of positive laws (from cases, statutes, and regulations) and of constitutional structures and rules that ensure democratic governance. Nevertheless, where interpretation of the

---

32. *Id.* at 1081 n.2.
33. Lujan v. Defenders of Wildlife, 504 U.S. 555, 576 (1992).
34. *Id.* at 577.

law ends and elaboration of substantive doctrine begins is highly contested. Although no one seriously contends that legal formalism—the notion that a judge simply declares what the law is and does not make law—is an accurate empirical account of judicial decisionmaking, the idea that judges should apply or "find" the law rather than make it continues to exert a powerful influence on legal doctrine and practice.[35]

This view of the judicial role is reinforced by the counter-majoritarian objection to judicial decisions that challenge politically popular decisions by the political branches.[36] This objection is perhaps well known in the human rights context. When a court strikes down a law or invalidates a political decision on the ground that it violates the rights of a political minority, an unelected, unrepresentative branch of government arguably frustrates the will of the "People" to govern themselves through the legislative process.[37]

Standing doctrine recognizes this tension and seeks to define the boundaries of judicial power in relation to the legislative and executive branches. When a court dismisses a climate change suit on standing grounds, the underlying assumption is that the exercise of judicial power would impinge on the democratic processes for making and enforcing laws. In the cases discussed above, the courts' message is clear. The Native Village of Kivalina should seek redress through the political process, not the courts. Environmental organizations should lobby Congress (or state agencies), not the courts, if they desire stricter emissions standards.

Upon closer examination, however, these conclusions do not appear quite so obvious. Interdisciplinary approaches within the fields of legal geography and socio-legal studies can uncover the assumptions behind these decisions and illuminate the different social and political forces that shape them. From a law-and-geography perspective, climate change litigation challenges legal and spatial categories that otherwise appear natural by highlighting how

---

35. For example, in defending the view that judicial decisions must be retroactive, Justice Antonin Scalia has drawn on the idea that judges "find" law, while at the same time acknowledging that judges "make" law:

> I am not so naive (nor do I think our forbears were) as to be unaware that judges in a real sense "make" law. But they make it *as judges make it*, which is to say *as though* they were "finding" it—discerning what the law *is*, rather than decreeing what it is today *changed to*, or what it will *tomorrow* be.

James B. Beam Distilling Co. v. Georgia, 501 U.S. 529, 549 (1991) (Scalia, J., concurring in the judgment).

36. Well-known developments of the counter-majoritarian objection include: ALEXANDER BICKEL, THE LEAST DANGEROUS BRANCH: THE SUPREME COURT AT THE BAR OF POLITICS (1962); ROBERT H. BORK, THE TEMPTING OF AMERICA: THE POLITICAL SEDUCTION OF THE LAW (1990); JOHN HART ELY, DEMOCRACY AND DISTRUST: A THEORY OF JUDICIAL REVIEW (1980).

37. Whether this is an "acceptable" use of judicial power rests, of course, on a given society's values and commitments.

they are constituted by and perpetuate power relations. Democratic values are arguably better served by allowing climate plaintiffs to proceed to the merits of their cases. Socio-legal theories of legal mobilization and social movements suggest that climate change litigation may not only further key democratic values, but also advance the objectives of the plaintiffs and the larger environmental movement with regard to climate change.

A.   Legal Geography: A Critical Assessment of Standing Doctrine

Scholarship at the intersection of law and geography frequently calls attention to the ways in which legal and spatial categories participate in social relationships. These accounts are therefore critical inquiries that understand law and space "as relational, acquiring meaning through social action, rather than objective categories that operate prior to social life"[38]; legal and spatial categories are products of power relations, which they in turn perpetuate by appearing "neutral" or natural. In addition, law and space often overlap in mutually reinforcing ways to produce particular "orderings" of the world.[39] For example, citizenship requires the spatial specification of the state, and property rights and concepts such as trespass and nuisance are tied to land defined by spatial boundaries and lines. Most salient for purposes of this chapter, legal doctrines of jurisdiction and separation of powers draw on spatial notions of institutional separation. Rather than viewing these institutional spaces as givens, legal geography seeks to uncover the social relations that underlie them so that they "will begin to appear less as objects in the world than as complicated effects."[40] From this perspective, we see the institutional spaces of the judiciary, the legislature, and the executive not as places or neutral categories, but as products of complex power relations.

Legal scholars who are skeptical of legal geography's critical perspective may nevertheless agree that it resonates with legal critiques of standing doctrine, which is notoriously incoherent and—many argue—susceptible to manipulation based on the ideological or political preferences of judges. A critical inquiry, however, looks not at individual preferences, but at social relations that shape and are shaped by legal language and categories. Critical accounts seek to "denaturalize" the categories of law and space that mask the

---

38.   Nicholas Blomley, *From "What?" to "So What?": Law and Geography in Retrospect, in* LAW AND GEOG-RAPHY 17, 22 (Jane Holder & Carolyn Harrison eds., 2002).
39.   *Id.* at 29.
40.   Irus Braverman et al., *Introduction, Expanding the Spaces of Law, in* THE EXPANDING SPACES OF LAW, A TIMELY LEGAL GEOGRAPHY 1, 18 (Irus Braverman et al. eds., 2014).

power relations that frequently work to marginalize those without material or social power.[41]

Legal scholars have long recognized the geographical nexus required by the injury-in-fact requirement for standing in the environmental context. In the well-known Supreme Court case, *Lujan v. Defenders of Wildlife*, spatial and temporal language reinforces the plaintiffs' lack of a "direct" injury in Justice Antonin Scalia's majority opinion. The plaintiffs challenged a federal regulation that excluded federally funded overseas projects from the consultation requirement under the Endangered Species Act (ESA).[42] Under §7 of the ESA, a federal agency must consult with the applicable federal wildlife agency before it engages in any action that may jeopardize a protected (i.e., listed) species or adversely modify protected species' habitat.[43] The plaintiffs argued that the regulatory removal of the consultation requirement for projects outside the United States was likely to jeopardize protected species of particular interest to them.[44] The Court held that the plaintiffs had failed to show an injury-in-fact; they had failed to show that they would soon travel to the places where these species lived. Language describing the plaintiffs' alleged injuries as "remote" and "distant" in time and space served to reinforce legal requirements of "imminence" and "concreteness."[45] In his dissent, Justice Harry A. Blackmun sought to unhinge legal injury from physical space by emphasizing how environmental injuries can cause harms across great distances.[46] Both opinions illustrate how law and space overlap to produce an understanding of "injury," which ultimately makes it easier to deny environmental plaintiffs access to the courts.

In climate change litigation, geographic ties are also important, but in slightly different ways. Plaintiffs allege injuries close to home—injuries to the land on which they live and the air that they breathe. Spatial categories of home, community, and property reinforce legal notions of direct and concrete injury. Spatial notions of remoteness and indirectness nevertheless appear in connection with legal concepts of causation and redressability. When

---

41. For example, Melinda Harm Benson has analyzed judicial gatekeeping rules, including standing, from a legal geographic perspective. Melinda Harm Benson, *Rules of Engagement, The Spatiality of Judicial Review* 215, *in* THE EXPANDING SPACES OF LAW, *supra* note 40. She argues that litigation is a "discursive" space and legal "rules of engagements" function as "barriers." *Id.* at 234. Moreover, "[t]he barriers themselves can be seen as discursive products of interpretation that can (and should) be contested. Access to the space of law (and therefore the law itself) is policed through the validation of rival narratives that underpin the applicability (or not) of exclusionary doctrines such as ripeness, standing, and final agency action." *Id.*
42. Lujan v. Defenders of Wildlife, 504 U.S. 555, 558-59 (1992).
43. 16 U.S.C. §1536(a) (2012).
44. *Defenders of Wildlife*, 504 U.S. at 563-64.
45. *Id.* at 567 n.3.
46. *Id.* at 594 (Blackmun, J., dissenting).

courts analyze the causal link between specific greenhouse gas emissions and these injuries, they look for a geographic and temporal nexus between the defendants' conduct and the plaintiffs' injuries. Similar spatial language—"remote," "attenuated," "indirect"—serves to reinforce the absence of legal categories of causation and redressability and perpetuate social relations that favor powerful interests at the expense of the most vulnerable.

These conclusions may be unsurprising to lawyers familiar with tort principles of factual and proximate causation, but standing doctrine is not designed to decide a case's merits.[47] Instead, it claims to be safeguarding the democratic separation of powers. The question we must therefore ask is whether climate change litigation threatens democratic values.

Even if we define democracy to mean majoritarian democracy (that is, a version of democracy that seeks primarily to further the popular will of the majority), climate change litigation does not threaten it. Allowing individuals to litigate their climate-related harms does not turn judges into lawmakers. Instead, by giving these plaintiffs an opportunity to argue their cases, courts can help mitigate the pathologies of representative democracy illuminated by public choice theory. The largest emitters in the energy and transportation sectors have the concentrated, well-funded interests that influence lawmaking, while Alaska Native villages and others injured by climate change lack the organizational and material resources to change public policies. To dismiss these cases as best left to the political process is empty rhetoric because the political process has failed them. Legal and spatial language regarding the separation of powers cloaks this reality by creating the appearance that all grievances will be heard in *some* space and at *some* time.

The social reality—that climate grievances are shut out of *all* governmental spaces—is at the heart of Judge Gould's frustration in *Bellon*. In denying climate plaintiffs access, courts do not simply dismiss *individual* complaints; they participate in social processes and relations that negatively affect the public welfare. Whether we think our democratic institutions should act as agents of the majority or whether we think they should independently deliberate toward the public good, our democratic visions incorporate some notion of the public welfare. When the judiciary allows individuals to expose the potential failings of the political process, it acts in the public interest and arguably serves democratic ends.

---

47. For an analysis of climate change litigation and tort law, see Douglas A. Kysar, *What Climate Change Can Do About Tort Law*, 41 ENVTL. L. 1 (2011). For an analysis that distinguishes standing's causation requirement from a merits determination of proximate causation, see Bradford C. Mank, *Standing for Private Parties in Global Warming Cases: Traceable Standing Causation Does Not Require Proximate Causation*, 2012 MICH. ST. L. REV. 869 (2012).

This potential dynamic is clouded by legal and spatial categories of the "individual" and the "public." As described above, standing doctrine privileges *individual* injuries, excluding suits by plaintiffs who seek to further *public* or collective interests. This individual-public dichotomy safeguards powerful interests in property and wealth, as well as negative personal liberties, while rendering other interests critical to human wellbeing invisible. For example, courts may characterize interests in environmental goods, such as clean air, as nonjusticiable public interests, while describing limitations on private activities that cause environmental harm as individual injuries properly within the courts' constitutional jurisdiction. This distinction masks the interconnectedness of individuals to each other and the natural world, a dynamic that ecology has long warned we should not ignore.

If these distinctions do not further desirable democratic ends, then courts should question whether they are proper components of the standing inquiry. An injury is no less of an injury simply because it is widely shared or "public." In both *Native Village of Kivalina* and *Bellon*, the plaintiffs could identify concrete, individualized injuries. Indeed, because these cases involve present (or imminent) climate injuries, they do not challenge standing's "injury-in-fact" requirement. Plaintiffs with climate-related harms do not seek to open the courthouse doors to suits based on a general public interest in the proper administration of laws, but instead seek specific remedies—damages or injunctions—for their individual injuries. Consequently, a decision on the merits would not challenge the view that Article III's case or controversy requirement bars courts from issuing opinions with only advisory or hypothetical effect.

The courts' application of the causation and redressability requirements in modern standing analysis similarly fails to serve the doctrine's underlying separation-of-powers purpose. In both *Native Village of Kivalina* and *Bellon*, the plaintiffs sued defendants with a causal connection to their harms, and in both cases the remedy the plaintiffs sought would address the harm in some way. The plaintiffs lacked standing because the courts found the connections to the defendants too "attenuated" and—in *Bellon*—the requested remedy too insignificant to affect the pace at which the planet is warming. In other words, the courts focused on the *extent* to which the defendants contributed to the harm and the *extent* to which the requested relief would mitigate the harm. Given the depth of analysis, these opinions look more like decisions on the merits than threshold determinations of constitutional jurisdiction.

Moreover, resolving questions of degree on the merits would not threaten the separation of powers. Indeed, the law regarding factual and proximate causation is primarily *judge*-made common law. Courts have a long history of adapting these tort doctrines to new challenges, including fault apportionment among multiple defendants and remedies for increased risk of harm. In mass tort litigation, for example, courts have created new ways of apportioning fault (e.g., market share liability)[48] and new remedies for addressing increased health risks (e.g., medical monitoring).[49]

This history of doctrinal adaptation does not mean, of course, that plaintiffs with climate-related harms will prevail on the merits. But it does suggest that difficult questions about the strength of causal connections and the efficacy of a given remedy are not jurisdictional questions. A decision on the merits is far from hypothetical or advisory, provided the plaintiffs can "fairly trace" their injuries to the type of conduct engaged in by the defendants and can identify a remedy that arguably addresses their present or imminent injuries in some way. Shifting these questions to the threshold determination of standing simply cannot be justified as a means of safeguarding the constitutional separation of powers.

B.   Legal Mobilization and Social Movement Theory: Productive Possibilities

The critical assessment provided by the perspective of legal geography reveals the undemocratic effects of the separation-of-powers rationale used to deny climate plaintiffs access to the courts, but it does not offer theories about whether and how climate change litigation might advance democratic ends. Even if we accept the critical account and think courts should not dismiss these cases on threshold issues such as standing, we might ask whether allowing plaintiffs to proceed to the merits matters in any meaningful way. Plaintiffs like the Village of Kivalina will have difficulty establishing the required legal elements of their tort claims, including the causal link between climate-related harms and the conduct (i.e., greenhouse gas emissions) of specific defendants. Moreover, challenges to state action (or inaction) like the one in *Bellon* will face a number of administrative law doctrines that favor state agencies' resolution of factual and legal questions.

Fortunately, accounts of legal mobilization and social movements within the socio-legal scholarship offer some insight into the productive possi-

---

48. *See, e.g.,* Sindell v. Abbott Laboratories, 607 P.2d 924, 937 (Cal. 1980) (holding that defendant manufacturers of the drug DES could be held liable in proportion to their respective shares of the market when the plaintiff could not identify the specific manufacturer of the DES that caused her injuries).
49. Ayers v. Township of Jackson, 525 A.2d 287 (N.J. 1987) (allowing plaintiffs with significant exposure to toxic chemicals to recover the costs of medical monitoring for the onset of disease).

bilities of climate change litigation in democratic societies. These accounts accept the idea that legal language and norms can perpetuate social relations and practices that disadvantage less-powerful groups, but they also seek to understand how social actors and movements use legal claims as mechanisms for social change in certain contexts. As Michael McCann explains, the objective of legal mobilization theory is "to analyze the constitutive role of legal rights claims as both a resource and a constraint for collective efforts to transform or 'reconstitute' power-laden relationships among social groups."[50] His work, for example, on the legal strategies of the pay-equity movement demonstrates how activists have used law to attract and galvanize movement participants and to gain leverage in negotiations with employers.[51] Legal mobilization theory therefore recognizes the potential for social change and may suggest ways in which climate change litigation may advance some of the plaintiffs' objectives.

By adopting a "decentered" view of how law operates in society, legal mobilization scholarship has called attention to the indirect, symbolic effects of judicial decisions.[52] For example, activists have used litigation to gain "leverage" with private and public actors and extract concessions that they would not otherwise obtain via political processes. Litigation is a well-known tactic for forcing informal settlements and resolution. The costs of protracted litigation are high, and powerful interests may fear the consequences of a judicial decision, including the loss of "decision-making autonomy . . . to outside parties such as judges."[53] In addition, litigation can often capture media attention and provide a means by which to communicate grievances to the larger political society, which can have a stigmatizing effect on powerful interests. These effects require a credible threat of judicial intervention, which means they are less likely to occur if litigants know that courts are likely to dismiss cases on jurisdictional grounds, such as standing. If courts were, however, to allow more climate litigation to proceed to the merits, climate plaintiffs would not necessarily need to win to be successful. In fact, "leveraging is most successful when it works as an unfulfilled [but credible] threat."[54]

When used along with other strategies for political change, litigation can also prompt policy reform by giving less-powerful interests a voice and added

---

50.   Michael W. McCann, *Legal Mobilization and Social Reform Movements: Notes on Theory and Its Application, in* LAW AND SOCIAL MOVEMENTS 3, 5 (Michael McCann ed., 2006).
51.   *Id.* at 4.
52.   Michael W. McCann, *How Does Law Matter for Social Movements?, in* HOW DOES LAW MATTER? 76, 80 (Bryant G. Garth & Austin Sarat eds., 1998).
53.   *Id.* at 91.
54.   *Id.*

influence in political debates.[55] Climate litigation can make climate-related harms more difficult for political actors to ignore, thereby helping to level the playing field and further the aims of representative democracy. As Judge Gould argued, legal challenges like the one in *Bellon* can prompt state and federal agencies to act when they otherwise would not. Furthermore, by providing a forum that furthers the political participation of underrepresented interests, climate litigation adds voices to the public conversation regarding climate change—a democratic benefit even if it does not lead to legislative reform and other policy changes.

In fact, even though the Village of Kivalina's lawsuit did not proceed to the merits, it may have helped draw attention to the present harms of climate change in the Arctic. The Village's story is often recounted in news articles and scholarly commentary, and in many cases, the focus is on governmental accountability, rather than private liability. For example, one news account quotes a Kivalina Council leader's description of the problem as one of political injustice: "'The U.S. government imposed this Western lifestyle on us, gave us their burdens and now they expect us to pick everything up and move it ourselves. What kind of government does that?'"[56] During his recent trip to Alaska, President Barack Obama became the first president to visit Arctic Alaska. On his way to the Native Village of Kotzebue, he flew over the island of Kivalina. In addressing his audience in Kotzebue, he recognized the U.S. government's obligation to the Village of Kivalina: "'If another country threatened to wipe out an American town, we'd do everything in our power to protect it. . . . Well, climate change poses the same threat right now.'"[57]

The president also promised additional governmental assistance, but the $2 million promised falls far short of what is needed.[58] A political solution to the imminent disaster facing Arctic communities will not materialize without broad-based support and mobilization. As the literature on social movements has documented, the success of a movement depends on social structures. Social conditions and changes that result in increased hardship can create "structural opportunities" for social mobilization, but mobilization also depends on resources in the form of leadership and ties to exist-

---

55. *Id.* at 93; *see also* CHRISTOPHER D. STONE, SHOULD TREES HAVE STANDING? LAW, MORALITY, AND THE ENVIRONMENT 74 (3d ed. 2010) (arguing that "GHG-related suits—and the publicity they generate—educate even when they lose").

56. Stephen Sackur, *The Alaskan Village Set to Disappear Under Water in a Decade*, BBC NEWS MAG., July 29, 2013, http://www.bbc.com/news/magazine-23346370.

57. Julie Hirschfield Davis, *Obama Takes Climate Message to Alaska, Where Change Is Rapid*, N.Y. TIMES, Sept. 2, 2015, *at* http://www.nytimes.com/2015/09/03/us/politics/obama-takes-climate-message-to-alaska-where-change-is-rapid-in-alaska.html?_r=0.

58. *Id.*

ing organizations and constituencies capable of mobilizing and engaging in varied social-change strategies. Often, the most vulnerable populations lack associational ties to the necessary networks and organizations.[59]

Though broad-based support is essential, litigation can help build it.[60] The symbolic power of a successful court challenge can mobilize supporters and reinvigorate a movement. This phenomenon appears to be playing out in response to the recent success of a challenge to Dutch climate policy brought by a nonprofit representing approximately 900 Dutch citizens.[61] This past summer, a district court in The Hague ruled that the Dutch government must reduce greenhouse gas emissions in the Netherlands by 25% from 1990 levels by 2020.[62] Drawing on IPCC reports, international law, and domestic law, the court concluded that the state has a duty of care to mitigate greenhouse gas emissions and that the state had breached its duty by committing to only a 17% reduction.[63] Reports suggest that the case will likely inspire similar litigation in other countries.[64] Moreover, the court's decision (the first of its kind) may give activists the credibility they need to use the threat of climate change litigation as leverage in their efforts to force political action and change climate policies.

IV.   Conclusion

Although litigation certainly cannot solve the complex problems presented by climate change, it may have a role to play, particularly in addressing the present harms to the most vulnerable populations on the planet. The photograph of the vanishing island of Kivalina taken from Air Force One on President Obama's recent trip to Alaska captures the truly imminent threat to the village's existence[65]; in approximately 10 years, the village's land will

---

59.   McCann, *supra* note 50, at 18-19.
60.   McCann, *supra* note 52, at 84.
61.   Joan Schwartz, *Ruling Says Netherlands Must Reduce Greenhouse Gas Emissions*, N.Y. Times, June 24, 2015, *at* http://www.nytimes.com/2015/06/25/science/ruling-says-netherlands-must-reduce-greenhouse-gas-emissions.html?_r=0.
62.   Urgenda Foundation v. Netherlands, No. C/09/456689/HA ZA 13-1396, ¶ 5.1 (The Hague D. Ct., June 24, 2015) (English translation), *available at* http://uitspraken.rechtspraak.nl/inziendocument?id=ECLI:NL:RBDHA:2015:7196.
63.   *Id.* ¶ 4.84.
64.   *See, e.g.*, Emma Howard, *Hague Climate Change Judgment Could Inspire a Global Civil Movement*, Guardian, June 24, 2015, *available at* http://www.theguardian.com/environment/2015/jun/24/hague-climate-change-judgement-could-inspire-a-global-civil-movement (noting support for a similar case in Belgium and possibly Norway and reporting that many environmental organizations are considering litigation according to one source).
65.   *See* Juliet Eilperin, *The Photo That Says More About Alaska Than All of Obama's Instagram Feed*, Wash. Post, Sept. 3, 2015, *at* http://www.washingtonpost.com/news/energy-environment/wp/2015/09/03/the-photo-that-says-more-about-alaska-than-all-of-obamas-instagram-feed/.

be gone.[66] The harm is actual and imminent, and it is the kind of harm that courts have long recognized as legally cognizable. Though tort doctrines may not perfectly resolve how to apportion causation and fault, courts should not deny injured plaintiffs an opportunity to make their best arguments. The democratic separation of powers does not require or justify judicial decisions that dismiss climate change litigation on standing grounds. Rather, these legal and spatial designations mask unequal distributions of power and serve to silence the voices of the most vulnerable. Allowing climate-related claims to at least be heard would strengthen, not undermine, the democratic rule of law.

---

66.   This is an estimate by the Corps. *See* Maria L. La Ganga, *This Is Climate Change: Alaskan Villagers Struggle as Island Is Chewed Up by the Sea*, L.A. TIMES, Aug. 30, 2015, *at* http://www.latimes.com/nation/la-na-arctic-obama-20150830-story.html.

Chapter 10
Promise and Peril: National Security and Climate Change

Inara Scott

In increasingly direct language, politicians, think tanks, government agencies, and researchers have identified climate change as a threat to national security. The 2014 Quadrennial Defense Review, a public document that the U.S. Department of Defense (DOD) released to describe current U.S. military policy, describes climate change as a "threat multiplier" that can "enable terrorist activity and other forms of violence."[1] A 2014 report by the Center for Naval Analyses (CNA) Military Advisory Board—the same organization that originally used the term "threat multiplier" in a 2007 report[2]—recently raised the stakes, now calling climate change a "catalyst for instability and conflict."[3] Following these reports, in October 2014, the Pentagon released its Climate Change Adaptation Roadmap, which states, "Climate change will affect the Department of Defense's ability to defend the Nation and poses immediate threats to U.S. national security."[4]

In his commencement address to the U.S. Coast Guard Academy, President Barack Obama made his position clear:

> I'm here today to say that climate change constitutes a serious threat to global security, an immediate risk to our national security, and make no mistake, it

---

1. U.S. DOD, QUADRENNIAL DEFENSE REVIEW 2014 at 8 (2014), *available at* http://www.defense.gov/pubs/2014_Quadrennial_Defense_Review.pdf [hereinafter QUADRENNIAL DEFENSE REVIEW].
2. CNA MILITARY ADVISORY BOARD, NATIONAL SECURITY AND THE THREAT OF CLIMATE CHANGE 7 (2007), *available at* http://www.npr.org/documents/2007/apr/security_climate.pdf.
3. CNA MILITARY ADVISORY BOARD, NATIONAL SECURITY AND THE ACCELERATING RISKS OF CLIMATE CHANGE 2 (2014), *at* https://www.cna.org/sites/default/files/MAB_2014.pdf [hereinafter CNA REPORT]. "'In the past, the thinking was that climate change multiplied the significance of a situation,' said Gen. Charles F. Wald, who contributed to both reports and is retired from the Air Force. 'Now we're saying it's going to be a direct cause of instability.'" Coral Davenport, *Climate Change Deemed Growing Security Threat by Military Researchers*, N.Y. TIMES, May 14, 2014, at A18.
4. U.S. DOD, FY 2014 CLIMATE CHANGE ADAPTATION ROADMAP 1 (2014), *available at* http://www.acq.osd.mil/ie/download/CCARprint_wForeword_c.pdf [hereinafter CLIMATE CHANGE ADAPTATION ROADMAP].

will impact how our military defends our country. . . . Denying it, or refusing to deal with it endangers our national security.[5]

Importantly, the U.S. military's acknowledgement of the threat of climate change to national security is not unique. Indeed, a review of relevant government documents and statements by high-ranking government officials suggests that over 70% of countries view climate change as a national security threat.[6]

Despite this assurance from a variety of U.S. and international sources, the Fifth Assessment Report by the Intergovernmental Panel on Climate Change (IPCC) (hereinafter AR5, or Fifth Assessment Report) states, "Confident statements about the effects of future changes in climate on armed conflict are not possible."[7] While the IPCC's caution in drawing a definitive correlation may be based on a lack of scientific certainty, caution may be warranted for public relations purposes as well. A recent study found that tying national security and climate change could create a "boomerang" effect in which individuals who were already doubtful or dismissive of climate change could become angered by linked coverage of the issue.[8] Having DOD further climate change initiatives has certainly not gone unnoticed by congressional Republicans, who passed legislation in 2014 to prevent DOD and the U.S. Department of Energy from using funds to implement climate change initiatives.[9] Thus, while many believe climate change presents a clear threat to U.S. security, deliberately linking the two is not without peril in the highly politicized world of climate change.

This chapter describes the impact of climate change on national and human security and the potential to advance mitigation and adaptation strategies by explicitly linking the two concepts. Finally, it presents a strategy of

5.   Remarks by the President at the United States Coast Guard Academy Commencement, *at* https://www.whitehouse.gov/the-press-office/2015/05/20/remarks-president-united-states-coast-guard-academy-commencement (May 20, 2015).

6.   AMERICAN SECURITY PROJECT, THE GLOBAL SECURITY DEFENSE INDEX ON CLIMATE CHANGE: PRELIMINARY RESULTS 3 (2013), *available at* http://www.americansecurityproject.org/climate-energy-and-security/climate-change/gsdicc/.

7.   INTERGOVERNMENTAL PANEL ON CLIMATE CHANGE, CLIMATE CHANGE 2014: MITIGATION OF CLIMATE CHANGE 773 (2014), *available at* https://ipcc-wg2.gov/AR5/images/uploads/WGIIAR5-Chap12_FINAL.pdf [hereinafter 2014 IPCC MITIGATION REPORT]. None of the four reports that comprise the IPCC Fifth Assessment Report (AR5) directly addresses "national security" but rather addresses "human security," and as a related issue, considers the effect of climate change on armed conflict and state stability. *See infra* notes 10-13, 31-36, and accompanying text.

8.   Teresa Myers et al., *A Public Health Frame Arouses Hopeful Emotions About Climate Change*, 113 CLIMATIC CHANGE 1105 (2012), *available at* http://link.springer.com/article/10.1007/s10584-012-0513-6/fulltext.html.

9.   *See* David Gutman, *McKinley Amendment Bars Defense Funds for Climate Change*, CHARLESTON GAZETTE, May 25, 2014, *at* http://www.wvgazette.com/article/20140525/GZ01/140529501#sthash.GyVBzbWx.dpuf.

advancing mitigation and adaptation activities that avoids the explicit pairing that may result in an unintended and disruptive backlash.

I.   Assessing the Climate Change Impact on National and Human Security

The Fifth Assessment Report does not directly consider the issue of "national security;" instead, it directly assesses the impact of climate change on *human security*, which it defines as "a condition that exists when the vital core of human lives is protected, and when people have the freedom and capacity to live with dignity."[10] Based on its review of relevant peer-reviewed research, the IPCC concludes that climate change can indeed threaten human security because it "undermines livelihoods, compromises culture and individual identity, increases migration that people would rather have avoided, and [can erode] the ability of states to provide the conditions necessary for human security."[11] More specifically, increasing drought, floods, erosion, and salinization associated with climate change can lead to a loss of livestock and arable land, increase poverty, and impair access to food and freshwater.[12] Extreme weather events, exacerbated in frequency and severity by climate change, are also likely to lead to increased displacement and migration of people and communities, which can in turn leave them more vulnerable to climactic conditions.[13]

When specifically examining the impacts of climate change on U.S. security,[14] military experts have concluded that many of the stresses identified by the IPCC—drought, extreme weather, salinization, mass migration—either enhance existing conflicts and vulnerabilities ("threat multiplier") or create catalysts for new conflicts.[15] These conflicts can threaten the security

---

10.   2014 IPCC MITIGATION REPORT, *supra* note 7, at 759.
11.   *Id.* at 762.
12.   *See id.* at 761.
13.   *Id.* at 767.
14.   The term "national security" is used in a variety of ways, and is not specifically defined in any of the sources consulted for this chapter. This can make it risky to directly compare the findings related to the ties between national security and climate change. U.S. military organizations appear to utilize a broad definition of national security that sweeps in any significant threat to U.S. citizens' lives, both domestically and abroad, threats to military personnel, and threats to military infrastructure. Other organizations and reports focus more narrowly on the integrity of state government and state borders. As previously noted, AR5 focuses on "human security" rather than national security. *See supra* notes 10-13 and accompanying text. The instant chapter describes the differences between these reports in order to highlight both the state of the research and the manner in which links between national security and climate change are described, discussed, and used to further activities toward mitigation and adaptation.
15.   *See* CNA REPORT, *supra* note 3, at 8. As President Obama put it in less than 140 characters on Twitter: "More severe weather events lead to displacement, scarcity, stressed populations; all increase likelihood

of the United States, particularly when they create conditions that support terrorism or terrorist organizations.[16]

A frequently cited example of the threat multiplier theory is the recent upheaval in the African nation of Mali. For several years, desertification and food scarcity exacerbated conflicts between ethnic groups in central and southern Mali. After a weak central government was overthrown by a coup in 2012, a variety of groups, including an Al Qaeda affiliate, moved in and fought for and exercised control.[17] Thus, while climate change did not directly cause the conflict, the argument is that it enhanced existing stressors and increased the possibility that conflict would erupt.[18] Other conflicts that may have been similarly impacted by climate stressors include the 2011 "Arab Spring" and the ongoing conflict in Syria.[19]

Research supports the assertion that many of the factors that increase the chance of civil war (including poverty, a history of violence, conflict in neighboring states, and weak government institutions) are sensitive to climate change.[20] In particular, struggles over the distribution of natural resources, when paired with weak governance, can increase the risk of armed conflict.[21] Looked at from a different perspective, societies that have undergone violent conflict are less adaptable and more vulnerable to poverty, famine, and other climate stressors.[22] A history of violent conflict has also been linked to environmental degradation.[23] Climate may therefore help to create vicious cycles of conflict, poverty, natural resource depletion, and further conflict.[24]

---

of global conflict." Rose Hackman, *Obama Ties Climate Change to "Likelihood of Global Conflict" in Twitter Q&A*, THE GUARDIAN, May 28, 2015, *at* http://www.theguardian.com/us-news/2015/may/28/president-obama-twitter-climate-change.

16. *See* Arija Flowers, *National Security in the 21st Century: How the National Security Council Can Solve the President's Climate Change Problem*, 11 Sus. Dev. L. & Pol'y 50, 51 (2011) (describing indirect effects of climate change and international security challenges). Another example of climate change supporting terrorist organizations can be seen in Pakistan, where the changing climate has limited available water for irrigation and power generation. Chronic power outages have generated protests within Pakistan, and emboldened the Taliban. *See* John Steinbruner, *Rising Temps and Emerging Threats: The Intersection of Climate Change and National Security in the 21st Century*, 15 Vt. J. Envtl. L. 665, 667 (2014); Richard Leiby, *Pakistan's Power Crisis May Eclipse Terrorist Threat*, Wash. Post, May 27, 2012, *at* http://www.washingtonpost.com/world/asia_pacific/pakistans-power-crisis-may-eclipse-terrorist-threat/2012/05/27/gJQAPhOSuU_story.html.

17. *See* CNA Report, *supra* note 3, at 13.
18. *Id.*
19. *Id.*
20. *See* 2014 IPCC Mitigation Report, *supra* note 7, at 772.
21. *Id.* at 773.
22. *Id.* at 774; *see also* Jon Barnett, *From Vicious to Virtuous Cycles*, Envtl. F., May/June 2015, at 42 ("The effect of violent conflict on vulnerability to climate change is a much bigger problem than the vague possibility that climate change may cause violent conflicts.").
23. *See* 2014 IPCC Mitigation Report, *supra* note 7, at 774.
24. *See* Barnett, *supra* note 22, at 44.

Another key stressor on national security identified by U.S. security experts is extreme weather and sea-level rise.[25] These factors have a number of potential impacts. Extreme weather events can disrupt international supply chains and cause extensive damage in coastal cities, which are doubly impacted by the combination of extreme weather and rising sea levels.[26] Military bases, many of which are located in vulnerable areas, can be directly threatened by these events, as can military personnel who train or live in such areas.[27] U.S. military forces can also be indirectly affected by the need to provide humanitarian aid and disaster relief.[28] U.S. security interests can also be threatened when floods, extreme heat, and storms damage domestic transportation infrastructure (rails, roads, and runways), or the electric grid.[29] Finally, extreme weather, armed conflict, and instability in developing nations can impact U.S. access to oil, undermining energy security.[30]

The Fifth Assessment Report, unlike some other sources, is careful to limit the conclusions that can be drawn regarding the impact of climate change on armed conflict and state integrity. While the IPCC has concluded that factors leading to armed conflict and civil upheaval may be linked to climate change and that there is "justifiable concern that climate change . . . increase[s] the risk of armed conflict," the IPCC could not conclude with confidence that climate change was a direct *cause* of any specific conflict.[31] Based on conflicting evidence and a lack of agreement among peer-reviewed scholarship, the report concludes, "Confident statements about the effects of future changes in climate on armed conflict are not possible given the absence of generally supported theories and evidence about causality."[32]

---

25. The DOD Climate Change Adaptation Roadmap lists four impacts from climate change most likely to require a response: (1) rising global temperatures; (2) changing precipitation patterns; (3) increasing frequency or intensity of extreme weather events; and (4) rising sea levels. *See* Climate Change Adaptation Roadmap, *supra* note 4, at 4.

26. *See id.* at 15; *see also* Michael B. McElroy & D. James Baker, *Climate Extremes: Recent Trends With Implications for National Security*, 15 Vt. J. Envtl. L. 727, 740 (2014).

27. *See* CNA Report, *supra* note 3, at 23-24.

28. *Id.* at 23.

29. *Id.* at 26.

30. *See* Marcus Dubois King & Jay Gulledge, *The Climate Change and Energy Security Nexus*, 37 Fletcher F. World Aff. 25, 29-32 (2013) (describing potential supply disruptions related to climate change effects).

31. *See* 2014 IPCC Mitigation Report, *supra* note 7, at 773.

32. *Id. See also* King & Gulledge, *supra* note 30, at 25-28 (2013). Marcus King and Jay Gulledge analyzed scholarship on the climate change/energy security nexus and found it made primarily of non-peer-reviewed "grey literature," authored by government agencies, military and security organizations, panels, NGOs and think tanks, and multilateral agencies. Within the academic literature, King and Gulledge found the relationships between climate change and violent conflict was "highly contested." *Id.* at 25.

Darfur illustrates both the tendency to broadly link climate change and armed conflict and the challenge of directly identifying climate change as a cause of any single struggle. In a 2007 *Washington Post* editorial titled *A Climate Culprit in Darfur*, U.N. Secretary General Ban Ki-moon directly linked drought, climate change, and the mass killing in Darfur[33]:

> Amid the diverse social and political causes, the Darfur conflict began as an ecological crisis, arising at least in part from climate change. . . . [I]t is no accident that the violence in Darfur erupted during the drought. Until then, Arab nomadic herders had lived amicably with settled farmers. . . . But once the rains stopped, farmers fenced their land for fear it would be ruined by the passing herds. For the first time in memory, there was no longer enough food and water for all. Fighting broke out. By 2003, it evolved into the full-fledged tragedy we witness today.[34]

By contrast, the Fifth Assessment Report asserts that multiple studies dispute that the fighting in Darfur was "primarily caused by climate change."[35] The authors of the report claim that studies suggest that "government practices [were] far more influential drivers than climate variability, noting [ ] that similar changes in climate did not stimulate conflicts of the same magnitude in neighboring regions, and that in the past people in Darfur were able to cope with climate variability in ways that avoided large-scale violence."[36]

The IPCC's reluctance to directly associate climate change and armed conflict is important. While multiple white papers from government agencies and think tanks directly tie national security and global warming,[37] these direct links may not be supported by peer-reviewed research. Several studies acknowledge that the interwoven, multiple causes of violent conflict make it difficult to find direct causal relationships from any single factor.[38] As one review of the literature notes,

---

33.   Ban Ki-moon, *A Climate Culprit in Darfur*, WASH. POST, June 16, 2007, *at* http://www.washington-post.com/wp-dyn/content/article/2007/06/15/AR2007061501857.html.

34.   *Id.*

35.   2014 IPCC MITIGATION REPORT, *supra* note 7, at 773.

36.   *Id.*

37.   *See, e.g.*, QUADRENNIAL DEFENSE REVIEW, *supra* note 1, at 8; ENVIRONMENTAL JUSTICE FOUNDATION, THE GATHERING STORM: CLIMATE CHANGE, SECURITY AND CONFLICT 11-13 (2014) (acknowledging academic disagreement over the role of climate change in armed conflict in Africa, while nonetheless concluding that climate change, human rights, and security are deeply intertwined and require analysis and planning by relevant stakeholders), *available at* http://ejfoundation.org/report/gathering-storm-climate-change-security-and-conflict; CHRISTINE PARTHEMORE & WILL ROGERS, SUSTAINING SECURITY: HOW NATURAL RESOURCES INFLUENCE NATIONAL SECURITY 5 (2010) (arguing that, in specific cases, "natural resources are closely intertwined with political stability and security"), *available at* http://www.cnas.org/files/documents/publications/CNAS_Sustaining%20Security_Parthemore%20Rogers.pdf.

38.   *See* ENVIRONMENTAL JUSTICE FOUNDATION, *supra* note 37, at 11; PARTHEMORE & ROGERS, *supra* note 37, at 9-10.

What is the evidence for climate change causing violent conflict? Our short answer is: So far, not much. . . . [T]here are many books, papers, and articles that . . . claim to present evidence for these links. But, many of these studies are based on assumptions and causal models . . . that are unexplored, unproven, or too simple.[39]

The Fifth Assessment Report highlights the potential weakness in overstating such arguments, while still supporting the link between climate stressors and a loss of human security.[40] A report by the Environmental Justice Foundation draws a similar conclusion:

[T]here is a strong relationship between climate change, fragility and conflict—but [ ] the links are mediated by a range of social, political and economic factors. . . . [P]olitical settlements, the availability of natural resources, patterns of human migration, and governance structures all have the potential to influence whether climate change, in one context, leads to conflict but in another does not.[41]

Thus, while we have extensive support for the proposition that climate change can create or intensify conditions like drought, famine, and human displacement, and lead to rising sea levels and extreme weather events, we do not have similar support for the proposition that climate change will be the direct cause of violent conflict or result in the collapse of vulnerable state governments.

II.   The U.S. Military and Climate

A.   The U.S. Military Plans for Adaptation

It is no accident that the strongest statements linking national security and climate change have been offered by military think tanks and DOD. As Section I describes, the U.S. military is likely to encounter a number of unique threats directly related to a changing climate that may also directly threaten the lives of U.S. citizens.[42] While it may be difficult to directly identify cli-

---

39.   TIM FORSYTH & MAREIKE SCHOMERUS, CLIMATE CHANGE AND CONFLICT: A SYSTEMATIC EVIDENCE REVIEW 30 (2013), *available at* http://eprints.lse.ac.uk/56352/1/JSRP_Paper8_Climate_change_and_conflict_Forsyth_Schomerus_2013.pdf.
40.   2014 IPCC MITIGATION REPORT, *supra* note 7, at 773.
41.   ENVIRONMENTAL JUSTICE FOUNDATION, *supra* note 37, at 33.
42.   Although U.S. military documents do not directly define the term "national security," DOD's "most fundamental duty . . . is to protect the security of U.S. citizens." QUADRENNIAL DEFENSE REV., *supra* note 1, at 13. DOD overall defense strategy is divided into the three pillars: (1) "protect the homeland;" (2) "build security globally," and (3) "project power and win decisively." *Id.* at V. Given this broad mission, it is not surprising that everything from the growth of pandemic disease to drought

mate change as a cause of any single armed conflict or the advancement of terrorist organizations,[43] it is not so difficult to conclude that rising sea levels create substantial physical threats to military infrastructure or that extreme weather events can directly threaten the lives of U.S. citizens and military personnel.[44] The U.S. military will also need to respond to changing conditions in the Arctic, as sea ice melts and countries vie for access to and control over new shipping lanes and fossil fuel reserves.[45]

DOD has generally pursued a strategy of responding to threats from climate change, rather than seeking to prevent it. Its 2014 Climate Change Adaptation Roadmap focuses on "integrating climate change considerations into our plans, operations, and training across the Department so that [it] can manage associated risks."[46] The specific actions that DOD plans to undertake in response range from the specific (reviewing and modifying, as needed, stormwater management and other utility systems at military installations)[47] to the general (initiating a review of existing directives and policies to determine which need to consider climate change impacts).[48] The Quadrennial Defense Review strikes a similar tone:

> The Department will remain ready to operate in a changing environment amid the challenges of climate change and environmental damage. We have increased our preparedness for the consequences of environmental damage and continue to seek to mitigate these risks while taking advantage of opportunities. . . . [W]e will complete a comprehensive assessment of all installations to assess the potential impacts of climate change on our missions and operational resiliency, and develop and implement plans to adapt as required.[49]

While the U.S. military is therefore incorporating climate change adaptation measures into its planning, it has not directly advocated for climate

---

and erosion have been identified as challenges to national security. *See* Climate Change Adaptation Roadmap, *supra* note 3, at 4-6.

43.   *See supra* note 31-36 and accompanying text.
44.   *See supra* notes 25-29 and accompanying text.
45.   *See* U.S. DOD, Arctic Strategy 2 (2013) (articulating a primary strategy of maintaining, "a secure and stable region where U.S. national interests are safeguarded, the U.S. homeland is protected, and nations work cooperatively to address challenges"), *at* http://www.defense.gov/pubs/2013_Arctic_Strategy.pdf. *See also* Navy Task Force Climate Change, United States Navy Arctic Roadmap for 2014-2030 at 6 (2014), *at* http://www.navy.mil/docs/USN_arctic_roadmap.pdf; *see, e.g.,* Mary Beth West, *Exploring the Legal and Political Future of the Arctic: Arctic Warming: Environmental, Human, and Security Implications,* 42 Vand. J. Transnat'l L. 1081, 1097-1107 (2009); Matthew Padilla, *The Great Thaw: National Security at the Top of a Melting World,* 8 Sustainable Dev. L. & Pol'y 52 (2008).
46.   Forward, Climate Change Adaptation Roadmap, *supra* note 4.
47.   *See id.* at 10.
48.   *Id.* at 11.
49.   Quadrennial Defense Review 2014, *supra* note 1, at 25.

change mitigation. However, many see the link between national security and climate change as providing fertile ground for support for mitigation. Some of those views are presented next.

B.   The U.S. Military and Mitigation

While DOD stops short of endorsing policies to mitigate climate change, President Obama has been vocal about the importance of making such efforts, partly, as noted above, because of the direct link he draws between climate change and U.S. security.[50] Other scholars and military consultants have similarly argued that climate change mitigation is necessary in order to prevent threats to national security.[51] The CNA Report advocates for direct U.S. involvement in efforts to mitigate climate change, but in a very specific manner. It recommends that "the U.S. should lead global efforts to develop sustainable and more efficient energy solutions to slow climate change."[52]

Here, arguably, is the most fruitful area for mitigation provided by the link between national security and climate change: *energy use and fossil fuel consumption.* The U.S. military, the single largest institutional consumer of fuel in the world, contributes significantly to overall U.S. greenhouse gas emissions.[53] Although a reduction in U.S. military GHG emissions will not, by itself, stop climate change, it would have a measurable impact on U.S. emissions. In addition, the U.S. military has a history of driving technological innovation, whether it is in the development of Navy vessels, nuclear weapons, or robotics.[54] Innovations in reducing the dependence of the U.S. military on fossil fuel through the development of new technology

---

50.   *See supra* note 5 and accompanying text.

51.   *See, e.g.,* ENVIRONMENTAL JUSTICE FOUNDATION, *supra* note 37, at 5 ("further and urgent action is needed to ensure the prevention of conflicts related to climate change. . . . [I]nvestment in mitigation now is [ ] investment in a safer and more secure future for vulnerable people across the world."); CNA REPORT, *supra* note 3, at 5; Flowers, *supra* note 16, at 50 ("The most politically feasible and compelling argument for addressing climate change promptly is the U.S. security depends upon it."); McElroy & Baker, *supra* note 26, at 742 (summarizing security risks caused by climate change and concluding that extreme events caused by climate change will affect "water, energy, food security, and critical infrastructure"). *See also* Joshua W. Busby, CLIMATE CHANGE AND NATIONAL SECURITY: AN AGENDA FOR ACTION, Council on Foreign Relations, CFR No. 32, at 18-21 (2007), *at* http://www. cfr.org/climate-change/climate-change-national-security/p14862 (suggesting that mitigation efforts create opportunities for diplomacy, but also create potential wedge issues).

52.   CNA REPORT, *supra* note 3, at 5.

53.   *See* Laura Horton, *Future Force Sustainability: Department of Defense and Energy Efficiency in a Changing Climate,* 4 GOLDEN GATE U. ENVTL. L.J. 303, 307-08 (2011) (estimating that the military produced of 1.5% of total U.S. greenhouse gas emissions in 2008); *see also* Editors, *The Pentagon's War Against Climate Change,* BLOOMBERG VIEW, July 18, 2014, *at* http://www.bloombergview.com/ articles/2014-07-18/the-pentagon-s-war-against-climate-change.

54.   *See* Siddhartha M. Velandy, *The Green Arms Race: Reorienting the Discussions on Climate Change, Energy Policy, and National Security,* 3 HARVARD NAT'L SEC. J. 309, 314-16, 319, 348-49 (2012).

could have a significant impact on its own and could also help lower prices, drive demand for energy efficiency and renewable energy technology, and create a virtuous cycle of lower prices and wider adoption of renewable energy technologies.[55]

Prof. Sarah Light has proposed the concept of the "Military-Environmental Complex" to describe the potential of the military to drive both public and private dollars to the reduction of fossil fuel use and the development of renewable alternatives.[56] She contends that the Military-Environmental Complex has the potential to "change individual attitudes and beliefs about climate change" by linking energy consumption and national security.[57] Her theory takes two parts: first, the U.S. military can serve to validate climate science.[58] Second, through the adoption of conservation and increasing use of renewable resources, the military has the potential to create "spillover effects in the sphere of values," such that those who would not otherwise have supported such efforts would do so because of the connection with national security.[59]

The danger of this strategy, which Professor Light recognizes, is that these explicit linkages between climate change and national security have the potential to alienate both climate change supporters and deniers.[60] The psychology of climate change beliefs and attitudes is complex and multi-faceted[61]; well-meaning efforts to further adaptation and mitigation may in fact create significant roadblocks to the accomplishment of climate initiatives, as has been seen in the attempts to pass legislation forbidding DOD from addressing climate change, even where it presents a risk to military personnel.[62]

An additional challenge to such efforts lies in the difficulty of identifying climate change as the primary cause of any single national security conflict.[63] As noted previously, research does not clearly support such a conclusion, and the IPCC has been unable to reach such conclusions.[64] While climate change does present a real threat to human security, and

---

55. "[I]f the Navy comes knocking, they will build it. The price will come down and the infrastructure will be created." Velandy, *supra* note 54, at 348 (quoting U.S. Secretary of the Navy Ray Mabus).
56. *See* Sarah Light, *The Military-Environmental Complex*, 55 B.C. L. Rev. 879, 884-88 (2014).
57. *See* Sarah Light, *Valuing National Security: Climate Change, the Military, and Society*, 61 UCLA L. Rev. 1772, 1778 (2014).
58. *See* Light, *supra* note 57, at 1778.
59. *Id.*
60. *Id.* at 1778-79.
61. *Id.* at 1782-86.
62. *See supra* note 5 and accompanying text.
63. *See supra* notes 31-36 and accompanying text.
64. *See supra* notes 31-32 and accompanying text.

certain issues—such as the impact of rising sea levels on military installations—create undeniable risks for the U.S. military, those who would link the concepts of national security and climate change must use caution not to overstate their case. Climate change may have been a *factor* in the Arab Spring, the conflict in Darfur, and the fighting in Mali, but one cannot confidently conclude that it was the primary cause of *any* of these events. Drawing unsupported conclusions can only provide fodder for climate change deniers and feed efforts to restrict U.S. government involvement in adaptation and mitigation efforts.

C. Addressing Climate Change Without Addressing Climate Change

Can climate change mitigation efforts be furthered without raising the specter of climate change? In fact, efforts to reduce U.S. dependence on fossil fuels need not to be undertaken solely, or even primarily, to achieve mitigation goals. The military's dependence on fossil fuels creates significant strategic and operational vulnerabilities and puts military personnel directly into harm's way.[65] Reducing U.S. dependence on fossil fuels could provide financial, operational, and strategic benefits, without even considering the impact of climate change.

One source of vulnerability associated with fossil fuel use is the U.S. dependence on unstable and potentially hostile governments, a vulnerability the United States has sought to reduce for years with a drive to become more "energy independent."[66] Another source of vulnerability relates to the U.S. need to constantly resupply troops—including those in hostile areas—with fuel. Supply lines are notoriously difficult to protect and defend, and doing so costs the U.S. government millions of dollars, much of which likely ends up in the hands of the very terrorist organizations the U.S. military is engaged in fighting.[67] It also costs lives: estimates suggest that of the casualties in Afghanistan caused by improved explosive devices, 10% occur on roads during resupply missions.[68] As a 2008 report by the U.S. Government Accountability Office states, "DOD's high fuel requirements on the battlefield can

---

65. *See* Velandy, *supra* note 54, at 313-14.
66. *See* Mark E. Rosen, *Energy Independence and Climate Change: the Economic and National Security Consequences of Failing to Act*, 44 U. RICH. L. REV. 977, 988 (2010) ("There is growing consensus in U.S. national security circles that American dependence on imported oil constitutes a threat to the United States because a substantial portion of those oil reserves are controlled by governments that have historically pursued policies inimical to U.S. interests.").
67. *See* Velandy, *supra* note 54, at 324-25.
68. *Id.* at 328.

place a significant logistics burden on military forces, limit the range and pace of operations, and add to mission risks."[69]

Reports also suggest that the military could save money by adopting a new energy strategy that prioritizes reducing energy dependence and developing new technological capabilities.[70] In a report commissioned by DOD, a consulting agency calculated that reducing energy use by 3% per year could yield savings of $43 billion by 2030.[71] Reducing fossil fuel dependence by increasing the use of renewable energy resources and improving efficiency could therefore save military lives, redirect money to more worthy causes, and create more flexibility in the way missions are carried out.[72] Climate change need not enter into the equation.

Major Siddhartha Velandy has suggested that the U.S. military start a "green energy 'arms race,'" using the military's power to drive technology and innovation, and its role as the single largest consumer of energy to "globalize the demand for clean and renewable energy and drive the development of technology and regulation."[73] Velandy's premise is that, much like the drive for nuclear weapons, once the United States begins a push for renewable technology and energy efficiency, it will pass along those innovations to our allies, and then force other nations to compete to that level.[74] Notably, the motivation for the green arms race, like the development of a new energy strategy, does not rest on preventing climate change. Rather, it is supported by a drive to reduce supply chain-related vulnerabilities, save money, and increase flexibility.[75]

III.   Conclusion

The Fifth Assessment Report concludes that climate change does present a threat to human security and that the factors leading to armed conflict and

---

69. U.S. Government Accountability Office (GAO), Defense Management: Overarching Organizational Framework Could Improve DOD's Management of Energy Reduction Efforts for Military Operation, GAO-08-523T, at 5 (2008), (Statement of William M. Solis, Director Defense Capabilities and Management), *available at* http://www.gao.gov/assets/120/119405.pdf.

70. *See* LMI Consulting Partners, Transforming the Way DOD Looks at Energy: An Approach to Establishing an Energy Strategy iii (2007), *available at* www.dtic.mil/cgi-bin/GetTRDoc?AD=ADA467003. While the report does not include an estimate of the cost of achieving these reductions, it asserts that the cost would be compensated by a "multiplier effect" in savings resulting from new technologies and processes that would be implemented. *Id.* at G-5.

71. *Id.* at vi, G-1 to G-5.

72. *Id.* at 313-14; *see also* Rosen, *supra* note 66, at 996 (describing the increasing "electrification" of combat, which threatens fuel convoys and limits military commanders by forcing them to remain within access of fuel supply lines).

73. Velandy, *supra* note 54, at 311.

74. *Id.* at 311-12.

75. *Id.* at 313-14, 323-28.

state instability are linked to climate change.[76] Numerous organizations, military experts, and academics have identified threats to U.S. national security from climate change, ranging from infrastructure made vulnerable by sea-level rise and extreme weather to threats to the safety of military personnel called in for disaster relief or engaged in armed conflict in failing states. DOD has outlined a strategy for adaptation that requires planning around these risks and utilizing climate science to identify future areas of potential conflict.

On the other hand, the Fifth Assessment Report also makes clear that the science is far from settled when it comes to the question of whether climate change is a direct cause of violent conflict or state instability. The complexity of the relationship between national security and climate change suggests a number of possible responses. First, the risks identified by DOD in the Climate Change Adaptation Roadmap and Quadrennial Defense Review can be addressed through adaptation planning and risk analysis, and the U.S. government appears to be making an effort to do so. The next step, of course, would be using the threat to national security to promote efforts at mitigation. President Obama has done exactly this, both by using the bully pulpit and by creating new regulations designed to lower the rate of U.S. carbon emissions.[77] Academics have also suggested creative ways to advance mitigation through the development of renewable energy technologies and energy efficiency, efforts that could originate within the U.S. military but spillover to both domestic and international military and civilian markets.

Using threats to national security to press directly for climate change mitigation has the potential to make significant strides in the reduction of carbon emissions. However, it should not be considered the only option for those seeking to advance mitigation strategies. As noted above, there are many non-climate related reasons for the U.S. military to engage in efforts to reduce its fossil fuel dependency. At the same time, the politicization of climate change in the United States may defeat such efforts by creating a backlash when the government chooses to directly link climate change and national security. It may be that while the politics around climate change remain so toxic that they create potential obstacles to the adoption of mitigation policies, a focus on the non-climate benefits of these policies may ultimately prove more

---

76. *See supra* notes 11-13 and accompanying text.
77. *See* Julie Hirschfeld Davis, *Obama Recasts Climate Change as a Peril With Far-Reaching Effects*, N.Y. TIMES, May 20, 2015, *at* http://www.nytimes.com/2015/05/21/us/obama-recasts-climate-change-as-a-more-far-reaching-peril.html?_r=0; CLIMATE CHANGE AND PRESIDENT OBAMA'S ACTION PLAN (visited June 30, 2015), *at* https://www.whitehouse.gov/climate-change.

effective. Changing the U.S. military reliance on fossil fuels could have the ultimate spillover benefit—helping the planet and mitigating the disastrous effects of climate change.

Index

Notes